Love: A Trail Worth Blazing

Norma Bent Johnson

This memoir is as factual as my memory allows it to be.
However, names of individuals have been altered to protect
their privacy.

Cover art by Adrian Kikuo Britton

About the author

Norma Jeanne Bent-Johnson was raised in Balboa, California, a beautiful beach town South of Los Angeles. Raised by a single mom, they were very poor, five people sharing a one bedroom cottage.

Growing up in Balboa during the 1950's was a simpler, but also a challenging time for the young impressionable girl whose role models were Marilyn Monroe and Lana Turner.

Believing that in order to find true love, she had to look like the famous movie stars of the era, led her to anorexia, excessive drinking and addiction to prescription medications. It may have been the lack of a father figure in her early life that caused her obsession with men and finding love.

She went to work for a local police department, leading to a career of four decades in law enforcement as a civilian investigator. She is now retired and resides in Southern California with her husband, spending much of her time working for animal rights.

She hopes her tale of obsession, addiction and anorexia, all in the name of love, will help other women avoid going down a similar path, leading to disaster.

Love can, and should be a beautiful thing; it does not have to be disastrous.

To my family and friends without whose support I would never have finished this book. I cherish them all.

Table of Contents

1 INTRODUCTION

I spent a great deal of my life searching for my Mr. Right. This search took me down the path of anorexia, and many dates and relationships that could only be considered weird, comical, and even sometimes disgusting and scary.

There was the doctor, who after only two dates, decided to remove his prosthetic leg while I obliviously brewed a pot of coffee in the other room. This wouldn't have been a problem were it not for the fact I had no idea he had a prosthetic leg and to walk into a room and see someone's leg sitting two feet away from them can be quite off-putting to say the least.

Then there was the date from hell who turned very hostile when I denied his advances. He began stalking and threatening me to the point I was literally afraid for my life. I'm convinced to this day that the only thing that saved me was the fact that I worked for the police department.

I dated more than one man with a drinking problem. They would be oh so charming and attentive and gentlemanly with the first couple of drinks but then things could go downhill quickly and many times I had to beat a hasty retreat by calling a taxi to pick me up while they were in the bathroom!

But none of my experiences deterred me from continuing my search for the perfect man. I grew up in an era where the movies depicted a woman's life plan as finding true love, leading me to believe I would not be a truly worthwhile woman until I found my true love. Heaven forbid a woman could be happy or satisfied without a man! I was young and impressionable and thought I had to look like Marilyn Monroe or Lana Turner to land my Mr. Wonderful. This is what led me to anorexia and to the brink of death. Everything I did centered on my search for that elusive true love.

But don't despair, I ultimately learned that if it is love and a soulmate you desire, you will find it. And you don't have to resort to the drastic measures that I did. I have a man in my life who accepts me with all my phobias and flaws; a blessing, as not many men would. And I ended up finding him when and where I least expected it. It was a long, hard, and oftentimes funny journey as you'll read about it in this book, but in the end it was worth it. I learned a lot about myself, especially that until I learned to love and respect myself, no one else would either.

So, happy hunting!

2 THE EARLY YEARS

I was born Norma Jeanne and grew up in Balboa, California, during the 40's and 50's, the best of times and a time never to be forgotten in history. The best because it was a time of innocence, when as a 13 year old girl I was singing in bars and hanging out with musicians twice my age, without any fear. The one exception was being caught by my mother. During the forties, the darkest side to this period was World War II, although I was too young then to know what that really meant.

One of my earliest memories is riding on the Red Car from Newport Beach to Los Angeles with my mother to visit relatives when I was about five years old and seeing all the servicemen dressed in their military uniforms. I was a cute child with golden curls and an angelic face and probably reminded many of the servicemen of their beloved children at home. They would ogle over me and hold me on their laps. That was my first real interaction with men since I had an absent father and I lapped up the attention. I believe that was when I became destined to be boy-crazy for the rest of my life, ever on a quest for the male attention missing in my younger years.

Even at the young age of five, if it wasn't male attention I was seeking, it was adventure. On occasion, I would stay with my grandparents in Los Angeles. Once when I was five, I decided I needed to go to the Sears store about a mile from their house. Feeling like a kid in a candy store, I grabbed a shopping bag, filled it up, and tried to leave the store with my bounty, having no clue they expected me to pay for my treasures! The salespeople who had watched my little shopping spree stopped me and asked where my parents were. When I told them they were at home; they said they were going to call the police. Traveling a mile alone hadn't scared me but the thought of my grandpa, who was an L.A Sheriff, finding out put the fear of God in me and I begged them not to call the police! Unfortunately I was still too young to have mastered the art of begging and next thing I knew, there was grandpa looking none too happy. My punishment was a spanking with the razor strap and at that moment I needed no further convincing that my traveling days were over. But kids have short attention spans and their memories fade.

It wasn't long after, that I went to visit them again and foolishly decided to set out on another adventure. I started out not really knowing where I was headed, although I knew it wasn't back to Sears. After wandering for a little while, a man approached me and offered to buy me the best ice cream cone ever if I got in his car and went with him to the ice cream parlor. His hand reached out for me and at the same time I felt someone grabbing my arm and pulling me away from him. A lady was yelling at him while steering me to safety. To this day I believe God sent an angel to save me from what could have been a terrible fate. Unfortunately the angel called the police and suddenly there was grandpa again, looking none too happy with me. This resulted in another spanking, but this one definitely left a lasting impression. My solo explorations ended for good.

I lived with my mother and grandmother and one of my brothers in a tiny, one bedroom beach cottage. My first recollection of that tiny house was the infestation of roaches. At night you could hear the intruders crawling up the walls and some would land in bed with me. This put me in a state of hysteria, screaming loud enough to wake up the neighbors.

Many a night I ended up sleeping on the front porch, where I had to contend with fleas only. I felt this was a better trade off. After many nights of terror with these creepy crawlers, the owner conceded and had the exterminators fumigate the place. To this day I have an extreme horror to these ungodly insects. We were fortunate, though, to have an indoor commode where you did your business and disposed of it by pulling the long link metal cord. On occasion, it would overflow. This, too, was very frightening to me. The john was enclosed in a coffin-like upright box. There were steps leading up to the discolored porcelain bowl and once she blew you never had time to run down the three or four steps and I thought surely I would drown. I also believed and envisioned serpents in their scaly snake appearance emerging from the cloudy water, grabbing me and carrying me away on an endless journey through the sewer system. Maybe this was the beginning of my journey working through numerous phobias to come!

Being poor in this very affluent area of the Balboa Peninsula, led to many embarrassing moments growing up. I remember around the age of 10, I attended a preteen swimming class hosted by the Red Cross. We had no money for a bathing suit so I wore my brother's swim trunks. Just swim trunks, no top! Even though I was developing slowly and wasn't any bigger than most of the boys, all of the other girls wore tops and the boys teased me mercilessly. And as if that wasn't bad enough, after one very embarrassing belly flop, I rose to the surface with the trunks down around my knees! After that episode, somehow my mother found the money to buy me a cheap one piece bathing suit. A few years later when I had developed in to a size 40D, these same mean boys did everything they could to get my attention short of doing hand stands in front of me, but I pretended I didn't know they existed.

In spite of being poor and the embarrassment that came with that, I lived in paradise. Birthdays and Christmas were such special times, as I knew I was going to get a gift of paper cut out dolls, which I loved. Being as money was so tight, I was thrilled just to have a package or two to open. Once or twice in my early years, I would get a ceramic doll with outfits my grandma would crochet for them. These wonderful treasures meant everything to me, and I appreciated them so much, even at that young age.

During my pre-teen and teen years, I took odd jobs around town. My goal was to earn enough to buy a new bicycle, because my old hand-me-down had fallen apart and had been welded back together so many times that my frequent falls became quite embarrassing, and painful. I cleaned beauty parlors and houses. It didn't take long for me to decide that manual labor wasn't for me. I was lucky enough, or so I thought at the time, to land a job as a helping hand to "Pop", one of the photographers in the Fun Zone. I would stand outside the photo booth and try to lure customers inside. It was much better than scrubbing toilets! Pop seemed to really like me and my friend Karen, and he would take pictures of us in our school dance costumes. One of the costumes consisted of a grass hula skirt. While Pop was helping to position us for the picture, his hands managed to wander between our legs. We were pretty naïve, but somehow we knew that this was wrong. When we told our parents what had happened, our feisty little mommas stormed down to Pop's and must have scared the daylight out of Pop, because a few days later he was gone, and his business was closed.

My next job was as a short order cook at the end of Balboa Pier. Even though getting up at 6am was torture, it was still better than cleaning toilets or searching for returnable cola bottles in the trash, and I loved being on the water.

"Pop" took this picture of me when I was 13 years old

The guy who ran the concession was about 50 years old, quite ancient to a 13 year old, with a dirty looking beard and clothes, but I tried to ignore this, and just focus on the hourly wage and tips I would make; soon I would have my new bicycle!

Even though I was only 13, one morning he grabbed my butt. There was no one around but the two of us, so the second time he tried to grab me, I pushed him really hard, causing him to lose his balance and burn his hand on the hot grill. He screamed and I ran! When I told my mom, she stormed over there and threatened to call the police. He begged her not to, he had a wife and a family and this concession was their only means of income. After much scolding, and apologizing and begging on his part, she decided to show him mercy and not call the police. The concession closed about a month later. I'll never know if this event had anything to do with it, or if he groped another unsuspecting child, whose parents did call the police.

3 GETTING INTO MISCHIEF

Around age 13 is when I really developed and looked much older than I was. I felt so much more mature than the teenage boys vying for my attention. I started hanging out at local bars, my favorite being the Blue Room which featured live jazz. It was my second home for a while, until my mother figured out what I was up to. I would go on stage and sing back-up for the musicians, and although I had mad crushes on almost all of them, there's one in particular whose face I still remember to this day; so rugged and handsome and sophisticated. I tried desperately to convince him that fate had brought us together, and I couldn't live without him, but he just humored me, telling me that we could talk about it in 10 years, when I was older. I think this was my first real experience of rejection and heartbreak. Like every other teenage girl, I thought I would die of a broken heart. As it turned out, this would be just the first of many heartbreaks.

Even though all of these men treated me with respect, like a daughter or a sister, and watched over me, when my mother discovered what I was up to, she was furious! I remember her storming the club with two police officers by her side and trying to grab me, but I was as fast as the Tasmanian devil, and flew out the back door before they could catch me. Eventually my mother won that battle, and I was no longer allowed to "bar hop". For the longest time I believed that it was the end of what could have been a famous singing career, although my true friends advised me not to have regrets because my singing can make a dog howl. Maybe those nice men really were just humoring me!

I always loved being in the spotlight, beginning with all the attention I received from the servicemen on the train. I thrived on it. I remember two other occasions when, I'm certain, my chance at fame and fortune slipped through my fingers. When I was five, I entered a baby beauty and personality contest. This was the Shirley Temple era, and I fit right in with my head of blonde curls and angelic face. I won the contest and was sought after by an agent from Paramount Studios who had attended the pageant. He wanted to schedule me for a screening at the studio, but my mother turned him down, declaring the entertainment world "decadent". I didn't find out about this until I was much older. I was devastated, believing I could have been dazzling on the silver screen!

When I was 10, I entered a talent contest at our local theater. When my turn came to sing, something went wrong with the sound system, and even though no one beyond the first row could hear me, I still came in second. My mother believed the winner, who just happened to be the act right before me, sabotaged the sound system so they would win. I'll never know if I would have been "discovered" and become rich and famous… but life goes on.

I had two close girlfriends, Karen and Dodi, who, during our pre-teen and teen years were just as boy-crazy as I was. Never was there a dull moment during our quest for male attention! I remember my first kiss at age twelve with Frank, a fellow student who was tall and had what I thought was a "gangster" look, very dangerous and romantic to a twelve year old girl. I almost screamed the first time he kissed me, because I was not prepared for the tongue being jammed into my mouth! But being a trooper, and not wanting to be labeled a "novice", I stifled the scream and let Frank continue.

Karen, Dodi and I

After a few of these tongue kisses, I finally started to relax and enjoy the experience, and, for the first time, I think I fell in love. Of course it didn't last long, I was twelve and there would be many more boys and men on my horizon.

Being raised in a beach town meant wild times. Balboa was crazy during the Spring Break at Easter. Lots of parties and, of course, lots of boys. These boys weren't safe from us; we were constantly on the prowl! I remember one year, when Dodi, Karen, and I met some boys who were renting a house on the ocean front. We partied with them during Easter Break. I connected with a guy named Nat, who introduced me to the anatomic difference between males and females. At first sight, I have to admit, I was not at all impressed with the male penis, and actually thought it was quite ugly. All I could think of was "is this what all the excitement is about? Yuck". Of course my opinion of this part of the male anatomy changed drastically as time went on, thank goodness! But I definitely enjoyed making out with Nat. We went at it hot and heavy and my lips became so swollen I could barely talk, and my neck was covered with hickeys. I just knew, that when I got home, my mother was going to beat the life out of me. But at the time, the excitement was worth the punishment that was sure to follow.

I remember that later Karen had a huge crush on Gene, who looked just like Montgomery Clift. And I had a huge crush on his friend, Bob, who was built like Mr. Atlas and had a smile to die for. Bob worked on the fishing boats, and I would watch him leaving the docks from my upstairs window. I would put Nat King Cole's "Red Sails in the Sunset" on the stereo, and I would dream of the day when I would be able to make out with my handsome hunk. Of course both these guys were much older than us, but that didn't matter, our hormones were raging.

One night Gene invited us to his cottage for a soda. Before we knew it, Gene was lying in the center of his bed between Karen and me, which, as I learned later in life, was called a "sandwich". At first it was pretty exciting, but then the excitement turned to awkwardness as I just lay there while Gene and Karen were making out hot and heavy. I tried to leave, but Gene pulled me back and started kissing me. This felt even more awkward because all I could think of was: "This is Karen's love, not mine." This didn't last long before we decided to leave. Karen and I discussed this for weeks, and we got many laughs from it.

Before old Pop closed his photo booth, I had him take a picture of me with Gene. I still have it to this day, a memento of my first, and only, "sandwich".

My mother and grandmother managed an apartment house right on the bay-front. During Easter Break and at summertime, we were always booked up. The property was owned by a Hollywood agent who managed such celebrities as Nat King Cole, Red Skelton, James Arness, John Forsyth, Johnny Weissmuller, and many others, whom I was very fortunate to meet as a consequence.

One of my most embarrassing moments in my lifetime was meeting John Forsyth. He knocked on our door, and when I saw who it was, my stomach started doing flip flops, and I let out two farts that were so loud that I thought the door would blow off its hinges! But he was a total class act, and showed no reaction, he just smiled and asked for his keys.

Our apartment house was aptly called The Grey Goose, as our mascot was a real gray goose, an old gander named Henry. Every morning at sunrise, like clockwork, Henry would wake up the whole neighborhood. That resulted in many a death threat against poor old Henry. On one occasion I think he feared ending up on someone's supper table and took off running down the main boulevard with my mom and grandma chasing him, stopping traffic and causing even more death threats! After about an hour, fatigue set in and we were able to catch him and take him home where he promptly fell asleep.

After that episode we tried to keep Henry in a safe enclosure. But he didn't know what was best for him and refused to remain in captivity. So he went back to splashing in the bay and entertaining visitors with his antics. Sadly, not long afterwards, Henry went missing for good. The town was put on alert, and flyers were posted everywhere, but we never saw Henry again.

Without Henry to wake me up in the morning, I found myself frequently being late to work. But something Henry did give me was the introduction to my very first lover. While searching for Henry, I met Jim, a Greek God, who could make me weak at the knees with just one glance! Jim was at least twice my age, but I didn't care. In all my teenage wisdom, I just knew he was "the one".

Jim and I dated a couple of times, and I was determined that he was going to be mine forever. I was in love, and he became my first lover. Unfortunately, Jim actually found my virginity a turn off. Not what I expected at all! I thought I was bestowing the biggest honor on him, and he would be falling at my feet with gratitude! Once he found out my true age, and that I was jailbait, all I saw was his backside as he flew out the door! I felt very betrayed and cheap after this experience. But, unfortunately, I can't say that I learned any lasting lessons from this experience.

I lived only a couple of blocks away from one of the best music centers of that time, the Rendezvous Ballroom. There was so much great live music in the mid-fifties, and the cost of a ticket was not much more than going to a movie, so everyone could enjoy it. It was not like today, when ticket prices are so exorbitant that many people miss out on the opportunity.

The first entertainer I saw there was Nat King Cole. I sat on the edge of the stage and just stared at him in awe. His voice was so mellow and he was such a great showman, that he brought the house down with his performance. On occasion, Nat King Cole also stayed at our apartment complex, and had his boat tied up at the dock. I still have a matchbook which reads, "It's a Match, Marie and Nat".

One night Desi Arnaz and his band were playing and I was singled out to go on stage, where I was cajoled into dancing the rumba with the Latin King himself. I was a "fluffy", a girl with large breasts, and I was very self-conscious as I thought my 40D's must have been bouncing all over the place as he swung me around. Of course he praised my performance, but I knew better.

All the great bands of that time, Duke Ellington, Count Basie, and my personal favorite, Stan Kenton, played at the Rendezvous. I never missed an appearance. Many of the famous rock and roll bands also rocked at the Rendezvous. Little Richard stands out in my mind, because I had never before seen anyone dressed in purple pants and a bright yellow polka dot shirt, gyrating the way he did. And I loved his platform shoes!

I decided to get a part time job serving food and drinks, so I could enjoy all the wonderful entertainment for free. I was hired, but my career as a food server was very short-lived. The very first night, while serving a cheeseburger to a customer, a large cockroach fell from the ceiling right onto his cheeseburger. I ran screaming from the counter, creating quite a scene, and that was the end of my food serving days. But the manager was a nice man, and gave me one more chance. But this time I would not be serving food; I would only be selling sodas, a job I was much more suited for.

One night, when Stan Kenton was playing, one of his saxophone players, Steve, came on my radar. My hormones immediately started raging, I couldn't take my eyes off him, and my emotions were just out of control. He had to be at least twice my age. Short, with a goatee, Steve was not the type to score a second look, but to me he had what the French call "je ne sais quoi", that certain something.

When I told my friend Sharon about these crazy feelings of mine, her advice to me was: "Don't get involved with a musician. They are whore mongers, who will use you and then dump you." This advice originated with Sharon's mother. I've often wondered what happened to her mother to cause her to have such negative feelings about musicians.

I tried to heed her advice. I really did. But my attraction to this man overwhelmed my resolve, and I couldn't stop staring at him whenever I had the opportunity. Steve finally came over to me one day and introduced himself, probably wondering who this crazy young girl was, ogling him constantly! His voice was low and sexy; those dark eyes pierced right through me. I was ready to follow him anywhere! But the reality was, he only approached me to let me know he appreciated that I was such an ardent fan. If he had been able to read my mind at that moment, I wonder if he would have taken advantage of the situation, or if he would have run for the hills! After this encounter, I stayed away for a while, but later Steve and I ended up having quite a history.

My friend Sharon was a strong willed Italian/Irish girl and she got me into more trouble. She was very bold and I was a follower at the time. Some of my favorite memories are of the insane situations we got ourselves into.

One afternoon Sharon and I had been at the beach, and we were heading home, when we heard this loud rumble, like nothing we had ever heard before. Before long, all the streets were filled with motorcycles and drop dead gorgeous men! Sharon and I had fallen hard for Marlon Brando in "The Wild One", we saw it 16 times! So we felt like our prayers had been answered when we found ourselves in the midst of about 100 motorcycle riders dressed in leathers, just like Brando! We zeroed in on a group called "The Speedy Shifters". We introduced ourselves to a couple of them, and soon found ourselves riding on the back of their bikes. The one I was with, suggested that we ride on the wet sandy beach, and off we went. We had barely hit the sand, when we hit a bump and off I went, sailing through the air. I didn't even mind the pain or the embarrassment, because I was living my dream!

We invited the two guys over to my house for coffee and donuts. Naïve, I know. Offering coffee and donuts to motorcycle gang riders is like offering a steak to a vegetarian. I knew that my mom and grandma were out for their daily walk; surely they wouldn't mind me inviting two guys over for coffee.

We picked up the donuts from the donut shop, and when we rounded the corner to my house, what we saw shocked us so badly that we dropped them all over the ground! The entire motorcycle gang of about 30 was in the parking lot of my apartment building, revving their engines and sending dirt flying everywhere! We immediately realized this was not going to turn out well for us.

Most of them were as drunk on Thunderbird as they could get, a drink of choice at that time, because it was cheap. Bottles started flying. They were yelling, and completely out of control and wreaking havoc. The guy I had been riding with suddenly tore off his clothes and jumped buck naked into the bay from our dock. He started screaming "wine is fine! and f**k anyone if they don't believe it!" It was Easter week and our apartments and cottages were filled to capacity; the Boardwalk was full of people out on a stroll, so, needless to say, he drew quite a large crowd!

About ten of these wild men came into our office, smoking, drinking, and shouting obscenities. They never had any interest in our offering of coffee and donuts; they only had partying on their minds! And they paid no attention to us as we begged and pleaded for them to leave before my mom and grandma got back.

We were sobbing and pleading with them when my 4'9" feisty mom and my grandma of equally small stature returned. It was a sight to see her whip in to action and chase those big burly drunk men right off our property. Once they were gone, we discovered cigarette burns on our couch, wine bottles thrown about, and cigarette butts everywhere. My punishment was to be grounded for the rest of Easter Break, and maybe for the rest of my life, which I probably would have deserved.

In order to minimize her embarrassment, my mom told our Easter renters that I was her visiting niece. She told them she hadn't been aware that I was so out of control, and this would be my last visit with her until I grew up. It really crushed me that she would disown me like this, especially after I explained that we had only invited two guys over for coffee and donuts and we had no control over what happened. She was unfazed and I was still grounded.

At last, I got my freedom back, and Sharon and I were out on the streets again, up to our usual shenanigans. We loved to party and have a good time, but the only really bad thing we did was to have an occasional drink. Sharon drank more than I did, and I can remember her puking many times. One of those most embarrassing moments was when we were riding the Ferris wheel in the Fun Zone. We were stopped at the top and that's when I noticed her starting to heave-ho. Sure enough, she leaned over the side and spewed vomit all over the cars and riders below. There were definitely no love connections for us that night.

One day, while visiting at Sharon's house which was located in Newport Heights, we took a walk and visited briefly with a neighbor. She said, a visiting friend of hers was trying to fix something on his Porsche. All we could see were a set of legs and feet adorned with cowboy boots. We heard a hello from him, but never did get a glance at this guy. Later in the week Sharon said her neighbor told her that James Dean was the guy under the car, trying to repair a leak. We were devastated to think that we had been that close to him, yet all we saw was the bottom half of him – well, not even that much!

My other two good friends, Karen and Dodi, did not approve of Sharon, and thought she was a bad influence on me. They would not hang out with me if Sharon was around, which was tough, because we had been friends for a long time. Dodi used to carry her bible and tell us we were both going to hell if we didn't change our ways. It used to keep me awake some nights, wondering if she was right.

On one occasion Hollywood came to town to film a movie, with a cast of mostly gorgeous men. Sharon and I managed to introduce ourselves. By this time we had gotten pretty smooth at approaching men. We ended up hanging out with two of the best looking actors. I was interested in Tony and we hung out for a few days. Unfortunately Tony treated me like a kid sister, not at all what I had in mind. He knew I was only 15 years old, and he didn't care to risk going to jail for that. I did my best to assure him that it wouldn't happen, but to no avail. In his book even cuddling and kissing was out, no matter how much I pleaded. We ended up having a good time, despite the lack of physical contact, and I think I learned a bit about how to control myself. Not an easy task.

It was time for me to get my mind off the boys and get a real summer job. I landed what I thought would be a perfect job for me, waitressing at a small restaurant in the center of Balboa Island. Unfortunately it only took two days to realize that it might not be so perfect after all, and getting my mind off boys might not be so easy, either.

On my second day, one of the most gorgeous men I have ever seen came in. Immature, boy-crazy teenager that I was, I literally could not keep from gawking at him. My timing also could not have been worse. I was carrying a crate of glasses and I tripped, sending glasses flying everywhere! The manager fired me on the spot, claiming that I had trouble focusing. In fact, I really had no problem at all focusing. The problem was what I was focusing on. I slunk out of there, embarrassed and mortified that I had lost my job after only two days; above all, that the hunky guy had witnessed the whole disaster!

The hunky guy turned out to be named Sam, and Sam felt so badly for me, that he asked me out for dinner. Sam was 6'2" with the most magnificent body, and a smile that just took my breath away. I stuttered and stammered until finally I was able to squeeze out a small "yes". Would my embarrassment over this man ever end?

Sam picked me up that night for our date. I had spent hours primping, and felt weak in the knees just hearing his knock at the door. He was even better looking than I remembered, and I felt like the luckiest girl in the world to be in the presence of this gorgeous man! It was very hard to contain my childish enthusiasm, and show him that I was a fully grown woman of the world. I'm sure I failed dismally.

At dinner I had no appetite, I could barely swallow. And speaking? That was out of the question! After dinner Sam invited me for a ride in his red Jaguar convertible. I should have wondered, why, since our conversation at dinner hadn't been exactly scintillating. But at the time I didn't care why. Although once he suggested driving out to Lover's Lane, I had

20

a pretty good idea why, I was still young and naïve, but I was starting to catch on.

Once we parked, Sam started kissing me, and it was beyond romantic. Out there in the wilderness, it seemed like we were the only two people in the world! I felt like I was in a fairy tale! But my fairy tale didn't last very long. His hands started to roam, and even though I was squealing with pleasure, I told him to stop; that kissing was as far as I was willing to go. He apparently wasn't interested in a night of nothing but kissing, and immediately started the engine and proceeded to take me home.

All the way home I was thinking, what have I done? I sat there wishing that I had never opened my big mouth. He dropped me off at home, thanked me for a nice evening, and off drove the most gorgeous man I had ever seen. Of course he made no mention of calling me again, and my teenage heart was crushed. I think this was when the realization came to me that the only way to keep a guy, was to give in to his desires. But then I remembered how Jim had dumped me so abruptly after I had given in to him. This was just all too confusing for a young girl to figure out!

About two weeks later Sam and I crossed paths again. I saw him leaving one of the local pubs and he approached me and asked if I would like to go listen to music at a club in Costa Mesa. I didn't hesitate to say yes, I felt so lucky to get a second chance with him! I jumped into his car so fast. I think he was looking around wondering where I went, there one second, in the car the next! Once on the road, I realized that Sam had had quite a bit to drink. At the club he continued to chug beer after beer, getting even more drunk by the minute. I was drinking cokes. No one even questioned my being there, even though I was underage.

After about two hours, we left the club and Sam assured me that he was okay to drive. He said that if I didn't trust him, I could drive. Little did he know that I was only 15, did not have a license, and had no idea how to drive a stick-shift. We took off and soon I noted the speedometer was up to 90 mph. I was holding on for dear life! I started panicking and yelling at him to slow down, but it was as if he never even heard me. It was about this time that I heard a siren, and saw the flashing lights of a police car behind us. I didn't think I would ever be so happy to see a policeman!

Sam could hardly stand up; much less pass a sobriety test. He was cuffed and off he went to jail. Even as he was stumbling and almost falling to the ground, he was apologizing, and I felt really badly for him, in spite of the danger he had put both of us in. I had to tell the officer the truth about my age when he asked me if I could drive Sam's car home. With tears gushing and lips quivering, I endured a very long lecture about the dangers of hanging out with an older man who would take me to a bar and endanger the lives of others by driving under the influence. I was sure that I, too, was going to be cuffed and hauled away to jail. But he took pity on me and drove me home, which was almost as scary as going to jail, because I would soon face the wrath of my mom!

My mom was not too happy to open the door and find her 15 year old daughter standing there with a police escort. Actually, "not too happy" is a huge understatement. On top of all that, the next day the police officer was sending a juvenile officer to our house to discuss the night's events. I think the officer sensed my fear of what my mom was going to do to me, because he proceeded to explain to her that I was an innocent victim, since I didn't know that I was being taken to a bar with someone who was going to get drunk. Poor judgment: yes, but he felt that I had learned my lesson and would never do something so foolish again. Those were well-meaning words, but he obviously didn't know me! During the entire encounter, I was a crying, trembling mess. But believe it or not, I still felt frustrated that I never got to make out with Sam that night!

I was obsessed with Sam, and I made a habit of watching for him at the local pubs. One night I spotted my friend Sharon's car out in front of one of Sam's favorite pubs. Sharon was a year older than me, and had her license. She would flaunt her independence; she could go wherever she wanted. Sharon was also very cute and had no trouble attracting the opposite sex. She was tall, slender, with long black hair and a great personality, and good looking men flocked to her, like iron filings to a magnet. I, on the other hand, was a little on the heavy side, with huge boobs, and I attracted a whole different element; translation: Losers.

I noticed Sharon was not alone in her car, and I knocked on her window. To my amazement I saw Sam sitting in the passenger seat with a puzzle of a U.S. map in his lap. She told me he was helping her with her geography class. My mind was reeling. All I could think, was: That BITCH! She knows how I feel about him! I wondered how long she had been pursuing this "friendship" with Sam; she knew that this was a cardinal sin in my book. I considered myself a pretty forgiving girl, but the one thing I could not forgive was a friend trying to steal my guy!

Sharon contacted me later that week and tried to convince me that they were just friends, and I had nothing to worry about. But I wasn't buying it. I felt betrayed by both of them, especially by her, because she was my close friend. I knew that men couldn't always be trusted, but I always thought that I could trust my friends! I told her that I wouldn't be hanging out with her anymore. I stuck to my guns for a few months before deciding to give her another chance. We reconnected and were back out on the town, wreaking havoc as only we could!

I later learned that one of my other high school friends, Abby, also had a fling with Sam, which she described as "pretty hot and heavy". He had abruptly stopped calling her and she was determined to find out why. I couldn't be mad at Abby, because she had no idea that I even knew Sam, let alone that I had gone out with him. But I was jealous that my "fling" with Sam had never progressed to the "hot and heavy" stage!

Abby asked me to go with her to Sam's mother's house to try and find out how she could reach Sam. Out of morbid curiosity, I agreed. When we arrived, Sam just happened to be there, and he was not at all happy to see the two of us. I can imagine what he was thinking, wondering if each of us knew about the other. He probably thought that we were there to gang up on him. But I just stood there speechless, while Abby read him the riot act. At the end of her tirade, he told us that he was getting married, and wouldn't be seeing anyone else anymore. Talk about having a bucket of cold ice thrown in your face! Obviously we meant nothing to him, because he had to have been in a serious relationship with his wife-to-be while he was enjoying his flings with us. On the way home, Abby asked me if I had dated Sam, because, she thought, he acted like he knew me. I told a semi-truth, that I had met him at the restaurant where I used to work and that was it. I didn't want to give her the satisfaction of knowing that she'd gotten much further with Sam than I had, because she was one of those girls who would go out with any guy, regardless of whom else they might be seeing. Even friendships didn't stand in her way.

I still felt like I needed answers from Sam. Why did he string me along, then dump me, and then have flings with two of my friends? I wanted him to know how much he had hurt me, and I wanted to know if he was really engaged, or was he just trying to get us out of his hair. But I didn't know how to find him. Fortunately, an opportunity presented itself to me when walking down the street, I saw Sam's Jaguar with the top down. I peeked inside and noticed a letter addressed to him at an address in Long Beach. I shouldn't have done it, but all self-control fled, and I reached in and grabbed that letter and ran!

I tracked down my friends Dodi and Karen and told them the whole story. They agreed to play detective with me and we headed off to the Long Beach address to investigate. Once there, the apartment was dark and it was obvious no one was home. We found an open window and jumped through, laughing the whole time, probably out of sheer terror of being caught! But it was also exciting, and gave us an intense adrenaline rush to be doing something so dangerous! We had a flashlight and started scoping out the apartment. We found women's clothing in the bedroom and cosmetic products all over the bathroom, confirming Sam's story that he was in a relationship with someone.

Suddenly we heard the door opening and then saw a light being turned on in the bedroom. At that moment I think we all might have peed a little in our pants! Somehow we managed to get out of the house undetected, and started running down the hill behind the apartment complex. Dodi slipped and went tumbling head over heels down the hill, and we just couldn't contain ourselves any longer! We started laughing so hard that Sam heard us and he started shouting that he was calling the cops! The word "cops" definitely lit a fire under us and you never saw three girls run so fast! We jumped into Dodi's car, still laughing hysterically, and peeled out of there. We got away without being caught. We probably should have gone to church the next day to give thanks, because we definitely had a Guardian Angel looking out for us that day!

Realizing Sam was living with another woman, and there would be no future for us, finally ended my obsession with him. As it turned out, it was a blessing. Shortly after our visit to his apartment, I picked up the local paper and there was a story about Sam. He had gotten drunk and gone over the edge, burning down the Orange Coast College Chapel! I never heard of, nor saw Sam again.

One of the teenage hotspots in the 50's was Merle's Drive-In. If you wanted to be one of the "in crowd", you had to hang out at Merle's! On any given night you could find Danny Flores parked there in his purple Oldsmobile. He was the king pin of cool. Being invited to sit in his car with him was not only the ultimate honor, but was also a big boost to your cool factor, and you could almost see the other girls turning green with envy.

I finally got my turn with the King of Cool! He sent one of his boys over to Sharon's car and Sharon and I both got a thrill when he said Danny wanted to see me, not Sharon. My greatest urge was to run like a shot over to him. Instead, I mustered every bit of self-control I had, and ambled slowly over to his car, making sure that all the other girls saw me, strutting like a peacock, and giving them a glance that said "look at me, eat your hearts out!"

He ordered French fries and cokes for us, never asking me what I wanted, which was standard procedure for a take charge kind of guy like him, something that I admired, back then. After we ate our fries, we started making out and managed to fog up the windows pretty quickly! I was hoping that no one could see us making out. While I liked them knowing that I was in the car with Danny, I preferred my make-out sessions to be private. After about an hour of hot and heavy smooching, I rejoined Sharon, and we headed home. I was definitely gloating, and tried not to give her too many details, because, as much as I hate to admit it, it felt good to see her jealous and dying of curiosity, for a change!

The next day at school, instead of seeing the expected looks of envy and words of congratulations for being "the chosen one", I heard people referring to me as cheap and a whore. I found out that the rumor was circulating that Danny had made it all the way to home base with me! I couldn't believe it, we were pretty much in plain view, and it would have been impossible for him to have scored with me. I was so stunned. I had never heard any of Danny's other girls being called such names. All I could think of was: why me? I was mortified, and Sharon became the gloater. That was the end of Merle's for me.

I was beginning to come to the conclusion that most men were egomaniacs with a scorecard to fill. I couldn't help but wonder why all the losers were attracted to me, and more importantly, why was I attracted to them?

One night when Sharon and I were out cruising, she decided that she was going looking for the Anesta twins, two very big and scary girls I didn't want on my bad side! Sharon wouldn't tell me why she was looking for them, but I told her to take me home if she was looking for trouble. I wanted no part of that! But she ignored me, and soon found the twins hanging out at a drive-in with about five other equally tough looking girls. One of those girls approached me and told me that Sharon was no friend of mine. She had told them all about my affair with Jim Bronius! I realized that it was true, because I had never confided that secret to anyone but Sharon. I couldn't believe that she had betrayed me again. And this time she didn't even bother to offer an explanation! I jumped out of her car, telling her that she was no longer my friend. One of the girls offered to drive me home, and we left.

The next day Sharon's brother called me and started screaming at me, basically blaming me for leaving Sharon alone, because some of the girls had followed her, pulled her over, and ripped off her clothes, even her Kotex, and threw them down a hill. Even though I was mad at her for spilling my secret, I still felt badly about it. No one deserved to be treated that way, and those girls were big and mean; she had to have been scared out of her mind! I asked to talk to her, but he told me to go to Hell and slammed the phone down.

In many ways, Sharon had charted her own course by going looking for them. For what reason, I still didn't know. Even after we made up a few years later, she never told me what she had done to incur their wrath. This event was a catalyst for me. I decided it was time to make some positive changes in my life. I joined the high school marching band and went back to hanging out at the roller skating rink; activities I thought would keep me out of trouble. But the best laid intentions can go amiss, and it wasn't long before I managed to find trouble, or you could say trouble found me.

So I set out on the road to turning my life around. No more scoundrels I told myself, no more bar hopping or boy-chasing, or breaking and entering, or being escorted home by the police, or hanging out with the wrong crowd, or pursuing men old enough to be my father, nope, it was time to stop the madness! There would be no more trouble of any kind for me. I was ready to walk that straight and narrow path! I really did have myself convinced, for a while.

So I returned to my old haunt, the local roller rink, where most of the good kids hung out. Strangely enough, the crowd hadn't changed much, and I was excited to reconnect with some of my old pals. As much as I hate to admit it, these pals were mostly boys, so I told myself: O.K., I can still be boy-crazy and walk the straight and narrow path. Again, I managed to convince myself, for a while.

Billy Maxwell was really cute, and full of mischief. He routinely tripped me while we were skate dancing, and while he claimed that it was his two left feet, I was pretty sure that he did it on purpose, so he could land on top of me! While I enjoyed the attention at first, after a while all the falling down and bruises pushed me on to what I hoped would be greener pastures.

Jimmy Thomas was the rink Casanova, and by now you know me pretty well: if there was a Casanova to be found within a 3 mile radius, I would find him! It was really odd, it just happened that way; I didn't even have to try. Jimmy was the king of the rink and all the girls followed him around like puppy dogs. I never dreamed that I would have a chance with him, because he was so handsome, and much older, and tended to go for the older girls. But again, you know me, when I set my sights on someone, I was relentless in my pursuit, and he was no exception! My pursuit was cut short by my complete and utter humiliation when an article was published in the skating rink newsletter, quoting me saying that if I had one wish, it would be to kiss Jimmy Thomas day and night! So my first try at walking the straight and narrow was not exactly a success story.

Next I decided I would concentrate my energies on music and go back to playing my old trumpet from grade school. I would have no time for trouble, I would be too busy practicing and playing and marching in the band, wouldn't I? Fate had other plans for me. I ended up getting stuck carrying a big old tuba in the marching band. That was just not the image I wanted to project. I didn't want to be known as a band geek. Plus, lugging around a tuba, or big bass drums, for five miles in the hot sun, turned out not to be so much fun. It didn't take long for me to figure out that this wasn't going to be my path to redemption after all. It was time I faced facts, I would never be happy, unless I just followed my heart and went wherever that took me.

I still couldn't get Steve, the saxophone player with the goatee, out of my mind. I had promised myself, that I would not return to the Rendezvous ballroom as long as Steve was still playing there, but breaking promises that I had pledged to myself was getting easier and easier as time went on. Even though I knew he was sexual dynamite and dangerous for me in every way, I couldn't help myself. Next thing you know, I found myself sitting right next to the stage, staring intently up at him as he played his saxophone. He finally looked my way and winked at me, and that's all it took to make me go weak in the knees! I just knew that this was the start of a great romance!

On his break, he approached me and asked where I had been. I rambled on about how busy I had been with my studies and my many social activities. Even though I was barely making it through school, I wanted to dazzle him with my intelligence and wit. Unfortunately, conversing with the next man of my dreams generally turned me into a rambling, dithering, incoherent mess. But I guess he was okay with a dithering mess, because he invited me out for coffee when he got off work.

Balboa is a small town; back in those days, all the locals knew each other. We went to a restaurant where my friend Karen's mom worked. I was hoping that she was gone for the day, because she usually worked the day shift. I was praying that I wouldn't run into anyone I knew, because I could visualize my mom barging in with that crazed look she got, and yanking me out by my hair, all the while yelling about me being a minor and Steve being a dirty old man. I really wasn't interested in being humiliated and being the talk of the town one more time! Karen's mom was working, but she turned out to be really cool, and actually spent some time chatting with us.

Steve and I really hit it off, and discovered that we had a shared love of music. He was such a gentleman that night, somewhat to my dismay, and I ended up with just a light goodnight kiss. He did say, though, that he was looking forward to seeing me again, and I went to bed dreaming about when that time would come.

It actually came sooner than I thought it would. The very next night after his show, he invited me to his apartment. And yes, I know what you're thinking, but I couldn't help myself, and off I went. I really was a good girl at heart and my intent was for our relationship to grow slowly, eventually leading to a physical relationship. But the best laid plans can go horribly wrong when dealing with a teen's raging hormones! And so our affair began that night, and lasted for several blissful months.

We became brazen in our relationship, and would even stroll down the streets in broad daylight. One day my friend Dodi ran up to us with a bible in her hand, telling us we were both going to burn in hell for having sex before marriage. She was screaming at Steve in full earshot of other people on the street, "How dare you defile my friend, you old bastard!" In my heart, deep down, I knew that what she was saying was true. Like I said, I really was a good girl at heart, and I didn't want to burn in eternity. So, even though it broke my heart, I ended our relationship.

Several weeks had passed, when I learned that the band was going on a world tour, and therefore I wouldn't have a chance to see Steve again for a very long time. I had felt sick the few weeks we'd been apart, and I just couldn't bear it any longer. One more time I went to hear him play, tears streaming down my face. We ended up at his apartment for the last time. Steve promised this would not be the end for us. Their tour wasn't starting for another month, and he had rented an apartment in Hollywood. He had lined up a gig to last until he left on tour, and he wanted me to be there with him.

As the time drew near for him to leave on the tour, he had one final Sunday jam session, and asked me to fill in for the female singer. Steve convinced me to audition, but when I arrived for the audition and envisioned myself on the big stage in front of all those people, I nearly fainted! I can't even call it stage fright, because I never even got near the stage! Backup singer: Yes; center stage spotlight: Not for me. I could tell Steve was disappointed when I told him that I couldn't go through with it, but I'm convinced that I made the right choice. I have no doubt that it would have been just one more humiliating experience on a list that seemed to be growing longer by the day.

Graduation time was nearing, and I was filled with excitement and happiness, happiness that high school was almost over, and excitement for what the future might bring! The last of my high school years had not been a particularly great time in my life. Once I became friends with Sharon, as mentioned before, Karen and Dodi would have little to do with me, and then when Sharon and I had our falling out, which was pretty ugly, I was out in the cold, feeling so much loss as to no longer have close relationships with my friends. I couldn't wait for the school days to end, so I could spend time with Steve before he left on his world tour. That was all that I could to look forward to.

On graduation day, when all the kids were partying and going out on the town, I was in Hollywood spending time with Steve at his new apartment.

This was the first time that I became aware of Steve's use of marijuana. Up until then he had kept it hidden from me; or maybe I just chose not to notice. I was very anti-drugs, and when I noticed the suspicious cigarettes in his ash tray, I told him how disappointed I was. This was a mood killer for sure, as much as he tried to cheer me up, I just couldn't snap out of my funk. For my graduation he gave me a copy of The Prophet, by Kahlil Gibran, which was considered a very cool gift at that time, but even that didn't help. I felt like this discovery was just a huge intrusion on what should have been my special night. To add insult to injury, he refused to take me out, insisting that we stay in and enjoy some "alone time". I did give Steve some credit for being protective of me. He never offered to share his marijuana with me, and he vehemently warned me never to try it myself! I couldn't help thinking how much more fun it might have been, had I gone out partying with the high school kids, especially with Leo, a guy in my art class. Yes, you guessed it, even though I was crazy about Steve, my eyes were already wandering!

Leo was much more mature than the other boys in high-school and easy on the eyes, too. We had a lot in common, and he especially loved to hear about my wild escapades! He was a little on the shy and quiet side. In a way, he was living vicariously through me, wishing he could be a little more free-spirited. He had hinted about taking me to the prom, and I secretly wanted to go, but being the mature woman about town, dating an older man who was also a jazz musician, I let him know that I was much too hip to hang out with high school kids. Too bad that I didn't follow my instincts this time, because he was an outstanding artist and went on to become very successful later in life. If I had only chosen him, my life path could have turned out quite differently.

Soon enough, I forgave Steve for not wining and dining me on grad night, and for using marijuana. The time had come for him to leave on tour, so the thought of not seeing him for a long time made all the bad stuff fly right out of my head. I felt that we had a true love connection, and I knew I was going to miss him terribly! As he traveled on his World tour he sent me letters from Europe and Asia. His favorite country was India. He loved the people and the culture, and the whole atmosphere of India. I found that a bit odd, since India was known to have a lot of poverty, and also their way of life was completely different from ours. But Steve was an artist, and as time went on, I learned that artists tend to view things very differently from the rest of us. Or could it have been the marijuana?

When Steve left on his world tour, I decided to go on a diet. I had lost 20 pounds and with my mom's encouragement and help she enrolled me in a modeling school. The loss of twenty pounds did make quite a difference and I was really excited about my new body. I couldn't wait for Steve to get back, and see the look of longing and admiration on his face when he saw the new me for the first time. But as things turned out, once the tour ended, Steve decided to stay in New York and start a new band, which he eventually did. He threw me what I considered a bone by telling me that I could come visit him after he got settled. I was pretty stunned, hurt and angry, after all of his letters expressing his desire to get back home and be with me. I hadn't yet learned that relationships traditionally take a back seat to a musician's art.

4   THE ROAD TO ANOREXIA

Michael Gerboni was the man who would change my life forever. He was an English professor at Long Beach State College. He was the epitome of the tall, dark, handsome Italian. And need I even say, he was much older than me. My first encounter with Michael was on the boat dock outside my house. He had just tied his sloop to the dock and was there to visit one of his neighbors. Within seconds of spotting me, he marched right up to me and said he wanted to get to know me if I was available. You can probably figure out what my answer was!

We started dating and I learned a lot from Michael, not just sexually but being a professor, he challenged me academically as well. He taught me about literature and the arts. I even read Oedipus Rex, never realizing such depravity existed before reading this book. He even got me to start Tolstoy's War and Peace, but it turned out to be a bigger investment of time and concentration than my teenage mind was ready for, so I never finished reading it; maybe someday.

The first night Michael and I spent together, we had wine by candlelight at his Corona del Mar cottage. He suggested we lie on the bed next to each other, without touching. He wanted to teach me about my sensuality, not just the physical act of having sex. As it turned out, I kind of ruined the whole sexual experience by promptly falling asleep, probably the effect of the wine. I woke up in the morning and my first thought wasn't about sex or Michael, it was about what terrible punishment my mom was going to inflict on me for staying out all night! Oddly enough, she went easy on me, and only grounded me for a week. Maybe she was starting to accept, that short of locking me in a windowless room, I wasn't going to be the perfect daughter every mother dreams of.

During the week I was grounded, Michael and I talked a lot on the phone, and continued to get to know each other on an emotional level. Our first date after my release was bicycle riding. I had been eagerly anticipating something much more romantic, like wine and candlelight, and sex! But he did surprise me with a very generous gift, a brand new racing bike. He was very athletic and conscious of his physical well-being, and he wanted me to make this a priority in my life also. He thought that if we exercised together, it would be more fun than working out. Unfortunately my first bike ride resulted in me wrapping myself and my new bike around a tree, painful and excruciatingly embarrassing! But to impress this man, I wouldn't give up! It took me a few more tries, but I did finally get the hang of it. Oh, the things I did for love and acceptance!

My next date with Michael was a day out on his boat. It was very luxurious, and sailing out to sea was oh! So romantic! Once we got back to dock, we popped open a bottle of champagne, and I decided to take the bull by the horns and let him know that I was ready to have a physical relationship with him. He didn't turn me down.

The first time with him absolutely took my breath away. It was everything and more than the stories I read about in True Romance magazine (how horrified Michael would have been to know that I read such trash. I kept that secret to myself). After a few glasses of bubbly, one thing led to another, and I experienced one of the most passionate nights of my life! He reminded me of one of those swashbuckling characters out of a Harlequin romance novel, and it was quite obvious that he was very experienced. I never wanted it to stop. I never wanted to go home! But way too soon, the rising Sun reared its unwelcome face, and once again I was thinking uh-oh, what's my mom going to do to me this time?

Chubby Days: Taken shortly before starting to diet

I was grounded for another week; I guess she wasn't quite ready to give up on me, and let me have free rein yet. But at least Michael and I got to talk on the phone, although he was reluctant to call me, because he was a little afraid of my feisty mother!

Michael and his ex-wife owned a modeling agency, and he encouraged me to lose a few more pounds, so that I could do a photo shoot for their agency. I was at 135 lbs., which I thought was a good weight for me, but he wanted me to get down to 120 lbs. as he thought that I would look better in photographs. He promised me that we could still go once a week to our favorite Mexican restaurant for cheese enchiladas, but the rest of the time I had to get serious about losing the weight.

Trimming Down

I was thrilled to think that I might become a model, and I was intensely determined to shed the weight to please him. Once I started dieting and began to lose weight, it became easier and easier. I learned that if I smoked cigarettes, drank a lot of coffee, and ate an occasional Hershey bar, I could lose weight very quickly. At that time, there was no negative stigma attached to smoking, in fact smoking not only helped me lose weight, but it also added to my cool factor.

During this time, I was working for Pacific Telephone in Orange. I had so much energy from the nicotine and caffeine that I outshone the other employees and was quickly promoted to a management position. I was very proud of my accomplishment, but Michael did not show much enthusiasm, nor give me encouragement. He thought that I was settling for mediocrity when I should be striving to challenge myself artistically and academically. But I needed a job; I never intended this to be my life-long career.

Michael decided to leave the teaching profession, because, in his words, he was tired of teaching idiots. He decided to study for the bar exam and enter criminal law. At the same time, he decided to move to Beverly Hills. I felt him pulling away from me. I couldn't understand why now, when everything had been going so great, or so I thought. Michael became critical of my appearance, telling me that I was becoming too thin to do fashion modeling. This really confused me because from the beginning he had stressed that thin was in, and encouraged me to lose weight. I was doing all of this for him! As it turned out, I never did appear in any of his fashion shows or photo shoots.

I started feeling strange, physically exhausted but still with so much nervous energy. People started expressing concern about my appearance and my health. By now I was down to 94 lbs. Looking back, that's borderline skeletal on a 5'9" frame! But I wasn't thinking rationally, I felt that as long as I could pinch a quarter of my skin, that was fat, and it had to go. I had become anorexic, but at that time anorexia wasn't a widely recognized illness, or even talked about, so I was clueless to the fact that I was actually suffering from an illness. I never found out about it until much later.

Anorexia days

I called Michael one day, and told him that I wasn't feeling well, and needed to see him. He said that he was busy with his studies, but would try to see me sometime soon. He also told me that I should stop dieting and start eating all the cheese enchiladas I wanted. I knew in my heart that this would be the last time I would ever hear from Michael. I felt devastated, I had done all of this for him, and now I was being unceremoniously dumped! I fell into a terrible slump, both mentally and physically.

I think now, that the reason Michael dumped me, was partly his guilt at having set me on this course of starvation and illness. It had to weigh on his mind as he watched me shrink to the point of becoming skeletal and to know that I was doing it for him. He did try to encourage me to stop dieting, but I wouldn't, and I couldn't, listen to any such advice because I was under the deadly spell of anorexia, an illness that not only causes weight to leave your body, but also causes all reason and common sense to leave your mind. You do not see what other people see when you look in the mirror.

I said that meeting Michael changed my life forever. That is an understatement. Becoming anorexic was the single most devastating event in my life, and it changed the course of my entire life. To this day, I still suffer the effects of this devastating illness.

5 MIXING WITH THE FAMOUS

Out of the blue, one day I got a phone call from my old friend Sharon. She said she missed me and called me "Booey", her nickname for me throughout our friendship. When I heard that term of endearment, I knew she was really ready to let bygones be bygones.

During our estrangement, Sharon had enjoyed great success in the music industry as a songwriter. I told her that I had been following her career and was very proud of her. We were both really excited to be talking again, and she invited me to meet some celebrities she had become acquainted with. Her call could not have come at a better time. This was exactly the medicine I needed to take my mind off my failed romances.

Sharon had written "Poor Little Fool" and she was determined that Ricky Nelson should be the artist recording her song. She was absolutely convinced that it would be a number one hit if she could persuade him to do it. Her determination paid off when one day she found Ricky at his parents' house playing volleyball and somehow got his agreement to do it; probably by hounding him mercilessly until he relented just to get rid of her. Sharon could be very persistent. This was one time her persistence paid off in a big way, just as she predicted; the song became a number one hit. Sharon was making so much money from royalties that she was able to purchase a beautiful Spanish style home in the Hollywood Hills.

A couple of days later, she called and said "get ready fast!" She was on her way to pick me up, and Ricky and David Nelson would be with her. She said Ricky would be driving and I could entertain David in the back seat. I didn't know what she meant by that.   My excitement sent me into a tailspin: What to wear? What to do with my hair? What to say so as not to sound stupid? Somehow I managed to put myself together but to say that I was nervous would be the understatement of the century! When they arrived, I was ready to hyperventilate! I opened the back door of Ricky's lowered and flame-painted Plymouth and sat next to David. Once seated, I started to calm down as both Ricky and David were down-to-earth, and genuinely friendly and welcoming, pretty much the same people you saw every day on the "Ozzie and Harriet Show".

Once we arrived in the city, Ricky suggested we should head out to Tiny Naylor's Drive-In. Sitting in the back seat with David, I was scared to even look at him. I didn't want him to think that I was staring at him like some star-struck teeny bopper! But boy, talk about temptation, that's all I wanted to do! I couldn't tell how he felt about riding in the back with me, because he was very quiet the whole time. It made me feel like maybe he didn't like me. Perhaps he was uncomfortable with the situation. Later I learned that he was that way by nature, just as he acted on their television show. I discovered then, that it was difficult to have a conversation with someone in the entertainment business if you weren't "one of them". There just didn't seem to be anything in common to talk about. I knew that my job at the telephone company wouldn't make the most titillating conversation. Not that anyone asked, anyway.

Once we got to the drive-in, the girls saw Ricky and started squealing. He was very gracious and signed autographs for them. I don't think they even noticed David in the back seat; all of their focus was on Ricky. I wonder how that made David feel. From his quiet demeanor there was no way of telling if he felt any jealousy. We ordered fries and cokes, just like all the "normal" people, but I was way too star struck to swallow a bite!

We cruised around afterwards, and Sharon and Ricky monopolized the conversation, talking business. I was actually quite grateful for their chattiness, because I had nothing to say that they would find the least bit interesting. The boys eventually dropped us off at Sharon's car, said it was nice to meet me, and we headed for home. My first encounter with celebrities was definitely not a glowing success, but that didn't stop me from being excited about the experience. I figured it was only my first time around a celebrity; I was bound to get better at it, right?

We went to Sharon's house, which was lavishly decorated with Italian furniture ordered from Europe. Although the evening had been exciting, it had also been emotionally draining, it can be quite nerve wracking to try and act mature and sophisticated and witty when you are really just a star struck tongue tied teenager! So I spent the night in Sharon's beautifully decorated guest room, falling asleep immediately, while thinking how I couldn't wait to go back to work and tell everyone about my big adventure. I knew the telling of the story would probably be more exciting than the actual event was.

The next morning Sharon told me we were going to meet the Everly Brothers at their home. I should have been a pro at this celebrity stuff by now, I thought, but nervousness struck immediately. I was very happy that Sharon was such a talker, because I could leave most of the conversation up to her. I figured, the less I said, the less chance that I would say something stupid. Sharon had known the brothers for some time, as they had attended several gigs together. She was also working on some songs that might have been of interest to them.

Their home was quite modest, for such big celebrities, and I wasn't sure if they both lived there, or what. They both were on the quiet side, although very polite; and of course: exceptionally handsome. Thank goodness Sharon kept the conversation going, otherwise there might have been that dreaded silence which I am always compelled to fill with useless prattling. We did not stay very long, and I was grateful when we left. At the time, I wondered: Are these people even happy? They seemed to be withdrawn and lacking any real joy. That was something I couldn't fathom, since being rich and famous was everyone's dream... wasn't it? Maybe the real reason was my being an outsider, which could have made them uncomfortable. We obviously had nothing in common, and I did not have any scintillating conversation to dazzle them with. Sharon was talking shop with the guys, and that suited me fine. I was anxious to leave, although grateful for the opportunity to meet Don and Phil. I know Sharon had a major crush on Don Everly. She was staking out that man in a most serious fashion. I'm sure this was the main reason for the visit! Eventually she got her wish, as they did become a serious item for a time. That girl definitely had a way with the guys, and they weren't just any guys; celebs were her forté.

I was still working my 9 to 5 job at the phone company while trying to decide what I wanted to be when I grew up. I felt my calling was to do something artistic, I just didn't know what exactly. The thought of modeling that was implanted in my mind by Michael was still there. I believed I had the perfect "Twiggy" figure, which was all the rage at the time. But I was still getting a lot of criticism about my appearance. Someone even went so far as to say I looked like a POW camp refugee!

I didn't take these criticisms very well, because as I said before, I didn't see what they saw when I looked in the mirror. I was very proud of all the weight I had lost and of the way I looked. I felt my appearance was one area in my life, over which I had total control, and I didn't want to lose that. Plus I felt that true love would no longer elude me, once I shed all those unwanted pounds. To someone who was always looking for love, this was enough incentive to keep me in weight loss mode forever. I felt such a "high" from what I thought was a huge accomplishment, going from an all-time high weight of 180 to 94 lbs. I didn't realize at the time that this was a not an emotional high, but a physical one: my nervous system was slowly starting to deteriorate because of my illness.

A very handsome Frenchman, whom I met through a friend, asked me out for a dinner date, affirming my opinion that I looked great in my new body. He was so sexy with a soft romantic voice, and I thought: uh oh, I'm in trouble... I know I'm going to fall in love; he's everything I look for in a man. Of course, I didn't even know him yet, so, obviously, it was his physical being that made me think that I could fall in love with him.

It was at this time that the realization struck me that I had a major character flaw; I was a very shallow person, something I wasn't proud of. I realized that I had always chosen my relationships based on appearance, never giving the less attractive guys a chance, probably causing me to miss out on some truly good men. I hoped I could change, but I wasn't terribly optimistic that I would be able to do it overnight.

After ordering our dinner, my handsome Frenchman spent half the evening lecturing me about my need to gain weight. He told me that I was beautiful, but I was ruining my looks by becoming too thin. He actually insisted that we would sit at the table until I finished my entire plate of spaghetti! I wanted to please him so I did try, but my stomach had shrunk so much that I was getting a heart burn and nausea. He asked me to put my hands in my lap when I was finished, telling me that they reminded him of a horror movie; they were so skeletal. I was crushed by his comments, and I thought that he was just being mean for some unknown reason. I did not believe that I was too skinny. He insisted he wasn't being mean; he was just trying to help me. After dinner, he gave me a hug and a sweet kiss and asked me to seriously think about what he said. In spite of our first date being somewhat of a disaster, I hoped I would hear from him again, but I never did.

My mom was constantly nagging me about my eating habits, as were all my family and friends. The one thing my mom knew I couldn't resist, was her homemade cheese sauce; so she made it for me quite often. And thank God she did. This was probably the one thing that saved my life.

I had stopped menstruating, and was scared that maybe I was pregnant. I had not been with anyone but Michael, and that had been over five months ago. My stomach was sunken in, my hip bones were protruding, so there were no outward signs of pregnancy, but I couldn't think of any other explanation. This is another symptom of anorexia, but I didn't know that at the time. I had never even heard of anorexia.

My old-time friends Dodi and Karen had re-united with me, which made me very happy. Karen had been my friend since we both were about five years old, and I thought the world of her. I had been so upset while she and Dodi stayed away from me, due to my relationships with others, but she and Dodi came through like the genuine friends that they were. Both the girls were worried about my appearance and tried their best to encourage me to eat, but it fell on deaf ears. I was at the point where I could hardly eat anything, even if I wanted to; because food upset my stomach so much. I still dreamt of the juicy hamburgers we used to get, visualizing the Thousand Island dressing running over the bun, with lots of cheddar cheese oozing from it. I really wanted to have just a few bites, yet I resisted the temptation. I feared that if I managed to get past the initial nausea, I would never be able to stop eating, and that wasn't a chance I was willing to take. I just learned to make the most of my few tablespoons of cheese sauce, and my Hershey bars, and the coffee, of course.

After high school, Karen, Dodi and I, all went our separate ways. I was heartbroken when Karen got married and moved away, north of Los Angeles. I just assumed that she would always be around. I really felt the huge loss. Karen's first marriage lasted only a few years. She had two daughters by her first marriage, which was the only redeeming feature of that relationship. She and her daughters ended up in Maryland, where she happened to meet the true love of her life, Emeric. This man worshiped her every move for thirty years, and took the best of care of her when she started having so many serious health problems. She passed away a couple of years ago and I know Emeric has never recovered from the loss of his Karen Sue. Karen and I had a life- long friendship; over sixty years. I miss her, too, knowing that she is no longer with us.

Dodi also got married, and even though she remained in the area, I rarely saw her. It seemed she had no time for her single friend, once she got married. Back then, I took it personally, and my feelings were hurt. Much later I realized that it wasn't that she no longer cared about me. Her priorities have changed. Dodi's and Karen's focus turned to their new husbands, and to their children, which is the way it should be. But for me, one who often walked a fine line between normal and abnormal, I valued my friends then and still do above all else, friends are a gift from God as far as I'm concerned, and I don't know what I would do without mine. The three of us did manage to get together from time to time, reminiscing about our wild antics, laughing and wondering how we survived, but we would never again experience the closeness we had in our childhood.

I tried occupying myself with my job, and working out. I became enthralled with yoga, which seemed to help ease my nervous spells. And I tried to walk several miles every evening. My nervous episodes were becoming more frequent and more pronounced, progressively getting worse no matter what I did. At the time I felt pretty lucky to have all that excess energy, little did I know what it would lead to.

About a month later, I got a call from Sharon. I was feeling lonely after what I perceived as my abandonment by Karen and Dodi, so I was very grateful to hear from her. The first words out of her mouth were "Prepare yourself, you are about to meet The King!" Hmmm, I thought, what king is she talking about, and what is she up to now? She told me that she was taking me to meet the one and only King, Elvis Presley himself!

At first, I think I was in a kind of shock, and it just didn't register. I mean, how could a poor little phone company toll sorter like me possibly be meeting the King of Rock and Roll, America's idol? He was staying in the penthouse of the Beverly Hilton Hotel, and she had arranged to take three of her girlfriends to spend the day with him. I was numb with fear. What would I wear? How would I do my hair? What would I say?

I ended up splurging on a pair of white sharkskin pants, the "in" thing at the time. And I couldn't possibly wear an old top and worn shoes with my new sharkskin pants, now, could I? So I splurged on those too. I probably spent a week's pay on my outfit, but I felt that I had no choice; this was The King, after all!

When I arrived at Sharon's house, she was busily primping. She had beautiful long black hair, and she had an annoying habit of constantly looking in the mirror and fluffing it. For some reason, when she did this, the expression on her face made me want to gag; it was so smug and self-appreciative. I suppose it was this confidence, which she wore proudly, that allowed her to become so successful in life. Maybe I was just jealous, because I so obviously lacked even an ounce of her self-esteem and confidence.

We picked up the other two girls, and headed out to Beverly Hills. Riding up in the elevator, I got a little dizzy from all the excitement, I suppose. I just couldn't imagine what to expect, or what I would say to the great Elvis Presley, without sounding like a swooning moron. Fortunately, when we first arrived, Elvis was still out riding his Harley, so we had time to relax and just hang out with some of his musicians. I was so nervous, I just grabbed the first seat I could find, which was on a long black leather couch. I was praying that Sharon or one of the girls would sit down beside me, but they were busy schmoozing with the musicians. I felt like I stood out like a sore thumb, sitting all by myself like some sort of leper. I was very uncomfortable, and I started to feel dizzy and nervous again.

After about fifteen minutes, the door swung open and in walked Elvis in all his glory, dressed in his leathers and looking every bit as handsome and sexy as I had imagined he would! He immediately sat down next to me, swung his legs over my lap, and said "Who might this be?" I could barely speak, but after an embarrassing bit of stuttering and stammering, I managed to finally tell him that I was Sharon's friend. This was the early sixties, when Elvis was in his prime.

I was extremely myopic, and could barely see my hand in front of my face without my glasses. I had to squint to see him, and between the stuttering and stammering and squinting, I'm sure he thought, he was fraternizing with some sort of nut case. Believe it or not, when he put his legs on my lap, all I could think was that he is going to get my new white pants dirty. Maybe I really was a bit of a nut case; I mean this was Elvis! Most girls would pray for Elvis' dirt on their pants, and would keep them forever as souvenirs! Maybe thinking of something seemingly rational and mundane, like is he going to get my new pants dirty, was my way of coping with a very stressful situation. This was the only other explanation besides being a crazy loon!

Sharon finally came over and formally introduced me to Elvis and to some of his friends. One of the girls, who came with us, had an on-again, off-again romance going with Elvis, and it was obviously an on-day, as they periodically disappeared into the bedroom. I was once again left sitting all alone on that big couch, feeling awkward, like a big lump, while the other girls kibitzed with the guys. My nervousness and fear of doing or saying something stupid kept me glued to my seat, probably looking even more stupid than anything I could have said!

After almost six hours of this, I thought I might go mad and leap out the window! But thankfully my life was saved when Elvis returned, and said that he would be sending out for pizzas. You would think that by now I had more embarrassing moments than any one person deserves. But no, there was more to come. Elvis announced to the room that he would be ordering a large pizza just for me, because "Girl, you be skinny, you're not leaving until you eat the whole thing; you need some meat on those bones". All eyes turned to stare at me, and if I could have fallen through a hole in the floor at that moment, I would have done it with a smile on my face!

After sitting for so long, my nerves were on high alert, and seeing those pizzas arrive didn't help! I knew that I would do my best to gag down some of it, because I would have done just about anything to avoid seeing Elvis and that room full of people looking at me again as though I were some sort of alien. I called upon every ounce of self-control I had not to gag as I sat looking at it. It had those hairy anchovies on it. Yuk! I mean, could this get any worse? I thought for a moment that maybe no one would notice if I ate or not. You've probably guessed by now, that this was not turning out to be my lucky day. I could see Elvis keeping his eye on me, so I tried to eat. He kept remarking that I wasn't making enough progress and I needed to eat more. After about an hour, I had managed to gag down a few slices, and I told him that I was full, and simply could not eat another bite, but in no way was I going to be a whiny little brat in front of him, so I pretended that I really appreciated his concern.

Elvis asked me where I worked. I told him, at PT&T. I had hoped to escape this question because people's eyes seemed to glaze over once they heard I worked for a phone company. I could see their eyes start to shift around the room, looking for someone more interesting to talk to. Elvis responded that he had never heard of that music label or music business. Obviously, he assumed that I must be somebody at least a little bit important in the music industry to be there. When I told him that it was a phone company, our conversation pretty much came to an abrupt end, as expected.

Elvis then stood up, grabbed his guitar, and told us he had just cut a new song, and wanted our opinion. Now this was exciting, and I immediately perked up. He started belting out "It's Now or Never" and was doing his gyrating thing, and it was one of the most memorable moments of my life. I'm still surprised to this day that I was able to keep from drooling all over myself or screaming out like a love-struck teenager. The song was spectacular, and we all agreed that it was going to be a major hit. To this day, every time I hear that song, I get a vivid image of that magical moment.

At last, the day came to a close. But now I could leave on a happy note, after watching him sing for us. He insisted that I must take the leftover pizza with me. Although I tried to decline, he insisted, telling me to "finish it off, you need it".

On the way home I was overcome by exhaustion, looking forward to crashing at Sharon's. But I still couldn't help thinking how exciting it was going to be to tell this story to my phone company co-workers. They would be so jealous! It isn't every day that someone like me gets the opportunity to rub elbows with the great Elvis Presley!

Still, there was no rest for me. That pizza did not stay with me, as I puked all night long. It had to be those hairy anchovies.

Thanks to Sharon, I have many fond, and some unusual, memories of celebrities, whom I would never have met on my own. Sometimes it really does pay to have friends in high places. What an exceptional few months it had been, meeting so many celebrities, especially Elvis. It's true what they say; there will never be another like him.

One day, while spending the weekend at Sharon's home in Hollywood Hills, I met her friend Will Hutchins. Will was best known for his portrayal of "Sugarfoot", a television series popular in the late 50's. We met him at a coffee house on Melrose Ave in Hollywood. The area was full of coffee houses frequented by the cool artsy people. When we exited the car, Sharon introduced us and he gave me a big bear hug and a kiss on the cheek. I tried to act cool, but inside I was swooning!

Once inside the coffee house, the female patrons recognized him and started shouting "Sugarfoot, Sugarfoot"! Before long, we were surrounded by girls asking for his autograph. He was so gracious and signed napkins and whatever else was offered to him. I could see them looking at Sharon and me, green with envy. I enjoyed every moment!

Will was one of my favorite celebrities. He was so unpretentious and had such a zest for life. I don't believe the man had a mean bone in his body, he just always appeared to be happy and enjoying whatever he was doing. Some of the other celebrities I met seemed to be dissatisfied with their lives, as though they were searching for something outside their grasp. My perceptions could have been wrong, but I felt a strong sense of loneliness in some of them. Maybe they had a difficult time developing and maintaining lasting relationships because of their celebrity, not knowing whom they could trust, or who cared for them, because of their fame or for who they really were.

Sharon had started dating a young handsome up-and-coming singer by the name of Eddie Cochran. He was best known for his hit "Summertime Blues", although he had other hits on the charts. He reminded me of Elvis. He had that sexy rebellious look that made girls go wild. Sharon told me that Eddie was the love of her life, and he was going to be her husband, no one could stand in her way!

Sharon invited me to a big rock and roll concert at the El Monte Legion Stadium. Eddie would be performing, so we would get backstage passes. I wasn't a huge rock and roll fan at the time but in no way was I going to pass up an opportunity like this. Plus, who knew what other handsome men might also be lurking backstage!

The night of the concert, Sharon and Eddie picked me up in a beautiful stretch limo. I had never been in a limo before, and I felt like Cinderella. We toasted with champagne. I thought I could really get used to living the good life!

At the concert, we went in through the performer's entrance. I wasn't about to wear my glasses, you know, just in case my Mr. Wonderful was lurking nearby, so I missed a lot. But I stood next to the curtain the whole night, and took in all the raw energy and excitement swirling around me. It was an incredible experience. Watching everything come together was quite an education, at least what little I could see of it.

After the concert, Sharon told me that she and Eddie had something they had to do, and she had made arrangements for Eddie's manager to take me home. I was uncomfortable at first, not to mention a bit disappointed not to be going home in the limo, but his manager turned out to be quite entertaining and likable. He wanted me to hop in his boat for a ride to Catalina, and under normal circumstances, I might have been persuaded. I always had a hard time passing up an opportunity for adventure. But I wasn't feeling very well, and I knew my mother and grandma would kill me if I hopped on a boat and took off with a stranger in the middle of the night. So he drove me home and that was the end of a very memorable evening.

In April of 1960, Sharon went on tour with Eddie and Gene Vincent. The three of them were on their way home when they got in to a deadly car crash. Their hired driver crashed at high speed, killing Eddie and seriously injuring Sharon and Gene. Sharon spent several months in a hospital in Bath, England, and endured several complex surgeries. She wrote me heart-wrenching letters describing how destroyed she was over Eddie's death. She said she would never recover, and she never did.

Sharon had invited me to go on the tour with them but at the time I had suffered my breakdown, and was too ill to travel. I will always wonder what my fate would have been had I gone with them.

Once Sharon returned to the states, she hit the booze hard, and was never the same again. It was difficult for me to be around her, her entire personality changed when she drank, she wasn't what one might call a "nice drunk". I always walked on eggshells around her, afraid I would say something that would upset her or set her off, and I didn't want to add to her misery.

Sharon eventually picked up the pieces of her life after a long period of time, and married a popular radio disc jockey by the name of Jimmy O'Neill. Jimmy was a nice man, and from the outside, they appeared to be happy enough. But I knew the truth; that she was still shattered inside. Poor Jimmy probably never really stood a chance, and before long, they were divorced.

She began another relationship and had a son. I never met either of them, and never even saw a picture of her son, although I was always bugging her to send me one. The last time I saw her, my friend Debbie and I met her at a restaurant in Newport Beach. It had been a long time since I had seen her, but not much had changed; she proceeded to get smashed. We tried to discourage her from driving in that condition, but as drunks too often do, she insisted that she was okay, and off she went. She had a guardian angel that night, because she managed to make it to one of her places in Newport Beach without hurting herself or someone else. I wish I had known at the time that this would be the last time I ever saw her.

We drifted apart after that event. I was uncomfortable with her heavy drinking, and we just didn't seem to have anything in common anymore. She chose to live her life on the edge, always unpredictable, and that wasn't me.

Sharon passed away several years ago, in her early 60's. I'm not sure what the actual cause was, but it wouldn't surprise me if it could be attributed to her broken heart, and years of alcoholism. I often wonder if things would have been different if I had been more supportive, if I could have helped her overcome her alcohol addiction. But unfortunately I had my own health issues to deal with during those years, so I was in no physical or emotional position to be of help to anyone else.

It was approximately three to four weeks after my incredible meeting with Elvis when my world came crashing down and my life as I knew it would never be the same. One night after a five mile walk, I started feeling very strange. I was hot and sweaty and was preparing to take a shower when I looked in the mirror and couldn't see my reflection! When I finally focused enough to see something, it looked as though my eyes were melting down my face and my mouth was melting down my neck. My head was distorted and misshapen, I felt like I was watching a horror film with me as the star! And I couldn't breathe or speak for what seemed like an eternity.

I vaguely remember trying to shout "I don't want to die, please God, don't let me die!" I felt as though I was no longer a part of my body, even though I could feel my lips moving and I could hear myself babbling incoherently. I think I was fading in and out of consciousness and there are no words to describe the fear and helplessness I felt. It would have been a blessing just to lose complete consciousness, rather than trying to comprehend what was happening to me. My heart was pounding, my body was shaking, but I felt numb at the same time. At that moment I knew I was on the brink of death.

My grandmother and youngest brother were home at the time. Once I was finally able to get their attention, the fear on their faces sent me in to even more of a panic. My grandma started trembling and turned deathly white and I was sure I was going to cause her to have a heart attack. My mother was on vacation and all I can say is thank God my brother was home on leave from the military. I could tell he was scared but he took charge, called an ambulance for me, and tried to calm my grandma.

Thankfully it didn't take long for the ambulance to get there, and they took me to the nearest hospital. I had never been in an ambulance before, and the blaring sirens and paramedics hovering over me only made me feel more scared. I could see their lips moving but couldn't comprehend what they were saying, but I could tell by the looks on their faces that it wasn't good. I started hallucinating and believed that they were taking me somewhere to die.

When I arrived at Hoag Hospital, I could see the emergency room doctors and nurses sharing puzzled looks. It was as though they couldn't figure out what was wrong with me. At the time of my collapse, anorexia was still a relatively unknown disease and they had no idea what had put me in this state. They prescribed sedatives for me and gave me a shot large enough to knock out an elephant. They told me to make an appointment with my regular doctor the next day, and sent me home.

The next morning I woke up, and my initial thought was wow, what a terrible nightmare I had last night! But when I tried to get out of bed, I realized that it had been all too real. I could hardly move, and started shaking violently. I was struck by a feeling of impending doom, which started me crying uncontrollably. I didn't know what was happening to me, I had never experienced anything remotely close to this; physically or emotionally. I wondered if I was going to die. I wondered why they couldn't help me more in the hospital. How long would this last? Would I ever get better?

I was finally able to get up enough strength to crawl down the stairs, although I felt like I was going to faint and throw up at the same time. I couldn't shake the veil of doom hanging over me and the tears started again, I just couldn't control it.

My brother laid me down on the couch and brought me some food. I managed to take a couple of bites between the uncontrollable crying. I was so depressed, that I just wanted to close my eyes and go to sleep in hopes that when I woke up, I would be back to normal.

I remember sitting on the beach in front of our apartment that morning, and not even being able to brush my own hair. My grandmother had to brush my hair and wash my face. And even as gentle as she tried to be, every part of my skin ached, almost as if the outer layers no longer existed. I cried every time she touched me, and pretty much every time I moved, there was just no comfortable position I could get in, lying down, sitting, standing. It all brought me to tears. I thought maybe I was losing my mind. I couldn't get a grip on reality, and felt like I was living in a state of hell. To this day I can't even find the words to express the anguish and pain I experienced, both physically and mentally.

Later, when I learned that I was suffering from anorexia, I made it my mission to find out as much about it as possible. At first I didn't believe that I could possibly be anorexic,

60

because I was just dieting, and I ate enough cheese sauce and chocolate bars to keep me filled up. I thought if I was eating, and I felt full, how could I possibly be starving? Wouldn't someone, who was starving, feel hungry? What I didn't realize was how little it took to fill me up, because my stomach had shrunk so much. It took a while for me to accept that I had done this to myself, all in the name of vanity and the hope that being thin would lead to the ever-elusive love I was searching for.

My mom returned from her vacation. Although she expected some fall-out from what I had been doing to my body, she was not prepared for what she found. But being the feisty strong woman that she was, she took charge and told me that I would start eating again, because eating and putting on weight was the only thing that could save my life. I could not have survived this time in my life, if not for my mother. I would awaken throughout the night shaking violently and crying hysterically. She would try and shock me out of these episodes by immersing my feet in freezing cold water and then very hot water. This seemed to help a little. My sheets were soaked with sweat every night, so she had to change them every single day. She coaxed me into eating, and would prepare special meals that at least sounded like something I might be able to gag down. I could still only take small bites and eat very small portions, because of the discomfort and nausea. Eating always resulted in stomach cramps and digestive problems, but my mother forced me to take these baby steps, she was determined to save me whether I wanted to cooperate or not.

My mom insisted that I go to the town physician, Dr. Monaco. He was a kind, charming man, and I had complete faith in him. When he saw me, he couldn't hide the look of shock on his face. He gave me his one and only lecture. He told me that he couldn't understand why a beautiful young girl would do such a terrible thing to her body. Keeping in mind that anorexia wasn't on the radar at that time, he took the best course of action he could, under the circumstances. He started me on a regimen of vitamins and a healthy diet. He administered B-12 shots and gave me insulin every day, and prescribed tranquilizers to help me get some much needed rest. I eventually became addicted to the tranquilizers, but I didn't care at the time. They were my escape from my horrible existence.

We didn't have money to pay Dr. Monaco for all these treatments. Being the kind man that he was, he only charged us $5 per day, telling us that when I was better I could work for him a couple of hours a week to cover the costs. He didn't think I would be ready to go back to work full-time for a long time, and suggested that I go on disability. Eventually I did help him out in his office, when the disability checks stopped.

I was still taking tranquilizers and wished I could get off them, because I was in a constant state of fatigue. I attempted to stop taking them for one day. The result was a panic attack. Dr. Monaco explained that I couldn't just stop cold turkey, and he felt that I still needed them in order to function.

Dr. Monaco told me that I had damaged the tissues that support the nerves in my body by starving them. Without the protection of these nerve cushions, he said, I could expect the continuation of the spells I was suffering through, the uncontrollable crying, the violent shaking, the feelings of despair and hopelessness. He thought it would be a long time before I would start to feel even a little normal again, but he couldn't predict for sure what was ahead for me. This was not very reassuring news. But he did tell me, that with hard work and determination, I could make progress. Now, when I didn't think I could sink any further, this sent me into an even deeper slump. My feelings of despair and hopelessness haunted me every waking moment. My only peace and solace was taking the tranquilizers and getting some blissful sleep.

I had also stopped menstruating, which I later learned was also caused by the anorexia. It was two years before I started menstruating again. My anxiety and depression and mood swings were partly caused by my hormones being out of control.

I tried to get some exercise by walking, but my equilibrium was completely screwed up. When I looked down, it felt like the floor was coming up and was going to hit me in the face. At other times I felt like I was on a roller coaster and was going to lose my balance. I grew afraid to go anywhere by myself, because I had the constant sensation of blacking out and melting away. I did fall a couple of times, but, thank God, I didn't break anything. It was so frightening to have lost control over my sensations, and I living in a constant state of terror, thinking I was always on the brink of death. When I woke up every morning, I was simply grateful and amazed to be alive, but dreaded facing another day of this madness.

I prayed constantly that I would recover and be able to go back to my new job, for which I had worked so hard. I tried to go to work a couple of times, but I started experiencing black-outs while driving. Fortunately I could tell when I was going to black-out, because I would see black wiggly things in my eyes, my ears would start ringing, and my lips would go numb. I was able to pull off the road until it passed and I got a grip on myself again. But as much as I wanted to return to work, my fear that one day I might not be able to pull over fast enough and I might hurt someone, led me to give up on driving alone.

My mother came to my rescue again. She was my security blanket, and when she was with me in the car, I felt a lot more confident and thought that I could drive without getting anxiety attacks. She offered to ride with me to my workplace in Orange. This was very brave of her, because she didn't know how to drive, and if anything happened, we would both be in trouble. After getting me safely to work, she would ride the bus all the way back to Balboa, and then she would ride the bus back to Orange again, in time to ride home with me when I got off work. This had to be grueling for her, but she never complained. We weren't able to do this for very long, though, because I just didn't have the strength to continue working. I made arrangements with my supervisor to hold my position open for me, although she couldn't promise how long she would be able to do that.

My supervisor (her name was Norma also) would stop by the house periodically to check on my progress. In my crazy way of thinking at the time, I thought that she would be kinder and more understanding since we shared the first name. This was not the case. With each visit she would tell me that she didn't think she could hold my position much longer. Her presence made me so nervous and apprehensive, that I would suffer a full blown panic attack the moment she left. The day did finally come when she came by to tell me that she had to give my position to another employee. This catapulted me into a deep depression, I felt like a failure, worthless. It's probably hard to imagine why hanging on to my job at the phone company meant so much to me, but to me it was my lifeline to a normal life. Losing that lifeline caused me to feel that maybe dying would be better than the life I was living. I know that's a contradiction to my feelings of wanting to hold on to life and being grateful for every day I woke up, but that was my life, a never-ending emotional roller coaster of contradictions.

As time went by, instead of getting better, things actually got worse. I started suffering from Agoraphobia, which is "fear of the open marketplace." In my case, it meant that I couldn't go anywhere I didn't feel protected. Open spaces made me dizzy and I would have panic attacks, hyperventilating uncontrollably. The feeling of not being able to catch my breath was horrifying. Every time it happened, I was sure that I was going to die. Between the anorexia and the agoraphobia, I became so weak that I ended up in bed for almost an entire year, and then, for another year, I was too fearful to even leave the house. The only time I dared to venture out, was to go to the doctor to get my shots, and only because I had to, and I could only manage it if my mother was by my side. She sacrificed a lot to see me through these dark days. She was my angel on earth. I thank God every day for her strength, love, and devotion, because if not for her, there's no doubt in my mind that I would not have survived.

I don't think that anyone who hasn't suffered from anorexia could fully understand the effects of this devastating disease. My words on these pages do not do justice to the actual and very real horror of this illness. And even once you are pronounced "cured", you're actually never really rid of the lasting effects of this debilitating disease. Many of the effects of this illness follow you for the rest of your life, altering the course of your life forever. I will explain more about how my life was drastically altered and irreparably damaged, it literally rocked my world.

During my long months of recuperation, my brother Stan would come home periodically from Vandenberg Air Force Base to try and cheer me up. He would go to all the local banks and purchase pennies and then we would set about going through each and every one, searching for collectibles. Every now and then we would discover a valuable one, and then he would sell it and purchase more pennies. It was entertainment and a diversion for me, which I needed badly, being confined to the house for so long. At times it wore me out, and I would get really stressed, but overall it was good for me; it took my mind off my troubles.

On one trip home, Stan brought a friend from the Base, to stay with us for the weekend. Henry was a tall handsome freckled faced man, with kind eyes and a warm smile. I liked him instantly, and sensed that he was a caring person, just the kind of man I needed to lift my spirits.

I had more fun that weekend than I had in the past two years. I still couldn't do very much physically, but I was able to sit on the beach in front of our apartment and enjoy the fresh salt air. Henry had a wonderful sense of humor, and he would sit with me and regale me with stories about their antics on the base. I felt very sad when he and Stan had to leave. For a short time, I had been lifted out of my morose mood and had actually enjoyed myself. Prior to their visit, I wasn't sure I would ever be able to do that again.

I wrote my brother several letters encouraging him to bring Henry back for a visit. The following month they both showed up, and my mood took an instant upswing once more. It was around the Christmas holidays, and there was mistletoe hanging in the doorways, and I had a pretty good idea whom I was going to discreetly steer towards those doorways! I had to be careful, though, for a couple of times I got so excited that I felt I was on the verge of having a panic attack, and I was fearful that a panic attack would be just the thing to send Henry heading for the hills.

66

Henry gave me a Revlon nail care kit for Christmas. It was full of beautiful nail polishes, a feminine gift, which made me feel as though Henry was looking at me as a woman, and not just as Stan's sister. I kept this kit for many years, and each time I would see it, I would wonder about what might have been, had Henry and I had the opportunity to develop a relationship. I felt badly for not having gifts for anyone, but I had not progressed enough physically to be able to go shopping. If only they would have had online shopping in those days! I told Henry how badly I felt, and vowed to make it up to him the following Christmas. He responded with a wide grin and a wink, a sign that he just might be around next Christmas. I felt elated. The next day one of my visiting relatives waited for Henry to leave the room, and then she winked at me and said "I'd set my cap for that one". At that moment I made up my mind, that I will do exactly that!

Unfortunately, outside forces were at work to prevent this from happening, specifically my brother Stan. When Henry stopped coming with Stan, I discovered that Stan had warned him about getting involved with me. Stan admitted to me that he had told him that I was too screwed up, and that he should be dating a wholesome "girl next door" type. I wouldn't have thought that Henry would be discouraged so easily, but who knows exactly what my brother said to him. The truth was, I did have more than my fair share of problems, but Stan ought to have trusted in Henry's judgment, letting him make that decision without his negative influence. He should have let things take their natural course, whatever that might have turned out to be. Between my brother selling me out, and no longer having Henry in my life, I felt myself going into a downward spiral once again.

Brothers are known for doing not so nice things to their sisters at times. Stan was no exception. One moment he could be very kind hearted, and the next he could turn to torturing me with a smile on his face. When I was so sick in bed and couldn't escape, he would recite Edgar Allen Poe's "The Raven" to me, which pushed me to the brink of insanity. One of his favorite pastimes was to curl his hand up like a spider, hang it over my head, and tell me horror stories. He would get very graphic about how the spider was going to enter my body and destroy it ever so slowly. I know in re-telling this story, it sounds silly. But you have to remember the emotional and physical state that I was in at the time. I was constantly on the verge of a breakdown and it didn't take much to push me ever closer to that precipice. I finally had to beg my mother to make him stop, and he would, but not for long.

I forgave my brother for destroying my relationship with Henry before it blossomed, because he was my brother, and I loved him in spite of his actions. But obviously, since I'm telling this story now, I never forgot it. Today he and I enjoy our phone conversations. We get carried away talking about religion and politics; two of my favorite subjects! He still enjoys telling me horror stories that he has read or heard about, which usually involves grisly murders and gory insects; creepy crawler types. Some brothers just can't resist tormenting their sisters regardless of how old they are!

I don't know how my mother gathered the courage to approach her boss about my illness, but she did. He was a big Hollywood agent and I would have thought he would have no interest in an employee's problems, but surprisingly, he was sympathetic and scheduled an appointment for me with his doctor at the Scripps Clinic in La Jolla, CA. He also told my mom that most of my expenses would be covered, so any expense we incurred would be minimal. This was truly a blessing, as I knew that my mother was very worried about how she would pay for my medical expenses.

We checked into a motel close to the clinic. Once at Scripps, I met with the doctor who would be running a series of tests on me. The testing lasted for two entire days. Upon the conclusion of all the tests he informed us that I had starved the cushions that protect my nervous system. A full recovery is not possible. This was also exactly what my hometown doctor had told me earlier! He found that there is a substantial loss of bone mass, also not fully recoverable. There were also some other minor problems of lesser concern. The only positive note was that with proper diet, he felt that I would start menstruating again. He prescribed more tranquillizers, warning me to only use them when needed. Unfortunately I felt I needed them quite often! I became addicted, living in fear that one day the doctors would take them away from me. I believed the tranquillizers were the only thing that kept me functioning.

6 SEATTLE WORLD'S FAIR

As time went by, I did become stronger and began to feel that maybe a change of scenery would lift my spirits. My brother had expressed interest in going to the World's Fair in Seattle. I asked him if we could go together on a cruise to the fair, believing that a relaxing cruise would be just what the doctor ordered. I expected that he would balk at the idea, but he surprised me by agreeing to do it. Was it guilt over the Henry fiasco? Perhaps... I'll never know.

We contacted a travel agent and learned that there was a ship that was a floating hotel, and it went not only to Seattle but also Victoria, British Columbia. The ship, The Yarmouth, would depart from San Francisco Harbor for a 10 day excursion. The price was within our budget, so I booked an outside cabin for us and eagerly awaited departure day.

I visualized a beautiful ship with a swimming pool, a gorgeous ballroom, and all the other amenities that you normally find on a cruise ship. The pamphlet provided by the travel agent depicted a first class ship with all these things and more! I packed plenty of casual and dressy clothes into five large suitcases. I was prepared for any occasion, plus there was always a chance that I would meet a handsome stranger and start a shipboard romance. I had to be ready.

We had to fly to San Francisco on a prop plane from L.A. International and it was quite a hassle with the six pieces of luggage I had to schlep around, with my brother's help. My brother was the typical guy, packing just one suitcase with the bare essentials. Back in the early sixties there weren't many jets available, and we ended up flying over the ocean in an old clunker that kept me on the verge of panic for the entire trip. As much as I loved the ocean, looking at it from that vantage point was not my cup of tea.

We survived the flight, arriving in one piece, eager to board our luxury liner. To say that we were in for a shock is a gross understatement! I use the term "ship" loosely, because what we boarded was more like a giant rusty tub, flying a Cuban flag! This was not long after the Bay of Pigs Fiasco. We were reluctant to even board, but we still had hope that once inside, conditions would improve. And the money was already in the hands of the travel agency, so on we marched like the good little soldiers we were.

Once on board, all our hopes were dashed. The "state of the art" swimming pool described in the brochure was rusted out and cordoned off by ropes. Even if it had been in working order, it was the size of a foot bath, and probably would have fit no more than three people at a time. We proceeded to our cabin, still trying desperately to hold on to a glimmer of hope that all was not lost. But our room was the size of a closet, not an outside cabin. Once the luggage arrived, we could barely turn around in it.

We looked at each other and said almost simultaneously: "We're not doing this!" We tried to find someone in charge, but most of the crew did not speak English. Panic started to set in, and we started raising our voices almost to the point of screaming, demanding to speak to someone who speaks English.

I'm afraid, good troopers that we were before, we now had been turned into raging demons. We finally found someone who could speak limited English. We unloaded our numerous complaints on him. We explained that I had been ill, and the stress of this situation might bring on a full scale breakdown.

We asked for our money back, since it would have been obvious, even to a blind person, that this ship was not the same ship as the one pictured in the brochure. He went and located his superior officer, and we had to explain to him everything all over again. We did not have much time left, as the ship was almost ready to sail.

At last, when all was said and done, the officer informed us that we could disembark, but we would be charged a fee. We told him it had better be a small fee, or we could sue, because they misrepresented the ship to the travel agent, and in their brochure which they provided to the agency. No comment was made to that remark. Surprisingly, he just looked at us and told us we'd better hurry if we wanted to get off the boat, because it was preparing to sail.

We hustled to our cabin and collected our luggage, my brother cussing me the entire time for bringing so much stuff. We managed to get off the ship within 15 minutes of departure. We were relieved and just stood there staring at each other, collecting ourselves for a few minutes, pondering what our next step would be. We didn't have much money to our names, most of it being spent on the cruise beforehand.

We called our mom and asked if she could wire some money to us. In spite of our fiasco, we still wanted to go to the fair. One more time, she came through for us, wiring enough cash to send us off and running again.

We made airline reservations for the following day to fly into Vancouver, B.C. My brother convinced me to ship half of my luggage home, because we wouldn't be able to lug around all of it. So after all my careful shopping, planning and packing, I ended up with just two suitcases to last the entire trip.

We found a hotel to stay in for the night. I was unhappy with the arrangement. Our room was on the 22nd floor, and this instilled an uncontrollable fear in me, another result of my illness. I think my brother had enough of me for the day; he had little sympathy for my plight, telling me to just toughen up. Stan ended up going out sightseeing that evening, while I stayed behind. I didn't want to go up and down in an elevator and be reminded how high up I was. I tried to sleep and forget how high up this room was, but sleep never came. Finally at around 3 AM, I woke up my brother, and told him that I could no longer stay in the room. We had to get to a lower level or I was going to have a full blown breakdown.

I called the front desk and explained my dilemma. They had one left on the fifth floor and I told them that we would take it. We were so exhausted, we didn't even get dressed for the move, we just traveled the elevator and halls in our pajamas, looking like a couple of bag people. The fifth floor was better, but I was still feeling a bit traumatized, so I took a couple of my tranquillizers and passed out.

When we picked up our tickets at the airport the next morning, we were cautioned that finding accommodations at this late date would be most difficult due to the fair crowds. We foolishly ignored this wise advice and pushed onward.

We ended up on a small prop plane again, and had to make four or five stops along the way. Each time we went up and each time we went down, my nerves jumped in sync. One of the passengers had apparently consumed too much of a mind-altering substance, because he jumped out of his seat and started mumbling incoherently about how we were going to crash and die. I actually found his antics took my mind off the bumpy flight for a short while; at this point any kind of distraction was welcome.

The pilot took charge, and forced the guy to sit down and be quiet, but once this happened, my mind started running rampant again. I ordered a drink so I could swallow my tranquilizer and attempt to calm down, but my mind started running rampant again. I started feeling suspicious of other passengers; one in particular. This one man was wearing a trench coat and sat tightly holding a black valise in his lap, never letting it out of his grasp, even when he went to the bathroom. I was sure it was a bomb, and maybe that was what the other man had been trying to warn us about with his ramblings. I drove my brother nuts with my conspiracy theories, until the villainous appearing man got off at the third stop, leaving the plane intact. But as each new passenger boarded, I checked them out thoroughly, until I was sure that none of them were mad bombers, or villains, as we called the bad guys in those days.

After enduring such a long and bumpy flight, our final descent and touchdown was once more white knuckle time. We weren't too sure that we were going to make it, as we were bouncing and skidding several times on the runway while the pilot was trying to get the wheels to stay on the ground. Once we made it, and finally got off that plane, I felt an overwhelming urge to throw myself on the ground and kiss it. But I didn't dare to give into it, as my brother surely would have pounded me through the pavement.

We stopped for dinner in Vancouver at a restaurant on the 10th floor. I wasn't thrilled with being so high up, but we were famished, and my brother was still a bit on the testy side, so I didn't dare complain. This was his choice, so I endured the altitude and must concede, that the view was awesome. Being so far north, there was daylight until 10pm. I just sat there, wishing that we had opted for a cruise to Alaska.

Finishing our dinner, we hailed a cab and went in search of a room. Our cabbie was not encouraging, and seconded our previous warning that most rooms had been booked months in advance, in anticipation of the crowds due to the fair.

After about an hour we stumbled upon a room for rent in a not so desirable part of town. The cabbie waited while we went in to check it out. A frumpy old guy, with a tobacco stained T-shirt and tobacco drool running out of the sides of his mouth, answered the door. So far, I was less than impressed, but we were feeling desperate, so we asked to see the room. I had barely set foot inside when a mouse ran right over my foot! I let out a scream and ran for the door, there was no need for my brother to ask me if I wanted to stay, I think he got the message loud and clear! I have always been a lover of most creatures, but there are some I love from a distance; I don't particularly want to sleep with them.

We continued driving around the city and started feeling rather hopeless, thinking we might be spending the night on a park bench. The cabbie took pity on us and offered to call a friend of his who worked at one of the older hotels in the city. When I say he took pity on us, one has to wonder why he didn't take pity sooner and call his friend. But he had two tourists at his mercy, and a guaranteed fare for the night, so I think he waited until he was either tired of our whining, or for his shift to end.

His friend told him, there had been a few cancellations at one of the older hotels, and if we hurried, we might get one of them. It was 2 AM, and after hours of riding around in the cab, we started to feel a slight glimmer of hope once again.

For the first time on this fateful trip, we had some luck, and got a room; it even had two double beds. I was weary of crashing on a single bed; not enough room to toss and turn. The room was on a lower level, which made me very happy. It appeared to be neat and clean. We were totally exhausted, and got ready for bed so fast, as if the Tasmanian Devil had invaded our room!

Shortly after falling asleep, I was awakened by an intense itching all over my body. I turned on the lights and saw what appeared to be bed bugs all over the sheets! My screaming startled my brother right out of his deep slumber. He was none too happy, similar to a grizzly bear being roused from its hibernation! But I could not stay in that bed under any circumstances. The only other option was the bath tub; there was no sofa and no other solution to my dilemma. The hard porcelain wasn't very conducive to a night's rest, and I tossed and turned fitfully all the night through.

The next morning I was exhausted and feeling wretched as we packed up and headed for Victoria. Once we arrived, it looked like paradise compared to what we had experienced so far. There was a beautiful bed and breakfast inn, where we were able to get a really nice room. I literally thanked God for getting us to this paradise.

The proprietor of the inn suggested that we contact his travel agent the next day and take a guided excursion, because there was too much to see on our own. We had a fantastic dinner at one of the local restaurants. We finally got a good night's sleep, and I awoke the next day feeling like a human being again, full of optimism that this was going to turn out to be a great trip after all! After a couple of days of wining, dining, sight-seeing and a restful night of slumber, I felt completely rejuvenated and my positive attitude and optimism returned. I was looking forward to the rest of our adventure!

Once we checked out of the bed and breakfast, we caught a ferry that would take us to Seattle. The ferry was huge and was actually transporting a train with lots of cars, very impressive! I started out feeling excited, but after several hours of sitting in very uncomfortable seats, I started getting tired and a bit irritable. We decided to have dinner and were planning to splurge on the best items on the menu, but were informed that they had not anticipated accommodating so many passengers, and had run out of food! My first thought was: Oh no, here we go again! At least they had some raisin and port wine left. The port tasted terrible but I drank it, after all "any old port in a storm" when you're tired and hungry!

It turned out to be a long, exhausting and grueling trip, probably exacerbated by the lack of food and the cheap port wine. Our only hope was that once we landed on shore, we would find a nice clean hotel. Our prayers were answered, and we found a room at a Holiday Inn. It even had a view of the harbor. It felt like things were looking up again. What a roller coaster we were on!

We were both exhausted, so we took our showers and went straight to bed. I was awakened in the middle of the night by what sounded like my brother throwing up. Sure enough, he said that he thought he was coming down with the flu. He had a fever and was throwing up. I couldn't believe that this was happening, after all we had gone thought to get this far! That nasty old roller coaster was rearing its ugly head once more!

For two days we had to forgo the fair, while my brother stayed in bed nursing his flu bug. The highlight of my day was going next door to the café to get chicken soup for him. While I commiserated with him, and felt badly for him, I secretly wished that he could speed up this getting well stuff. Once again, I was going a little stir crazy. Being cooped up for two days in a small hotel room, with a sick man for company, time was passing oh so slowly. Never in my life had I seen a clock move at such a snail's pace.

After two days finally had passed, we headed off to our destination, the World's Fair! I could barely contain my excitement to be so close after all we had been through. But once we entered the gates, what came to mind was "is this it? We travelled all this way, and went through so much for this?" I suppose maybe I just wasn't really the fair type, and maybe all along, my real goal had been the luxury cruise and a shipboard romance. In fact, that ship had definitely sailed away without me. Regardless of my disappointment, Stan seemed to be having a great time, and I was determined to put on my happy face and make the best of it for his sake. It was the least I could do after all I had put him through.

Other than the space needle, the fair didn't seem much different from the fairs we had at home. We traveled an awful long way to jump on a few rides and eat cotton candy. Stan did enjoy riding to the top of the space needle; without me, of course. I'd already had my fill of high places! The poor guy wanted so badly to eat dinner at the top, but I just couldn't do it, and he refused to go without me. The best part of the fair, in my opinion, was people watching. There were enough "characters" to keep me entertained, but one can find this in any crowd of tourists, anywhere.

After a couple of days sightseeing at the fair, I was relieved that it was time to head home. Instead of the relaxing luxurious vacation I had envisioned, our trip had consisted of one miserable mishap after another, with our final destination being a fair no different from any other. There was nothing spectacular about the event. After all we had endured and anticipated, we did expect at least one thing that would stand out, but it was not to be. I was totally ready for home sweet home!

We did received notice from the cruise line that they were going to withhold $50.00 for each of us. We felt pretty fortunate to get most of our money returned to us, because actually we would have given it all to them if that's what it took to get us off that traveling rusty tub!

Interestingly enough, about a year later, I read that the U.S. Yarmouth had sunk at sea. I was surprised that it had lasted that long! Fortunately, there were no lives lost at sea, and no one was hurt, which was a miracle!

After almost two years of not having a job, and feeling somewhat better and fully recovered from our World's Fair jaunt, I thought it was time to venture out into the world. I was afraid that if I didn't get myself motivated and seek employment, I might never be able to work again; that my affliction would keep me housebound. I was still reluctant to go anywhere by myself, or go too far from home on my own, even with the medication. I was so fearful that I would have an attack. People would think that I was crazy, and men in white coats would come haul me away in a straitjacket. I had to be very creative at thinking up excuses for not being able to go places, and it was exhausting. I felt that I had to hide from everyone my phobias and attacks. I didn't think they would understand. As I've learned throughout the years, I was right; many people just don't understand, preferring to label me as someone with a mental illness; a nut job. Nor did I expect to have a long life ahead of me.

But I did survive, and so far have made it to age 70 plus, a number I never dreamed I would see during those dark days. Obviously, God had some purpose for keeping me here, but to this day I'm still not sure what this purpose might be.

I got to the point where I started looking for work closer to home. I found a bookkeeping job but not knowing the first thing about balancing a checkbook, let alone complicated ledgers, it didn't last long. Next, I applied for a position as a librarian, maintaining the technical library at a business close to home. I was beginning to regain some of my old confidence, and this sounded like it would be a challenge. Instead it turned out to be tedious and boring, and I have never had the patience for tedious and boring tasks, so this one didn't last long either. I grew very weary half way through the work day, and found that taking a snooze in my car at lunch time would help me survive the rest of the work day. This was a life saver, until one day I forgot to lock my car, and woke up with this pervert next to me, who was trying to undo my blouse. I screamed like a banshee, and leaned on the horn until this creep jumped out. Later after relating my misadventure to my boss, describing this guy's appearance as best I could, she said that she was pretty sure who he was, and assured me that the matter would be addressed. I never found out who the culprit was. Probably it is better that I was not aware, because I would have confronted the sleaze, giving him a verbal lashing, and maybe punctuating it with a size 10 kick to the groin!

7 KARAM'S

My friend Dodi worked as a bookkeeper and hostess for an exclusive restaurant in Newport Beach, called Karam's. The clientele was the elite of Orange County; many Hollywood celebrities frequented the establishment. Dodi was taking on more duties and wanted someone to take over the bookkeeping and cashiering. When she offered it to me, I was thrilled.

Karam's was considered Orange County's equivalent to the upscale 21 Club in New York. The décor reminded me of a high end brothel, with its overstuffed black leather chairs, walls covered in red embossed velvet, intricate glass chandeliers, and candle wall sconces.

Mr. and Mrs. Karam were delightful people and I knew they would be wonderful to work for. On my first day of work they sat me down and told me that I need not buy groceries because I would be well fed at their restaurant. Every evening at six they invited the staff to dine in the Vintage Room, a beautiful dining room filled with expensive wines and champagnes. The food was mostly epicurean and much fancier than anything I was accustomed to, and best of all, it was free! I learned to appreciate fine dining and still do to this day. No fast food for me!

All the waiters wore tuxedos with a white shirt and black bow tie. They looked quite dashing in their tuxes, but their real talent was making crepe suzettes, my favorite dessert item on the menu. We were always excited when a large party ordered them after drinking all night, because 9 out 10 times they would be drunk to even touch the dessert. Once the waiter rolled the cart back with those untouched crepes, we would scoop them up faster than a seagull scooping a fish from the water! One night we really hit the jackpot when the waiter brought back 20 of those rich decadent crepes! I managed to gobble down quite a few all by myself, which was wonderful while I was doing it, but boy did I pay the price! The booze in them made me dizzy, and the richness caused my stomach to heave, sending me on multiple trips to the bathroom, drawing a lot of attention on me, the unwanted and embarrassing kind of attention. That was the last time I ever ate a crepe suzette.

My first duty of the day was to make coffee, and figure out which pastries to order for that evening. Mrs. Karam told me to be sure to order enough for me, too. I couldn't believe it; they just smiled when they saw my eyes open wide, my mouth starting to water. I was also responsible for computing the charges and sending out the bills for the regular customers who ran a credit tab. Some of these charges equaled my paychecks for an entire month. Pricey as these were, the customers never batted an eye, they could well afford it.

June Allyson who was married to actor Dick Powell was a regular at Karam's, as was Claire Trevor. Ms. Trevor was an avid artist; a few of her oil paintings adorned the restaurant walls. She always was most reserved and lady-like. June Allyson was the "girl next door" type on the silver screen, but not in real life; at least not one night when the staff and I witnessed her slam a bottle of champagne, breaking it on the dining table and splashing everyone seated. She obviously had too much bubbly and from the tone of her voice, she was extremely agitated. It was surprising to hear the foul language that was coming out of her mouth, for such a petite and sweet looking person.

A real heart throb was Tyrone Power who was also a regular at the original restaurant on the Balboa Peninsula, before it was moved to Newport Beach. I caught a glimpse of him once. What a gorgeous man!

One of my favorite celebrities to frequent the restaurant was Jeffery Hunter. He was an up-and-coming actor who showed great potential. The role I recall most is when he portrayed Jesus of Nazareth. I had seen him in other movies also, but this was my favorite. He had the most startling blue eyes I had ever seen, and thick black hair that framed his handsome face. He was not just a handsome man; most importantly, he was a very nice man. He saw me smoking one day and told me that I should quit. He said that he had quit with the help of a plastic shaped cigarette, and he pulled one out of his pocket and gave it to me. It was quite thrilling to have someone of his stature take an interest in me, offering his advice. Too bad that I didn't jump on the band wagon and take his advice at the time.

Months later I was so sad to learn that he had a fatal accident at home, falling and hitting his head, which resulted in his death. He was much too young, with such a great future ahead of him to have lost his life in such a tragic manner. Meeting someone in that profession who was so unpretentious and so caring was rare. I think, it is even more of a rarity these days.

My favorite celebrity encounter was "The Duke" himself, John Wayne. When we saw that he had reservations, we were all filled with excitement; even the Karams who had known him for years. One day he noticed me and said "You're a new one, aren't you?" And then he actually reached over and gave me a firm slap on the butt. He was a big man, and I was almost knocked to the floor! Dodi came over and properly introduced us. I was practically speechless, in awe of this giant man with the giant personality. He had such a booming voice and so much charisma, and a strong hand; my butt was still stinging! I remember going to the ladies' room, which was quite soundproof, but I could still hear his loud and clear voice, coming through the walls. No one else had a voice that could boom its way right through that wall!

He, too, was a very considerate and down-to-earth man. I wanted to ask him for his autograph, but I didn't want to infringe on his evening out. In hindsight, I wish I had thrown caution to the wind and just asked him, I'm sure he would have been happy to accommodate another star-struck fan.

Karam's attracted the Orange County eccentrics also. One multi-millionaire lived on the Balboa Peninsula and had a bay-front home, but when it came time to tip, he would pull out his little black leather change purse and leave a few coins on the table. None of the waiters wanted him at their stations; so, to be fair, they took turns. He eventually married a much younger woman and mysteriously ended up dead shortly thereafter. His wife was arrested and was tried, but she had all of his money to buy the best attorneys available, and she ended up being acquitted. The cause of his death was never determined. How ironic, and sad, that he scrimped and saved his money his whole life, only to be murdered for it, which was most likely the cause of his demise.

And then, there were the wealthy patrons of the place, who seemed to find it beneath them to have to pay their tabs on time. I would send out notice after notice with no response, but they would still have the audacity to continue coming in for dinner. After this would continue for months, the Karams would instruct me to send a "pay or die" notice. This was usually enough encouragement for them to dust off their checkbooks and pay. Fortunately, these were the exceptions; most of the patrons were generous and gracious.

My job at Karam's was one of the best jobs I ever had, and one of the most interesting. I was treated very well, fed like a queen, and got paid for it! The bookkeeping was simple, and I always had plenty of extra time to settle back until dinner service, put the TV on, put my feet up, and enjoy some of their wonderful coffee and pastries. All of the good food and pastries were finally putting some much needed pounds back on my thin frame, and life was good again!

But as was par for the course, the good times didn't last long. I soon met the man who would later turn out to be the Husband from Hell.

8 MARRIAGE

I hadn't dated for several years due to my illness, and I really didn't have the desire to jump back in to the dating world. But I had a friend named Jessie who was determined to set me up.

I had known Jessie all through high school and had been a bridesmaid in her wedding. She was a big girl, but despite her weight and marital status, men still flocked to her, for she had a delightful, outgoing personality. In school her nickname was "Boobs", which fit her perfectly since she had been generously blessed in that department, and she didn't mind showing them off.

Jessie had a girlfriend who was going through a divorce, and she wanted to set me up with the soon to be ex-husband, whom she described as very handsome and ready to date again. I was hesitant, but when she reminded me that women who didn't marry by age 25, were likely to end up as "old maids", no twisting of my arm was needed.

Jessie set up a meeting at her home. She hadn't exaggerated when she said that he was attractive. He was tall, with a low, sensual voice, and my first impression was wow! As an added plus, he drove a red Porsche. I was so easily swayed by good looks and sleek cars, (shallow, I know) but I just couldn't help myself. At the end of the evening, Don asked me out to dinner. If only I had said no! But I couldn't resist his charm, or his red Porsche.

At the time, I was renting an apartment with a friend, Dusty, who later ended up marrying my brother Stan. They have been together now for 40 plus years, so at least something good came out of that time in my life.

Don started spending nights at our apartment. He would leave early in the morning for his job as an electrician, and I would be able to sleep in, since my job at Karam's didn't start until 4pm. We were having lots of fun "playing house"!

I should have seen the red flags when he started showing up at my job unannounced, waiting in the parking lot until I got off. I had my own car, so there was no reason for him to be there, other than to keep a watchful eye on me. He became very possessive, and started grilling me about my activities and whereabouts when we weren't together.

Mrs. Karam saw the red flags and warned me about him. She called him a "nut" and tried to convince me that I deserved much better. She even offered to fix me up on dates with a couple of guys she knew, who were professionals and not "stalkers". Unfortunately I was convinced that his jealousy and possessiveness were just signs of how much he loved me. If he didn't love me so much, he wouldn't care what I did or where I went, would he? A foolish mistake so many women make, and I was still just a young girl.

One night, when he miraculously didn't show up in the parking lot to wait for me, a few of us decided to go out to a club. The group consisted of guys and girls from work, and we were all socializing and dancing and having a great time, all innocent fun. Somehow Don tracked me down and started to make a scene, accusing me of cheating on him. There was no reasoning with him in his angry state, and when he demanded I leave with him right then, I decided to go; I was afraid of what he might do if I refused. He immediately began yelling at me, accusing me of being unfaithful, while at the same time telling me that he loved me so much that he couldn't stand the thought of anyone else touching me! Being gullible and wanting to believe so much that he only behaved this way because he loved me, I stayed when all my senses screamed at me to run.

Not long afterwards, Don asked me to marry him. Again I said yes when every part of my being told me to say no, but my fear of becoming an "old maid" overcame my fear of marrying the wrong man. I wanted the fairy tale, and I foolishly thought that once I married him, he would no longer have any reason to be jealous and possessive, and we could have that perfect love and marriage I so longed for.

One of the saddest days of my life was telling the Karams that I was leaving my job to marry Don. Mrs. Karam made one last desperate attempt to change my mind, but I was determined that I was going to have my fairy tale marriage. It was a very emotional departure. I had grown to love the Karams like family, as well as my co-workers. It took a long time before I would stop missing them.

Don and I went to Las Vegas and we were married by the Justice of the Peace. It was a very cold, unemotional ceremony. The minister had one eye on a baseball game on TV while he performed the ceremony, and when he finished, he summoned his secretary to come in and sign the marriage license as a witness. That was it! A pathetic start for a fairy tale marriage. I walked out of that building more depressed than I had ever been in my life, even worse than when I was ill and bedridden. I wonder now, if I would have gone through with it if I had not been addicted to tranquilizers at that time, or was it the fear of being an "old maid" what drove me to make one of the biggest mistakes of my life.

As we exited the building, Don was proudly telling everyone that I was his new bride, and how happy he was. I tried to be a sport, and plastered a smile on my face, but inside I was ill, and all I could think was "what have I done?"

Our wedding night was a fitting ending to that star-crossed day. I had a panic attack, but that didn't stop my loving husband from satisfying himself.

We moved into a small, depressing apartment in Westminster. Shortly thereafter, his two children were sent by their mother to live with us. His son Steven was 8 and his daughter Darla was 6. I was only 22 years old and was not really emotionally prepared to become a full time mother of two kids, nor was this quite how I had expected my fairy tale marriage to begin. But I felt sorry for them because their mom didn't want them, and even though Don said he was thrilled to have them, his actions spoke differently. He was very moody, had no patience with them, yelling at them constantly. His son had a learning disability and Don's ego would not allow him to accept it. He was incessantly tormenting the poor child, trying to force him to learn things he was simply not capable of learning because of his disability. He was terrified of his father, and lived in a constant state of anxiety when Don was home. It was very sad, and I tried to be a calming, caring presence in their lives, as much as Don would allow it.

I was offered a job by a friend to manage an apartment complex in Costa Mesa. In exchange we were offered a 3 bedroom 2 ½ bath apartment at a reduced rate. It turned out to be a good move, for a while. They each had their own bedroom, which at least gave the kids someplace to go and find solace, and get away from their father.

I recall one Christmas time, when I was out shopping for Don's kids. I got stuck in traffic and was about an hour late getting home. In those days there were no cell phones. As soon as I walked in the door, he went into attack mode, accusing me of cheating on him and just bringing home the gifts as a cover-up to my affair. His jugular veins started bulging, his face turned bright crimson, and I knew that this was not going to have a good ending.

I tried to remove myself from the confrontation by taking the gifts upstairs. But he just followed me up the stairs, screaming the whole time. Once in the bedroom, he abruptly grabbed me and roughly pulled me down on top of him on the bed. The Good Lord was looking out for me that day because when we fell on to the bed, he apparently hurt himself and started yelping in pain. This gave me the opportunity to grab my purse and flee. I wanted the kids to come with me, but they were too afraid of the repercussions later. I hated leaving them there, but I couldn't force them to come with me, so I ran out the door and sped to my mom's house.

Later that evening Don called me, very apologetic and begging me to forgive him. He actually started crying, and swore that nothing like this would ever happen again. Always being a sucker for a sob story, once again, I fell for his lies. But I did warn him that if there was ever another incident like this, it would be the last; I would be gone for good. He told me that he got what he deserved, two broken ribs, and I didn't disagree. I was secretly pleased that he would have to suffer some pain and discomfort for what he had done.

I knew that I should pack my bags and leave, but he was a masterful manipulator. I was probably a victim of Battered Woman Syndrome, although it didn't have a name back then. He knew how to manipulate me, control me, play on my sympathies; basically con me in to believing whatever lies he told. It was emotional battery and he played it to the hilt. After every episode, he could convince me how sorry he was, how much he loved me, and all he needed was one more chance. And I would give him that one more chance, believing that I had made a commitment to him and to our marriage. I just had to try harder. Of course after each episode, he would be on his best behavior for a while. But he was never able to control himself, or hide his true nature for long. It wasn't just me he fooled; he could be most charming and charismatic, and there were many who were surprised when they eventually found out what went on behind our closed doors.

He remained on good behavior for quite a while after that last incident, and we were able to maintain a semblance of normalcy. We moved into a large home in Fountain Valley and there was enough to keep him occupied. It diverted his attention, away from me and the kids.

During this time Don and I even took some trips to the mountains, to Lake Tahoe, and actually had a good time together. He was much more relaxed when his kids weren't around. But once we were home again, his tension returned. He was constantly berating his son for his bad grades, but he wouldn't even consider allowing him to attend classes for kids with special needs. His ego caused him to make some disastrous decisions in his life, and this was one of the worst. Instead of allowing his son to attend classes with kids of his own limited learning ability, where he might be able to thrive, he just continued to threaten him and belittle him. The poor kid tried so hard, but normal studies were just beyond his capabilities, and he regularly suffered the wrath of his father.

His daughter didn't have any learning disabilities, but she definitely suffered from laziness. She was an average student, but she had the capabilities to be an outstanding student. While she was very smart scholastically, she did some crazy things, as though she was going out of her way to irritate her dad. One time she was in the bathroom that she and her brother shared, and she took two cans of baby powder and poured them all over herself. I discovered her when I saw baby powder pouring out from under the door. She was covered from head to toe, and looked like Casper the Ghost. I could barely breathe, or see her through all the powder flying around. Her dad was due home any minute, so I asked her why she would do such a thing, knowing that it could mean a spanking with the belt. She just laughed and started cleaning up, and I helped her. It seemed as if I wanted to avoid a confrontation between her and her dad, more than she did!

As soon as Don walked in the door, he demanded to know why the house smelled like baby powder. I made up some story, I don't even remember what it was now, and thankfully he bought it; another crisis averted. She pulled antics like this on a regular basis, and seemed to enjoy sitting back and watching me try to clean up her messes, or hide it from her dad. And even when she did get caught, she seemed impervious to Don's wrath, or to the pain of the belt. Over time it became clear to me that she suffered from some sort of psychological problem, as did most of his family.

Don's mother was victimized by his father, and that's what shaped the man Don became. His father was a mean, foul mouthed drunk, who enjoyed tormenting his wife. But his mother always made excuses for him, like most abused women do, and tried her best to please him and her family. One incident that stands out, is when his father threw a large kitchen knife at her while she was cooking. There was no provocation for his actions. Later he said he just thought of something that she had done earlier that pissed him off, and he needed to "scare her in to shape".

I hated going to Don's parent's house, I was tense and on edge, wondering what his dad might do. Don insisted that the kids and I go to his parents' house every Saturday night to watch

Lawrence Welk. I hated that music and was miserable until it was time to go home. But his mother did prepare delicious dinners for us every week; that was the one saving grace of the evening.

Trying to be Cinderella 24/7, taking care of two kids and a husband and a home, was wearing on me. I decided that I needed some sort of outlet; something that would be a source of relaxation and maybe provide me with a sense of achievement, too. I suggested oil painting to Don, and was surprised when he actually agreed. Of course this was something that I would be doing in the house, where he could keep a watchful eye on me, so probably that had something to do with his quick consent. My mom wanted to take a painting lesson with me, and I had to lie to Don, and tell him that she was paying for mine. I had managed to hide away a little money, but if he knew that I was using his money, he might not have allowed me to go.

Through the lessons, I became interested in painting ships, and actually I became quite good at it. I won second place in a local contest, and felt elated that I had accomplished something worthwhile on my own. I found myself staying up until the wee hours of the morning working on my paintings, which really wasn't the best thing for my health. Sometimes I pushed myself so hard that my nerves would get the best of me, and I would have a panic attack. It was difficult to learn to pace myself. I became addicted to painting, and I was such a perfectionist, that I simply couldn't stop until things were just right. But I was still excited at achieving something worthwhile, besides scrubbing toilets and taking care of the unappreciative members of my household. Through the next few years, I even sold all of my ship paintings, some of which I wish I had never let go. One still hangs in a former co-worker's home.

One day out of the blue Don's mother confessed to me that she had spoiled Don as a child. This was not exactly a huge revelation; it was quite apparent that he was used to being spoiled. She even went so far as to warm the toilet seat for him, so that sitting on it would be more appealing. I brought this subject up once, and he told me that having a bowel movement was almost as enjoyable for him as having sex. This admission sickened me, and I seriously thought about packing my bags, but I decided to try and put it out of mind instead.

His mother also told me that she would peel the skin off his grapes, and any other fruit or vegetable, if he wanted her to. And if she didn't starch his shirts just right, he would erupt in anger. Boy did I know that was true! I had experienced the same thing. I believe it's true, that mothers can ruin their sons for their wives and for future relationships.

One day my old friend Abby from elementary school phoned, saying that she had no place to live, and asked if I could help her out. Abby had been married and had five children, lived in a nice home in a good neighborhood, and appeared to have had a loving relationship with her husband. I was shocked to learn that she had walked out on her family. We had an extra bedroom, and I thought that it would be nice to have some adult company. Maybe she would even serve as a peace buffer, since Don was big on keeping up appearances, impressing strangers. Don agreed to let her stay until she could make other arrangements.

Once she moved in, I found myself not with a wonderful new companion, but with another person to take care of! I was doing her laundry, cooking for her, cleaning up after her, and growing angrier by the day.

My grandmother had been ill, and was in the hospital after gall bladder surgery. I was very close to her and went to visit her often. She was improving, and was supposed to be going home, when I received a call from a nurse, informing me that she had taken a turn for the worse. I wasn't sure exactly how bad things were, but I wasted no time getting to the hospital. I ran to her bed and was getting ready to hug her, when a nurse told me that she had passed away about an hour ago. She had already been dead when they called me. I was devastated and just fell apart. It had never occurred to me that she might die; she was recovering nicely, expecting to go home.

Don finally showed up at the hospital with Abby in tow. The two of them were just chattering away, and even laughing at times. I couldn't believe that my husband and my friend could be so callous, so indifferent to my pain and sorrow. He didn't even offer me a shoulder to cry on, didn't even put his arms around me; nothing at all. This just confirmed what I already knew: he was a cold-hearted bastard, a selfish, poor excuse for a husband.

At the time of my grandma's funeral, Don made the excuse that he had to work, and couldn't go. By then I was just relieved that he wouldn't be there, his presence would have tainted the ceremony for me, and it's not as though he would have been there to offer me comfort.

I kept hanging in there with this doomed relationship, partly because I couldn't afford to leave. I needed a good job and enough money to support myself. I started taking some evening classes on business, in hopes of finding a job. One evening I got home early from class, and noticed that Abby's door was partially open. I said hello, and when I got no response, I pushed the door open and found her and Don sitting very close to each other on her bed. They both acted flustered as they tried to quickly straighten up their disheveled appearances. Then they started making excuses, which only an idiot would believe about why Don was in her bedroom in the first place. I was infuriated and ordered Abby to get the hell out of our house! I picked up some of her clothes that were lying around the room, and threw them out the front door. Don had the nerve to tell me that I was overreacting, but he didn't try to stop me from throwing her stuff out the door. I think he knew better than to interfere with me at that moment. Apparently he had heard the stories about a "woman scorned", and he knew he had been caught. I was totally amazed at my reactions being the devout coward that I was.

For me, one of the worst sins is for a friend to not only blatantly lie and deceive you, but to become romantically involved with your partner, even if you had no use for him. This is one of the worst betrayals in my book, and one that I have never been able to forgive. Even if you're not crazy about your partner, it is still hands off, if the person is truly your friend. Abby knew that she had been caught red-handed, so there was no need to hang around. She hurriedly threw her personal belongings in her car and left. That was the last I heard of her until several years later, when I ran into her at a restaurant. That story will come later.

After the incident with Abby, my marriage continued to deteriorate even further. I even started spending more time with friends, going out to dinner and sometimes even going dancing with them. I later learned, that the reason Don didn't object to my absences was because he was frequenting a bar a few blocks from our home and was quite open about having the hots for one of the bartenders. Even our next door neighbors knew about it.

One night I went out with a good friend, Margie, and another friend of hers named Sue, to a hotel in Anaheim that had good entertainment. I ended up spending most of the evening dancing with one guy in particular. He was nice looking, clean cut, and seemed pleasant enough. As the night wore on, I had too much to drink and became disoriented. My friends decided to go upstairs to check out another musical group, and they would meet me around 1AM to head home. When 1AM rolled around, I had forgotten where I was supposed to meet them, and I couldn't find them anywhere, as I wandered around the hotel. I went to the parking lot, thinking that they might be waiting by the car, but I couldn't find the car, nor find any sign of them.

The parking lot wasn't very well lit and during my search, I tripped over one of the cement parking barriers and went flying. I landed hard on my left foot and even the massive amount of alcohol I had consumed earlier did not mask the intense pain. The guy I had been dancing with suddenly appeared, and saw me lying on the ground, and came to my rescue. He offered to help me find the car and my friends. He was going to bring his car around and drive me around the lot. I figured that he was okay, no Jack the Ripper. I had spent most of the evening with him, and he seemed normal. My foot was throbbing and already swelling; my tail bone, where I had landed, was hurting, too, so I was grateful for his help.

We drove through the lot and there was no sign of Margie's car. I had forgotten his name in my state of alcohol-induced confusion, but he told me not to worry, he would drive me home. I felt, I had no choice, since I couldn't find my friend's car, and figured that they had left without me.

Once we drove away from the hotel, he became very quiet, not at all the friendly talkative person he had been all night. Then

I noticed that we were going in the wrong direction. I asked where we were going and he said not to worry, he would get me home safely. Between the excruciating pain in my foot and back, and a sudden sense of fear, I immediately sobered up. I told him to stop the car and let me out but he said that he just had one stop to make, and then he would take me home, and I should just sit back and relax.

Terror was starting to take over, and my mind was racing with ideas of how to get away from this maniac. We pulled up to a shack and he shut off the motor. He exited the car and went inside the shack without a word. I'm sure he thought it was safe to leave me in the car because my foot had swollen to the size of a football and it was obvious that I was in excruciating pain. But he underestimated my fear, which was even more intense than the pain in my foot!

I quietly opened the car door, got out, and started running, going as fast as I could, while dragging my left foot. I saw that I was in an industrial area, where there were no homes, no people, not a car in sight. I knew if he caught me, there would be no one there to save me. So I just kept going as fast as I could without screaming from the pain.

I heard an engine start and knew it had to be him. I quickly dove behind some bushes just in the nick of time as I saw his car slowly driving by. I stayed hidden behind those bushes, barely breathing, careful not to make a sound, as I watched him drive by again and again, obviously looking for me. I knew that if he caught me, I was going to be raped and probably killed, so when some time went by without him driving past, I left the bushes and took off running as fast I could, sheer terror pushing me forward through the pain.

By this time, it was about 3AM. Not a good time to find people out and about, especially in an industrial area. I don't even know how far I went before I came to an apartment complex and saw a light on in one of the apartments. I was flooded with relief just to be in a place where there were people! I knocked on the door and told the man who answered what had happened. I asked if I could use his phone, since he didn't look like a derelict. Of course, that could have turned out to be another bad move, since the predator I just escaped from didn't look like a derelict either. But fortunately he was OK. I felt even more relief when I entered the apartment and saw a female sitting there. They told me that I was in the city of Orange, and the only person I could think of close by to call for help was Don's sister, who lived in Anaheim.

I called Priscilla and gave her a brief rundown of the night's events and asked her to pick me up. She showed up about a half hour later. As we were driving, I told her the whole sordid tale. She was amazed that I was able to escape with what looked to her to be a badly broken foot. But I knew the terror of a terrible fate awaiting me overshadowed all and everything else! I understood then how people in fear for their lives are able to do things that seem impossible, and find mental and physical strength they never knew they had.

Once home, Don did not appear too happy, as he explained that Margie had been calling for the past two hours, frantic and on the verge of calling the police when I showed up. I thought about calling the police myself, but I didn't think I could identify where he had taken me, and between the alcohol, the pain, and the fear, I didn't think I remembered enough about the guy and his car to give a decent description anyway.

I was just grateful to be alive, relatively unharmed, and home. My foot had grown to the size of a watermelon by now and the pain was so intense, I was nauseous, almost to the point of blacking out. I despised hospitals though, and didn't want to go, but Margie insisted. Don bundled us in the car and drove us to the emergency room, grumbling and groaning the whole time.

On the way, Margie told me that she and Sue had looked everywhere for me, and were out of their minds with worry when they couldn't find me. I knew that they felt really badly for leaving me alone and going upstairs. I told her how sorry I was for scaring them, and she gave me a big hug, which I honestly needed right about then, and told me that she was just glad that I would be okay.

They no sooner got me on the examining table than I passed out. The pain and fatigue had finally gotten the best of me. When I woke up, the doctor was preparing to cast my foot, which ended up almost reaching my hip. He gave me a powerful shot, told me my foot was broken in several places, I would have to wear the cast for quite some time, and I was going to have a lot of discomfort.

After several weeks, I was able to get around fairly well using crutches. Believe it or not, the thought foremost in my head during this time was going back to that Anaheim hotel in hopes of finding the maniac who had put me through such hell. I thought if I could get a good description of him, I could still report the incident to the police. I was worried about what he had done, or might do, to other unsuspecting women.

About a month later, at my insistence, Margie and I headed for the Anaheim hotel. After scouring the crowd, I saw who I thought was the guy. My recollection of him was fuzzy but he seemed very familiar. I was still on crutches so I couldn't just get up and take off after him, but that only slowed me down, it didn't stop me! Once he noticed me heading in his direction, I knew that I had the right guy, because he took off and was out of sight within seconds! My plan was to hit him with one of my crutches if I could get close enough, but at the least, I wanted to get a better description of him for the police. Unfortunately he disappeared too quickly; I wasn't able to do that. He never returned to the club that evening, although we waited just in case. We went back to the hotel numerous times over the next month, but I never saw him again. Finally had to give up my search.

Don and I made an agreement to continue living under the same roof for the time being, trying to give the kids some stability, for whatever it was worth. Truth be told, he probably didn't want to lose his housekeeper, babysitter, and cook.

But, I began to enjoy this arrangement. I had plenty of freedom to come and go as I pleased, as long as the household chores were done. I know, that sounds pretty pitiful, as though I had to buy my freedom, but at the time it was an improvement over the way things had been. My mom was a great help to us during my recovery. Having her around was a blessing, because Don was on his best behavior; for a while, at least. He resented that my family was always so good to me. On one of my birthdays, they bought me a beautiful new dress that I had been wanting. He said that I didn't deserve it and the kids deserved more than I did. This was a birthday gift from my family; it had nothing to do with the kids, it took nothing away from them, but this was just one of the many crazy things he came up with out of nowhere. He wanted everything to be on a schedule, too, and if something was out of sync, it pushed him to the brink of violence.

I was beginning to really loathe Don. I knew that I had to formulate a plan to escape the situation. I felt very torn at times, because I had become close to his kids, and I knew that without me there to offer some protection, life would be harder for them. They were actually the reason I hung on as long as I did. That, and not having a means of supporting myself. But I knew for a long time, that there was going to be no way but out.

I was getting better, but still in a cast and using crutches. One morning, while I was making breakfast for my mom and the kids, Don looked at the dishwasher and exploded, shouting "are these dirty or clean?" You would have thought he was asking if the world was coming to an end, he was so intense. I told him I would have emptied the machine if they were clean. He shouted "I hate this thing; I should just rip it out!" I guess I had reached my breaking point, because I told him to "go for it", knowing the wrath this would incur, and preparing to make a hasty departure. He furiously tore the dishwasher from the wall, and heaved it through the open door leading from the kitchen to the garage. It caused such a racket that some of the neighbors came out to see what he was up to now. He was cursing loudly as I was grabbing my mom and the kids to flee from the house. I was so thankful that I hadn't broken my right foot, and could still drive.

At the time of his tantrum, I had been making homemade syrup, something Don's mother made for him and which he still insisted on. He was in such a rage that he picked up the boiling hot pan from the stove top and was going to throw it out the kitchen window when the hot syrup started running down his arm. He let out such a squeal of pain, it probably alarmed the whole neighborhood. We were just on our way out the door when this happened, and I hate to admit it, I was actually glad that I got to witness it. Once again, I found some small satisfaction in his self-inflicted pain.

I later learned from one of the neighbors, who was brave enough to enter the garage, that Don was tearing dishes out of the cupboards and breaking them on the floor, and then throwing them out into the garage. I guess it was better that he was breaking stuff than bodies; he saved that for his girlfriend, which is another story! But how stupid was it to break his own stuff, stuff he paid for and would have to pay to replace. Not that it bothered me. It would be some small consolation that he would feel the pain of having to write those checks to replace everything he had broken!

We had been hiding out at my mom's when Don called, tearful and all full of his usual remorse. He apologized profusely, and promised that he would never let his temper get out of control again. He told me that we needed a new dishwasher anyway, and that he would replace it immediately. He also told me that I could pick out whatever new dishes I liked. He was trying to pacify me, but I told him I didn't think I could trust him not to lose his temper again, and I needed time to think about whether I could forgive him again.

I felt so badly that I hadn't been able to grab our cat Gussie when we left. She was my saving grace. She was one of the few things in our dysfunctional household that made me happy. I told Don that he had to take care of her while we were away, and he promised that he would. I wasn't worried that he would hurt her. We had found her in a trash can, full of fleas. We worked together to bathe her and pick the fleas off her. He appeared to care about her, except for the time she knocked some ornaments off the Christmas tree, for which he scolded her extensively, as if she knew what he was saying.

I had a hard time rationalizing why I stayed with this man, knowing that I didn't love him and probably never had. In the beginning, I thought that I did. Beginnings are always such a romantic exciting time in a relationship. But I came to the conclusion that I was a needy person, I didn't want to be alone, and after my illness, I wanted to feel protected, and have a steady, normal and predictable life. I thought that I had found this with Don, so I settled. I should have learned my lesson about settling from this experience, but some people are slow to learn their lessons.

I tried to find a job that I would enjoy, even though I knew that nothing would compare to Karam's. I finally opted for temporary work as a Kelley Girl. It was interesting and never boring, because I was constantly moving around. And I could select for whom I wanted to work, and when. I did this until Don started yanking my paychecks out of my hand. Then I figured: why work if I can't keep any of the money anyway? So I decided not to work unless I'm doing something I really love. Don was not pleased with this decision.

9 BREAKUP

Being the master of mental manipulation, Don convinced me one more time to forgive him and come home, promising that this had been his last display of rage; from here on out he would be a model husband. And I was still young and naïve enough to believe in fairy tales.

Life rolled along predictably. Then one day I got a call from Steve. He was back in Hollywood and wanted to see me. He had talked to my mom who was more than happy to give him my number. I explained to him that I was married, and unhappy, and as soon as I found a steady job, I intended to get divorced. We made arrangements to meet that evening at the ferry landing, which was close to my mom's house. I was so excited to see him after so much time had passed. I knew that Don had a meeting that night, so I told him that I was going to visit my mom who wasn't feeling well. A good plan, until Don insisted that I take the kids with me.

Once we arrived at my mom's, I told the kids that I needed a little time to myself, and was going for a walk. When I first spotted Steve, all of those old feelings came rushing back, as though we had never been apart. The first thing he said to me was "You are really skinny, not like the voluptuous girl I once knew, regardless, you are still a lovely lady." I was a little disappointed. I had expected him to feel the same way as I did, and gush about how much he had missed me and wanted to be with me. That night I had a hard time reading what he was feeling, and wasn't sure where we stood, until he asked if I could get away and go to Vegas, as his band was going to be playing at Caesar's Palace. I really wanted to spend some time with him, so I told him that I would think of some way to get out of the house. I had to cut our meeting short because I didn't want the kids to get suspicious. It was a good thing, because Don had decided to show up, and I got back just before he got there. It was interesting that first he made me take the kids with me, and then he showed up at my mom's, which was not something he normally did. It made me wonder if something in my demeanor made him suspicious, maybe it was the silly grin I couldn't seem to wipe off my face?

Don had been having an affair with the bartender who worked at a local pub around the corner from our house. I finally found out, when my next door neighbor Margie's husband got drunk and spilled the beans. She was my friend and felt it was her duty to tell me. I didn't take the news well, even though I didn't want him. I didn't want him cheating on me while we were living under the same roof; it was a matter of respect. I felt I deserved some small show of respect for hanging in there with him through all the ups and downs, mostly for the sake of his kids. I decided I could at least make things as uncomfortable for him as possible, so I started going with a friend, to the bar where she worked. We would make sure we sat within earshot of her working the bar, and then we proceeded to trash Don. I didn't know if it would be enough to make her dump him, but it sure made me feel better.

I thought this would be an opportune time to ask Don if I could go to Vegas for a couple of days with my mom and maybe Margie. I told him, my mom was feeling down after the loss of my grandma and she really needed a getaway and a bit of fun. It took some convincing, but I wore him down, and eventually I got my way. Plus I knew that he wouldn't mind some time alone, so he could see his girlfriend.

Right before I left for Vegas, Don told me that he and the bartender were just friends. He said he would stop in after work occasionally for a beer and would talk to her. He said she was having a problem with her dog being confined in a small apartment and she asked Don if he could help her out. I was not happy about the idea. I mean who needed a constant reminder of their husband's philandering? But next thing you know, we had inherited her dog Sheltie. From the moment that poor dog arrived at our house, all he did was run incessantly in circles around the picnic table in the back yard, only stopping when exhaustion overcame him and he had to sleep. I wanted to take him to the vet but Don, always the scrooge, wasn't about to spend a dime if he didn't have to. It broke my heart to watch him running in circles day in and day out and I told Don that as soon as I got a job, I was taking Sheltie to the vet. I didn't care if it did belong to his bimbo girlfriend, I forgave the poor dog; after all it wasn't his fault.

Margie was very excited about going to Vegas, and invited her friend Sue to join us. It worked out well, because I shared a room with my mom and they had an adjoining room. I phoned Steve and told him that we were on our way. All I could think of was reconnecting with him. I just hoped his feelings would come flooding back, like mine already had.

When I hooked up with Steve at Caesar's palace, my heart almost stopped beating. He just took my breath away, as he always had. He gave me a hug and then escorted us to the lounge where he was playing backup for Bobby Darrin that night. Being guests of the band, we had spectacular seats. I still couldn't read Steve's emotions. Truthfully, I was disappointed again that all I got was a little almost-friend-like hug from him. I guess I had been reading too many romance novels, because I was expecting him to sweep me off my feet and profess his undying love, right then and there. But I hoped that it was just because he was busy with the band, and had a lot on his mind.

I was very nervous just being in the same room with him, excited but nervous, too. I knew I needed something to calm my nerves, so when the cocktail waitress came by, I asked her what "would get me there fast?" She said "Do I have just the thing for you, hold on, you won't be disappointed!" She returned with a martini, telling me it was the answer to my prayers. I had never had a martini in my life, and made the mistake of taking a big swig, and barely kept from spitting it out! But I told myself to hang in there, after the first few sips it would taste better; unfortunately, that prediction came true!

I lost track of how many martinis I had, and soon also lost track of where I was or what I was doing. I remember looking up at Bobby Darrin, who was singing Mack the Knife, and then my curtain came crashing down and everything was a blur. I recalled the girls saying they were going to check out another casino but I wanted to wait for Steve. Bad move on my part, I would have much rather made an ass of myself in front of my friends than in front of Steve!

I headed back to the bar to wait for Steve, and somehow managed to down two more martinis! I blacked out once or twice, and when I came to, I was sobbing and telling the bartender how in love I was with Steve. I was drawing a crowd when Steve finally arrived and whisked me away. I recall him telling me that he was not pleased with me, and that I needed to shape up. I was pretty drunk, but not too drunk to be mortified! I tried to walk in a straight line but was staggering all over the place. Poor Steve was doing his best to keep me upright and balanced, but I could tell by the stares we got that he wasn't having much success.

Steve said that we were going to a club to have coffee, and we would possibly see Tom Jones, because it was one of his favorite hang-outs. Sure enough, Tom was there, but all I got was a brief glimpse before the curtain came down for good, and I had no more memories of that evening. Next thing I knew, I was in Steve's car and the sun was blazing. I couldn't understand how it could be morning already. Hell, I wasn't even sure where we were, or where we were going! Steve decided to drop me off at my hotel; we would talk later. I felt totally heart sick. I just knew, I had blown it with Steve. He did not sound at all encouraging about wanting to see me again. I assured him that I had never gotten so drunk before in my life, I just hadn't realized the dangers associated with drinking martinis, that they were almost 100% alcohol. I promised him that I would never do anything so stupid again. He said he understood, but he didn't sound completely sincere. I knew that it was bad when he didn't even offer to walk me to my room. As if the pounding in my head wasn't bad enough, I now felt like I had a knife through my heart.

When I walked through the hotel door, the first thing I saw was a large cigarette urn. I immediately ran to it, got on my knees, grabbed hold, and started vomiting my guts out. When I thought my insides were thoroughly cleaned out, I felt someone hoisting me up. Turns out I was wrong about being cleaned out, because I heaved one last time, which missed the urn! Two maids found out what room I was staying in, I suppose, by finding my key in my purse, and escorted me down the long winding halls to my room. I saw my mom, and then I blacked out once more, until that evening, when I awoke wrapped in towels, with a cold cloth on my head. I smelled wretched, like old stale vomit, even though I knew that my poor little mother had tried to clean me up as best she could. But if you think I smelled wretched, the way I felt was even worse, between the hangover and being heart sick, and being completely embarrassed, I just had a horrible feeling of being doomed.

It was actually a miracle that I didn't die from alcohol poisoning. Thank God my mother was such a wonderful caretaker or who knows if I would have made it. I'm sure she was getting tired of cleaning up my messes, but she never showed it. To add to all of my other ailments, I felt intense guilt at ruining what was supposed to be a fine getaway for my poor mom. Instead of having some fun to take her mind off my grandmother's passing, all she ended up doing was taking care of a puke soaked sobbing depressed disgusting mess of a daughter.

As I was sprawled out in that hotel bed, more miserable than I had been in a very long time, I kept having flashbacks of the evening's events. One of them was of the bartender telling me that Steve was married. But I wasn't sure if I was hallucinating or having a real memory.

Steve never phoned me at the hotel, so I called him at Caesar's. I had to know if I had really heard what I thought I heard; I couldn't leave it alone. It wasn't easy getting through to him, but my persistence finally paid off. In some ways I regretted that I did get hold of him that night, because he confirmed that he had recently gotten married. That news was just another dagger in my already broken heart. I asked him why he had invited me to Vegas and he couldn't, or wouldn't, give me a direct answer. He said that when he first saw me again a couple of months ago, he assumed that I was in a marriage that I was in no big hurry to walk away from. He had known his wife for a few years and one night they got together and one thing just led to another. My impression from what he did and did not say was that maybe he had just been looking for a "fling" with someone who was also married and therefore "safe", someone he already knew and could trust not to rat him out. I hung up the phone, and at that moment, I prayed to just pass out again. It would have been a merciful ending for that day.

The next morning I couldn't get out of there fast enough, I needed to put as much distance between us as I could. I didn't hear from Steve again for many years. One day I received a phone call from him. He was back in Hollywood, quite ill, and wanted to see me. Unfortunately, because of my driving/traveling limitations due to my own illness, I never did make it to see him before he passed away. It was some comfort to me though to know that he still had memories of us to want to see me before he died.

When I arrived home from my disastrous trip to Las Vegas, Don was in his usual sour mood. From what the kids told me, he and his girlfriend were not doing well. They told me that she came to the house one night, and may have spent the night. They had a big fight and the kids suspected he may have hit her. I wasn't surprised to hear this news. I always believed the only reason I was safe from physical attack was because I had three big brothers who would have knocked him from here to eternity, had he physically abused me.

Our relationship was obviously spiraling downward and I knew the time was drawing near when I would have to leave if I were to leave with a shred of self-respect, not to mention my sanity. I was repelled by Don's very presence, by the very act of him breathing or speaking. It doesn't get much worse than that. I truly believed that I had given our marriage all I had to give, until I was just simply drained, with nothing left to give. Living with someone who made you feel so unhappy, and so scared that anything you said or did could incite him to anger, was exhausting and was definitely taking a toll on both my mental and physical well-being.

My only regret was leaving his kids behind. I knew that life was going to become even more difficult for them, without me there to offer at least a bit of a buffer between them and their father, and a sympathetic shoulder to cry on. I thought of the many times Don beat his son with the belt until it opened his flesh and left large welts on his back and legs. He not only threatened them with the belt, but almost always carried out his evil threats. Beating them was how he alleviated his frustrations over Steven's learning disability and Darla's silly stunts. And it probably helped alleviate frustrations he had with me, too, since he was afraid of what my brothers would do to him if he physically abused me, plus I think he was smart enough to know that I wouldn't hesitate to have him arrested. It was heartbreaking to be a helpless onlooker with no means to stop his brutality against his children. On the occasions when I did try to intervene, it only fueled his anger and the beatings were even more severe. Don should have gone to jail for the abuse he inflicted on his children, but unfortunately they were so afraid of him that any time anyone questioned them about possible abuse, they would deny it. On one occasion one of Steven's teachers even questioned him about a bruise in the shape of a handprint on his face. But Steven made up some story and that was the end of it. In today's climate, that teacher would most definitely have contacted the authorities but way back then, child abuse was not at the forefront of people's consciousness the way it is today.

My friend Jessie felt a terrible responsibility for having introduced me to Don, so she was trying to help me find a good job that would give me the independence to move out on my own. She told me that they were hiring at the Huntington Beach Police Department. I told her that I would rather work at the Fire Department or at City Hall. I didn't have a warm and fuzzy feeling about cops and their rather elitist attitudes. I didn't think that I would fit in with them.

Jessie really wanted to introduce some happiness into my life. She had a good friend who was a police officer at the Huntington Beach Police Department, to whom she wanted to introduce me. I was pretty fed up with men at that point, plus he was a cop, so I declined. She tried her best to talk me into it, telling me that he was an exceptional guy, nothing like the stereotypical cop with an intimidating demeanor and arrogant attitude. She assured me that he was nothing like Don. She would never make the same mistake twice! But I still resisted. I felt that as long as I was still married and living under the same roof, I could not even consider going out with another man. Especially since I had already tried that once with Steve; just look how that turned out... disastrous!

Several weeks went by, and with each passing day, life with Don became more intolerable. Jessie told me that there were several openings at the City of Huntington Beach, and she finally convinced me to submit an application. I knew that she was right. I could not end my dysfunctional marriage until I found a steady job, and achieve some level of independence. Once I learned that the only openings were for Records Clerks in the Police Department, I was very disappointed and discouraged. I just didn't believe that I would be a good fit in that environment. But I tried to remain optimistic that an opening somewhere else in the City would come up.

My depression was deepening over what seemed like a hopeless situation, so I decided to take Jessie up on her offer and meet her cop friend. I thought maybe a little male attention would lift my spirits, which had hit rock bottom. However, once I had committed to meeting him, my insecurities started preying on my mind. How could I ever hide all my phobias from another man? How could any halfway normal man put up with my panic attacks and agoraphobia? Why would they even want to? Even though I took medication, it didn't always prevent attacks; attacks that made me feel like a fool; scared, that I was going to end up in the loony bin. Again, this was in the 60's and there was very little known about these illnesses, so it was understandable that someone witnessing the panic attacks or the seemingly unreasonable fears resulting from agoraphobia might assume that I was "crazy". It wore me out thinking of plausible excuses for not being able to do certain things or go certain places outside my comfort zone, places that most people wouldn't think twice about. And, as I had learned from Don, my weaknesses were a strong tool that could be used against me, to psychologically beat me down, and fuel all of my insecurities, until I felt like a worthless human being who perhaps really was crazy. Every time I ventured beyond my comfort zone, I just prayed that my medication wouldn't fail me! But finally, I decided that it was time to confront these demons and throw caution to the wind. I would meet Jessie's friend.

Jessie arranged for the three of us to meet at a local bar that was a popular cop hangout. She warned me that Fred was a babe-magnet, even though he wasn't the best looking guy. He apparently had enough sex appeal and charisma to make up for whatever he lacked in the looks department. When we first met, I found him cute in a boyish sort of way, and I was enchanted by his soft spoken voice and laid back manner. As the night wore on, I became enamored of this charismatic man and was excited to have such a nice guy to go out with, even if it turned out to be for just one night. Jessie had cautioned me about him though, warning me that his MO was to get a woman in bed and then promptly dump her, once the deed was done. I hoped maybe he was at a point in his life, when he was looking for a woman who would be more challenging, not so easy to seduce; that woman just might be me. Having a physical relationship with another man at this point in my life was not on my radar anyway, so I didn't think that I would have a problem resisting any physical overtures he might make.

After only two dates with Fred, he had me hook, line, and sinker! Never had anyone kissed me the way he did! To this day I can't come up with adequate words to describe it, or to describe the passion and longing I felt for this man. To say that he knew all the right moves, would be a gross understatement, let's just say, if he had written a book on how to hook a woman, it would have been a national bestseller, and a handbook that every man could have used to render us women helpless under their spell!

By our third date, it took every single ounce of willpower in my being to resist succumbing to him physically. He already had me emotionally! The fear of blowing this relationship by becoming just one more of his conquests kept me in check. That, and a lot of praying to God for strength!

On our fourth date, Fred told me he had a surprise for me and we would be gone most of the day. By now, Don was pretty open about his affair with his bartender bimbo. Even though I was happy to have him out of my hair, I was still insulted that he was so blatant about it. As for myself, not out of any sense of loyalty to Don, but just for my own self-respect, I tried to be very clandestine and discreet about where I was going, and with whom, usually saying that I was going out with the girls. I did not want to sink down to his level. And I didn't think his kids needed to see bad behavior from the adults in their life.

So I agreed to spend the day with Fred, and told Don that I was going on a day trip to Catalina with the girls.

We headed out on Saturday morning, heading south. I was so excited and couldn't wait to see what surprise Fred had planned for us! It seemed we had been driving a very long time and I had no idea where we were headed, until we reached the Mexican border and crossed into Tijuana. Immediately my excitement turned in to trepidation, carousing around Tijuana was not my idea of fun! I felt that I had been duped, and couldn't imagine why he would think that Tijuana would be a pleasant surprise for me. Back in those days, as now, Tijuana had a reputation for all kinds of debauchery, not the kind of place you took any self-respecting woman on a date! Thank God I had taken a healthy dose of my medication, otherwise I would not have been able to travel so far. I did feel very comfortable and protected with Fred, which helped tremendously with my feelings of panic. We had also stopped before hitting "T" Town and had a couple of beers with lunch, which relaxed and calmed me, even though I still felt somewhat uptight.

I literally gasped in shock when we entered the first club, and there were men and women actually engaging in sex acts on stage! I honestly couldn't believe what I was witnessing, and I told Fred that I wanted to leave immediately! I never considered myself to be a prude in the sex department, but what one does in the privacy of their own home with their partner is a whole different story; this public display going on in front of our eyes was beyond the pale! He was very nonchalant about the whole thing, telling me to sit back and relax; we would go window shopping in a few minutes.

I thought I would be the good sport and stick it out for just a few minutes, but when the emcee approached me and solicited me to engage in a group sex act, I didn't care anymore if Fred thought that I was the worst date he ever had, I stood up and told him that we were leaving right now! He mumbled something about me being too sensitive, but at least he agreed to go.

Fred did apologize to me once he realized how deeply offended I was, and offered to take me home. He promised me that the next time he wanted to surprise me, it would be something more to my liking. I actually felt as though Fred got some sort of perverse enjoyment out of my shock and horror, and suspected all along how I would react. I started thinking that maybe my Prince Charming had a dark side, which he usually kept well hidden.

I arrived home earlier than anticipated. I headed for the bedroom, wanting to shed my clothes and jump in the shower to scrub off the filth of that day. I swung open the bedroom door, turned on the light, and voila, whom did I discover, but a naked Don and his scuzzy bartender having sex! She started shaking and crying and acting as though I was invading her privacy, she actually had the nerve to act offended that I had walked in on them! I don't remember what I shouted at them but I can most certainly guarantee it wasn't ladylike. I slammed out of the room, leaving them to compose themselves and get dressed, all the while thinking: how much more debauchery must I witness in one day?

I stared at the whore as she exited the front door, still playing the teary eyed victim to the hilt. What nerve she had, jumping into my bed, in my house, with my husband, in broad daylight, with his kids present in the house! This was the final nail in the coffin that was our marriage. I told Don, he had disrespected me for the last time; I was moving out. I asked him what he was thinking. He just said he hadn't expected me home so early, plus, since we were planning to split up anyway, He didn't think it was that big of a deal. He said, he hadn't planned for it to happen, one thing just led to another. At that moment the only emotion I felt was complete and total disgust for this man, whom I had once vowed to love and honor for the rest of my life.

I threw together an overnight bag, and headed to my mom's in Balboa, expecting to stay there only until I could make other arrangements. On the way, I had a full-blown panic attack. I didn't know what to do. It scared the hell out of me! All the stress and tumult of that horrible day reared its ugly head and came rushing at me! I stopped at the first house I came to and pounded on the door. I told the man who answered that I was ill and needed to use his phone. He did not hesitate to invite me in and point me to the phone. I couldn't call my mom, because she didn't drive, so I called Fred, believing that he cared enough about me to come to my rescue, believing that he would feel that his actions contributed to my plight, at least in some small part.

I reached him, but as it turned out, it would have been better if he had never answered the phone. I explained my dilemma to him and asked if he could come and pick me up. He said he didn't understand what was wrong with me but he would come.

When he arrived, it was clear that he was not happy to be there. I told him what had happened at home, and that I was going to stay at my mom's. He agreed to take me to Balboa. I explained to him that I would be okay if he would just follow me to my mom's, I didn't want to leave my car overnight in a strange neighborhood, and I didn't know if I could find someone to help me retrieve it the following day. His facial expression said all I needed to know. He could not comprehend why I could drive myself to my mom's if he was following me but couldn't do it on my own. I tried to explain that it was a security thing, that if I was struck suddenly with another attack, someone would be close by to help me. I didn't go into too much detail, because I was still trying to hide the fact that this was a recurring problem. Rather, I tried to pass it off as a nervous reaction to the day's traumatic events.

He followed me most of the way. When we were almost there, I waved him on. I think I was deluding myself again, that Fred would be my Sir Galahad, sent to rescue me from the tyrannical husband from hell. Even though I waved him on, I was secretly hoping so badly that he would continue following me the entire way, making sure that I arrived safely. But he did not; he went on his way without hesitation. I berated myself for having called him, for letting him witness my secret shame. Although I understood why most men would not want to get involved with a woman who periodically freaked out, knowing that unless one experienced this illness first hand, one could never understand it, I still held out the naïve hope that Fred would be different, that he wouldn't be like most men. But sadly, I never heard from him again.

The next day I called Don and told him that I was going to come over and pack up some of my belongings. He replied that everything in the house was his property; that he had paid for it. How easy and convenient for him to forget that I had worked and contributed to the household, not to mention taking care of his kids and the household during the entire time we were together.

I decided to go to the house anyway, and attempt to pick up my belongings. When I arrived, the kids were standing at the door. They both ran into my arms and begged me not to leave them, or better yet, to take them with me. I told them how much I cared about them, and tried my best to explain why they couldn't come with me.

At the same time, Don approached me and asked if I would stay with the kids for a couple of days so he could go on a fishing trip. I agreed, as it gave me an opportunity to sort through my belongings and spend some quality time with the kids before I moved out.

Right after he left, I received a call from the personnel office of the City of Huntington Beach. There was an opening in the Fire Department, and they wanted me to come in and complete an application. I completed the application and scheduled some screening tests. This couldn't have come at a better time. I really needed a steady income and good benefits.

10 HUNTINGTON BEACH POLICE

By the time that Don returned from his fishing trip, I had packed up what belongings I needed, and loaded them in my car. I saw that his hand was bandaged and I jokingly asked him if he had a run-in with a shark. Without blinking an eye, he told me he and Babs had a fight and he slugged her in the jaw, breaking her jaw as well as his hand. He said that she learned fast, who was in charge. I thought to myself that if he had ever done that to me, he would have been behind bars. I know I had foolishly put up with his mental abuse, but I never would have tolerated physical abuse. I later learned that they kissed and made up, but it happened again, and they both ended up in the emergency room with broken bones. I hated to think how much his poor kids had witnessed and what effect it would have on their lives.

As I was about to leave our home for the last time, Don's final words to me were: "If ever you attempt to take me to court to get any of my property, I will chop you up in fine pieces and drop you on your mother's doorstep." Knowing what a psycho he could be, I took this threat very seriously, believing he was perfectly capable of killing me. And only a very sick person would threaten such a horrible death, shooting me would be much too mundane for him! I didn't want anything from him anyway, all I wanted was to get away from him, and I couldn't do it fast enough! The minute I threw my car in reverse, I heard a loud sound. My transmission had chosen that very inopportune time to blow up, and there I was, stuck in his driveway after just being threatened with a violent death! I was on the verge of another panic attack, so I called the towing company and rushed next door to my friend Margie's house.

Margie offered to drive me to my mom's house, but she said that we could no longer be friends. Her husband Lanny, another abusive creep, had ordered her to cut all ties with me if I left Don. I was heartbroken at losing her friendship. We had gone through so much together. I asked her if she wouldn't reconsider, and at least call me occasionally, or go to lunch with me once in a while, but she said that if Lanny found out, he would explode and she would end up in the hospital. As close as we were, our friendship wasn't worth taking that kind of risk. I recalled a couple of times when she had black eyes and I thought Lanny had done it. She always denied it, but I knew that he was responsible. I told her, I understood, and would never want to be responsible for putting her in a compromising or dangerous position. I couldn't help asking her why she remained in an abusive marriage. Her response was the typical one: she stayed for the sake of her two kids. I thanked Margie for being such a good friend to me over the past few years and wished her well. That was the last time we ever spoke.

Once I learned how much it would cost to fix my car, more than what I could possibly come up with, I told the mechanics they could blow it up if they wanted to. I borrowed enough money to buy another old clunker, and headed to the City of Huntington Beach Personnel Department. I learned that the Fire Department position had already been filled, but there was an immediate opening in the Police Department's Records Bureau. Of course, was there ever a doubt?

A couple of weeks later I received a phone call from the City of Huntington Beach. They had scheduled an interview for me with a Lieutenant in the Police Department. As I sat down for my interview, I became extremely anxious when I realized that I would be interviewed by a panel of three police officers. I was used to one on one interviews, not three people staring at me, rapidly firing questions at me one after the other. Their uniforms and guns contributed to my anxiety also. Cops tended to freak me out because I had had some bad experiences with them in the past.

I had been stopped by one of Huntington Beach's finest one night while on my way to visit a friend. When I saw those lights behind me and heard that siren, my heart practically stopped beating from fear, which was probably irrational, since I knew that I wasn't doing anything wrong. He asked me where I was going. After I told him, I asked him what had I done wrong. He said that he thought I was attractive and just wanted to meet me. I told him how much he scared me and he immediately started fidgeting, apologizing for offending me as that was not his intention. I'm sure he was worried that I would call his supervisor and make a complaint. I know lots of women are enamored of a man in a uniform and badge and he probably fully expected that I was one of them, flattered by his compliment. And truth be told, I was a little flattered. But I still told him that being stopped by a cop with sirens blaring and lights flashing was not a pleasant experience, and definitely not the way to impress a woman!

Later, once I started working at HBPD, I learned a lot about this officer. He had a colorful history of womanizing, and an approach to policing that at times was totally unethical, and sometimes borderline criminal. Interestingly enough, he later was promoted to sergeant, and then lieutenant. How times have changed! His type of behavior would never be tolerated today.

One of the questions I was asked during my interview, still stands out in my mind to this day. It came from a lieutenant who was absolutely revered by everyone in the Department. He asked me, in his words, if my soon-to-be son of a bitch ex-husband would storm the PD and cause a scene. I was shocked by the question, because I certainly hadn't discussed Don with them, so where were they getting this information? I wondered if he really knew about Don; or was just guessing, kind of playing with me? I answered that I didn't anticipate anything like that "…but you know, you have the guns, so there shouldn't be a problem". He laughed at my answer and said that he liked my attitude. He told me that he thought I would fit in just fine, in spite of my "sophisticated appearance". They said, they would get back to me in a couple of days. After that interview, I started thinking this just might be a fun place to work after all.

A short time later I was contacted and told that I would be hired on a temporary basis until they could do a thorough background check on me. If they found no skeletons in my closet, I would become a full-time Records Clerk. I still had reservations, but I was in desperate need of a job, so I accepted the offer. Men in uniform just seemed so militant and cold to me, not to mention all the guns! Again, I wasn't one of those women who swooned over a man in uniform, quite the opposite.

I started out working on the day shift, for a woman who had been with the HBPD for over 30 years. I found her to be almost as intimidating as the officers, but I needed the job.

I had only been working there about two weeks when a riot broke out in the downtown area. About a hundred bikers, mostly Hell's Angels, were indeed raising hell, and ended up spending some quality time in our fine jail. Numerous motorcycles were also impounded. Once the bikers were released, they wanted their bikes released too. At that time the Hell's Angels were notorious bad guys, and were a constant target of law enforcement. So, needless to say, they were not in the best of moods after spending a night in jail. One very mean old dirty biker came to the counter, just oozing hatred. There was nothing separating us but a short counter, and he glared at me and whispered, "You better get your ass in gear, or I'm going to fuck you, and then kill you". He was deadly serious, and knowing their reputation, I took his threat very seriously. I immediately went into shock, losing my voice and visibly trembling. I couldn't even tell anyone what had just happened because I couldn't speak. I quickly retrieved his paperwork and handed it to him with shaking hands. There were other scary bikers that day, but none compared to him. This was my first real encounter with the criminal element of our society, and what an eye opener it was!

By the end of that day, I couldn't help thinking: what have I gotten myself into? I should have held out for a position in the Fire Department, where the worst encounter I might have would be with a grumpy co-worker! I wasn't sure if I was going to make it in the Police Department. I wondered if I had the nerve and the courage to deal with the worst society had to offer. As it turned out, I was glad I stuck it out because I had no more encounters like that for a very long time.

Things were going along smoothly, but I should have known that it wouldn't last; nothing in my life ever went smoothly for long. I soon learned that I would be assigned jail duties, including matron duty and transporting prisoners to county jail. I thought I had signed up to be an office clerical worker, not to work in the jail with real prisoners!

Almost daily, we would hear an announcement over the loudspeaker "Matron to the jail... Now!" At the time I started working there, there were no female police officers, so civilian personnel were utilized. We had no formal training, and were subjected to many abuses by the prisoners, both verbal and physical. When I would hear that announcement, I would run to the restroom as fast I my feet would carry me, to try and avoid being the one sent to the "dungeon". Oddly, there were some girls who didn't mind the jail duties, so I happily let them do it whenever possible.

But I still had my share of encounters with an assortment of unsavory characters, as much as I wanted to, I couldn't always shirk my responsibilities. I decided that I needed to work really hard, to be promoted to supervisor, so that I could be the one sending the girls to the jail, instead of the one being sent.

Huntington Beach only had a temporary holding facility at that time, so prisoners were held there only until they could be transported to the county jail. Matrons had to do strip searches; that was the most dreaded of all duties. Some of the women were so filthy that even wearing gloves didn't keep me from wondering if I was going to catch some disease, or if bugs were going to jump on me! And the smell, putrid is the only word that comes close! When I would get a particularly nasty one, I would think this is it, I have to get out of here!

One night I remember in particular, I had to accompany Harry, a narcotics officer, to transport a female prisoner to the county jail. When we arrived, he thought he would be funny and told intake that I was the prisoner. He carried it so far that I'm sure if I had reported him, he would've gotten in trouble. But he thought it was great fun, and when I lit into him, he just laughed hysterically. The real prisoner seemed amused, too. It was the only time all night that she actually laughed.

On our way back to the station, Harry spotted a car approximately 1½ miles ahead of us. He looked at me and said "Norma Jeanne, that car is carrying two druggies and they are smoking pot. He hit the lights and siren and off we went in pursuit. It was Department policy that officers could not go in pursuit, regardless of the crime, when civilian personnel were in the car. But Harry had a bad habit of ignoring policy. In his opinion, his gut feelings trumped Department regulations. If he thought that there was a crime in progress, nothing and no one was going to stop him from pursuing the bad guy!

He caught up to the car and pulled them over, and sure enough, there were two males inside, and they reeked of pot! To this day I don't know how Harry could have known, when he spotted their car, they were too far away to see with the human eye! He got them out of the car, handcuffed them, and had them sit on the curb next to the freeway. All of a sudden he shouted: "Norma Jeanne, I have to take a leak, and you have to keep an eye on these two dirt bags." He shoved his gun into my hands and off he went down the embankment. I had never handled a gun before and this must have been evident even to the prisoners because they started laughing hysterically. Next thing I know, County Highway Police pulled up with their lights on, jumped out of the car, and pointed their guns at me! Talk about a deer in the headlights! I started screaming for Harry to hurry up because we had a big problem! With guns pointed at me, the chippies asked me what I was doing. I was wearing civilian clothing and in no way did I even remotely resemble a police officer. I could barely speak but managed to stutter that the officer was down the embankment "doing his business". I told them he had handed me his gun and told me to watch the prisoners for him. They didn't look convinced, but thankfully, Harry came bounding back up the embankment, zipping up his pants and explaining to the chippies what had happened. The chippies just shook their heads and told us to be careful and then departed with no further comment. No doubt we gave them a good story to share, and probably a good laugh!

After the chippies left, Harry asked me if I wanted to keep his gun or take his night stick, because I had to sit in the back seat with one of the prisoners. Obviously I opted for the night stick, although I really didn't know how to use that any more than I did the gun, but at least there was no chance of accidentally shooting someone with a night stick. I didn't think the guys were going to be a problem; they were high and laughing hysterically, apparently thoroughly enjoying their time with us. I'm sure they couldn't wait to tell their story to their friends, but I wonder if anyone even believed them! If I hadn't been there, I wouldn't have believed it!

Once we arrived back at the station, I told Harry that this was an event that would forever be etched in my memory. I also told him that I would like to punch his lights out for what he put me through. I really loved Harry, but you just never knew what was going to happen when he was around.

On my first Halloween night at HBPD, Loren and I were the only two working in the Records Bureau. I was looking out the window when I saw a large brown blob and wondered what it was. I turned away from the public counter and next thing I knew, over the counter came a huge gorilla, grunting and flaying his huge furry arms at us! We both screamed in absolute terror and started running towards the back of the building, but we weren't fast enough to get away! One of those big hairy arms reached out and grabbed me and I thought I was going to faint from fright! The gorilla started laughing hysterically, a familiar sound to us, none other than our pal Harry! He ripped off his grotesque mask and yelled "gotcha!" I wanted to smack him. His "gotcha" almost gave me a stroke. I thought some madman was going to kill us! Well, the madman part was correct anyway.

One night I was asked to accompany the Narcotics Unit on a stake-out. I was instructed to walk around the mall with one of the undercover detectives until they spotted the suspects making a buy. Well it happened so fast that I was shoved to the side and came perilously close to falling in the gutter. Harry came barreling out of the trunk of the undercover detective car so fast, he was practically flying! He jumped in front of the suspect's car, a VW bug, and almost ended up on the hood. He was able to reach in and grab the driver by the neck which caused the driver to lose control of the car. The VW veered in my direction. Somehow Harry managed to gain control of the VW before it plowed me down, and he dragged the driver out of the car. The passenger attempted to flee, but was tackled to the ground by several other narcotics detectives. If not for Harry's superhuman acrobatics, the bad guys might have gotten away. But not for long; bad guys rarely got away from Harry.

Harry was definitely what one would call a "loose cannon", á la Dirty Harry, doing whatever it took to get the bad guys, and to heck with the rules. He was like no other cop on the force, and there would never be another one like him. Harry pulled a few more antics, and then, to no one's surprise, was asked to take an early retirement. Things were never quite the same without our crazy Harry. We later learned that he was hired by an exclusive club in Newport Beach as a tennis instructor. I'm sure the ladies enjoyed Harry's quick wit and his bag of stories.

When I first got hired in the 1960's, HBPD's Chief of Police had the reputation of an eccentric. I did find him to be quite a colorful character, but also a very caring man. His pride and joy was his mare whom he spent hours grooming and caring for. During the annual 4th of July parade, you could count on seeing him proudly riding down Main Street, tipping his hat to the crowd and grinning from ear to ear. It was not unusual to find on-duty police officers brushing and cleaning the mare if the Chief was preoccupied with official business. The officers dreaded getting this assignment, and you could hear them groaning and complaining throughout the Department, out of earshot of the Chief, of course. No one would dare insult his beloved mare. Along with the grooming and feeding came clean up, and it was common to hear stories of the unlucky officers who accidentally stepped in the horse dung, screwing up their highly polished black uniform shoes. The officers were meticulous about their shoes, especially the motorcycle officers who wore the tall shiny black motor boots. They did not appreciate having to tread through mud and poop in their macho boots.

My immediate sergeant had learned that I was a painter, and asked to see some of my work. After viewing some of the photos, he asked if I would be willing to display some of them in the Records Bureau. I was happy to oblige him, thinking I might even get lucky and sell a few. He also scheduled a local paper to write an article, featuring me standing next to one of my paintings of a ship. Once the article came out, the Chief summoned me to his office, something we all dreaded, because oftentimes it meant we were in trouble. I was very nervous, but once he started talking, I realized that he was just a regular down to earth man, and I was able to relax. He asked if I would paint a portrait of him sitting atop his precious horse. He opened a filing cabinet filled with photos of the two of them. We spent several hours going through a few hundred photos, while I tried to explain to him that I had never done a portrait before. He wanted me to at least give it a try, and since I was a fellow animal lover, I agreed. I took several of his photos and started sketching every chance I got. My immediate sergeant was pushing me to get it done, looking for an "attaboy" from the Chief for "discovering" me. Every organization has its butt kissers and ladder climbers. Apparently, he was one of those.

Not long after my meeting with the Chief, he was out brushing his horse, and just fell over, dead. He had died of a heart attack while doing what he loved most. I never started the painting of the two of them and regretted not at least showing him my sketches before he died, I think he would have really liked them.

The next Chief of Police was Earle Robitaille. This man was revered by all. Without a doubt, he was one of the best in that position. In all the years of my employment I never heard a negative word about him. He was all for his men, and stood up for them. He also cared and treated the civilian employees with the utmost respect and fairness. It was a very sad day for all of us when his retirement date came. No one wanted to see this man leave. To this day, he has been remembered and honored by the department. We organized a surprise party in his honor, held at the facility, where it was packed to overflowing. The sentiment expressed was that this is his police department and it will always remain his.

At the time when I was hired, the police building was located downtown, at 5th and Orange Streets. It was old, sitting on sinking sand. Safety issues notwithstanding, the old building had a lot of character, as well as a lot of occupants who were characters. My friend Loren and I worked the swing shift; we laughed every time the sands shifted, and our chairs started rolling back and forth. You had to wedge your leg or foot between the chair and the desk to steady yourself. The Engineering Department attempted many times to level it out, but it never stayed that way for long. We eventually moved to a new and modern facility, and unfortunately lost a lot of the comradery that we experienced at the smaller facility.

As things turned out, I was totally enjoying my job at HBPD. After all the brow beating and mental abuse I took from my husband, I was starting to regain some of my old self esteem. I no longer felt like a worthless human being who had nothing to offer society. It was an exhilarating feeling. I wondered how I had ever survived under the reign of such a cruel and controlling man, or why I had stayed so long.

Loren and I loved checking out the officers. There were a few who were movie star good looking. One in particular, Evan, came in to visit me on a regular basis. I heard that he was one of the Department Casanovas, who had broken many a heart. I would become all flustered whenever he started talking to me; my mind would go blank. At times, beads of perspiration would appear on my quivering upper lip, and I thought I would topple over from a combination of embarrassment and sheer joy that he found me worthy of his attention. I'm sure he was quite used to the effect he had on women, but he was kind enough to pretend not to notice. When he finally asked me out, I was elated. I said yes without hesitation, in spite of his reputation of a Casanova. I mean, doesn't every woman think that she could be "the one" to change such a man? Anticipating our date gave me a rush of adrenaline and I became Superwoman at work, tearing through my work with a silly grin on my face, and loving everyone, even the obnoxious public coming in to file a complaint.

Evan had a sleek red Corvette, another testosterone booster and babe magnet, something else to attract women, not that he needed the help with his good looks. On our first date, Evan had to try and impress me with how fast his Corvette could go. We went flying down the Pacific Coast Highway at over

100mph with me screaming the whole time, like a little girl on a scary roller coaster, who wants to get off. When he realized that I was screaming from fright, and not exhilaration, he did the gentlemanly thing, and immediately slowed down. But it was too late, he had to pull over to the shoulder so I could get out of the car and throw up! Not exactly my idea of the perfect first date. We had to skip the dinner we had planned, and opted to park at the beach, trying to settle my churning stomach with a 7UP. Still, we ended up having a nice discussion, particularly about his life at the PD and how much it meant to him to become a police officer.

During our conversation, he mentioned that he had a very bad pain in his groin area and he was concerned about it. I asked him what the doctor said. He told me that he had been raised as a Christian Scientist and his family did not believe in doctors. I told him that I didn't mean to be disrespectful, but he needed to get to a doctor right away. I told him God had meant for some people to be healers and he should not look upon going to a doctor as a sin. He said he would think about it. My heart went out to him because I sensed that it was truly an issue of conscience for him.

Evan and I went out one more time after that, and I could sense that he was not feeling well. He ended up taking a leave of absence from work, but would come in to visit periodically. We all watched with a heavy heart as this beautiful man's health and appearance started rapidly deteriorating. His hair was thinning and he was almost bald in spots. His skin turned a pasty yellow-gray. He lost that spring in his step, and that special charismatic charm that so many insanely handsome men have. It was difficult at times to even recognize that this was the same man who took me on a 100mph ride in his red Corvette such a short time ago. Every time I talked to him, it took all my self-control not to break down in tears. Probably the only thing that kept me from crying as I witnessed his health deteriorating, was not wanting him to see how scared I was for him. He was only 25 years old when he died of prostate cancer. His funeral was one of the saddest I ever attended.

Driving back and forth to my mom's house in Balboa every day was becoming a grind, so I decided to find an apartment close to work. One of the officers directed me to an apartment complex a couple of miles away from the PD. For some reason he didn't bother to warn me that the apartment complex was in a high crime area. After moving in, all I had money for was a black and white TV. I got to enjoy my new TV for about three days before I came home one day, finding that my apartment was ransacked, and my new TV was gone. I have always despised thieves. They intrude in your private, personal space, leaving you feeling as if you had been physically violated. The thought of a stranger rummaging through my lingerie drawer made my skin crawl. I ended up throwing all of my personal items away and replacing them with new ones, untouched by strange hands.

After the break-in, I knew that I would never again feel safe and comfortable in my apartment, even though the officer who told me about the apartment would come over at night and sleep on my couch, with his gun at hand. He was feeling a bit guilty, I presume. This turned out to be a bad arrangement. We became more than close friends, and I felt horribly guilty, because I knew that he was engaged, planning to wed in the near future. I tried to end our arrangement, but eventually realized that the only way I could do that was to move. One of my co-workers, Marilyn, had rented a condo and was looking for a roommate. I jumped at the opportunity. Just prior to moving, I came home one night to find my street blocked off. There were cops from all different agencies in Orange County and they had their rifles drawn. It turned out that a biker gang had fired shots and one person had been hit. It was like watching a scene out of a movie, with all these cops with their weapons drawn. It probably would have been somewhat more exciting had it not been happening where I lived. It was the middle of the night before I was able to return to my apartment, and then I couldn't sleep because of all the adrenaline still flowing through my body.

I had one final party at my apartment before I moved. I decided to prepare Thanksgiving dinner for the officers who had to work on Thanksgiving day and could not be with their families. My friend Jessie helped out, and we worked tirelessly, preparing multiple turkeys and all the other traditional Thanksgiving dishes. We never anticipated so many officers would show up. I later found out that many of them had Thanksgiving dinner with their families, but came to my house to enjoy a second meal. Cops can be bottomless pits, and rarely pass up a free meal. Regardless, it was a good feeling to offer some holiday cheer to those officers who had nowhere to go. I was most surprised when one of our married captains showed up and proceeded to make suggestive advances towards me. At that time, being married did not seem to be as much of a deterrent to cheating as it does today, but that was before the Aids epidemic. I won't deny that my ego thrived on the attention; I mean, he was a captain, the highest ranking officer beside the Chief, and that was kind of a thrill. But I knew better than to even entertain the idea of a relationship with him. I was very diplomatic in letting him know that I wasn't interested. You had to be careful whose toes you stepped on, because stepping on the wrong toes could become a career suicide. I was proud of myself for doing it with finesse and in good humor.

One night I heard the dreaded "female to the jail" blaring over the loudspeaker. As usual, my first thought was: on whom could I shirk this off? I would not be able to hide in the ladies' room this time! As I frantically looked around, I realized that I was the only one.

As soon as I entered the jail, I heard a female screaming and swearing like a drunken sailor. Her arms, which looked shrunken to the size of broomsticks, were bound together with adhesive tape. Because her wrists were so skinny, the handcuffs slipped right off her. I was told that she had liver cancer, which caused her to have scabs all over her arms and body. She was screaming "Take this tape off me now, damn you all!" Considering the agitated state she was in, there was no way that I could approach her and try to get the tape off, so I asked the officer who brought her in, to try and remove it, hoping that would calm her down. Much to my amazement, he grabbed her stick thin arms and yanked the tape so hard that her skin came off and blood started squirting everywhere! She was yelling profanities like I had never heard, and I really couldn't blame her. I thought the officer could have at least tried to remove the tape gently, a little at a time. The officer then said to me "Now you can search her. You wanted me to take off the tape and that's what I did." I told him there was no way I was going near her; I did not get paid enough to deal with this kind of crap. I believed this officer really crossed the line, and should have been disciplined, but nothing ever happened to him. He had a reputation for being sadistic, and now I saw firsthand how he got that reputation.

Since I refused to search her, they called in one of the dispatchers to do it. While attempting to do the search, the suspect grabbed the dispatcher's wrist so hard that she fractured it, also causing some permanent damage. The dispatcher ended up having to medically retire after two surgeries failed to correct the problem. Most people thought she milked the system, getting a medical retirement, but I was not one of them. Having seen firsthand the state the suspect was in, I had no doubt that she was perfectly capable of inflicting great bodily harm. For some reason many people blamed me for the dispatcher getting injured, when in fact it was probably the officer's sadistic actions that caused the suspect to turn physically violent.

I moved into the townhouse that Marilyn had leased. It was in a decent neighborhood, and above all, close to the beach and close to work. It was such a huge relief to be away from my apartment in what sometimes seemed like a war zone, to be able to sleep at night, without an armed police officer snoring on my couch.

Marilyn was a tall, attractive redhead, with a very strong will and a great personality. She was separated from her husband and family, working the night shift at the PD while trying to pursue a career in decorating. She fell for one of the officers, who had the reputation of being borderline crazy. Not only did his reputation not dissuade her, it actually intrigued her. He also was very attractive, tall, dark, and you know the rest. She and this officer became romantically involved, even though he was still married. He and his wife had an arrangement where he would stay at home, but could do his own thing. It seemed his kind of life style was quite commonplace at the time, married officers having affairs with female civilian personnel. Even I had succumbed with my sofa guy, although he was not married at the time, but engaged to be in the near future.

Their affair had been going on for a few months, and their relationship was blossoming. She was hoping that he would leave his wife and they could have a future together. He led her to think that this just might become reality. Haven't we all heard this one?

One morning she woke up extremely sick to her stomach. She started throwing up a lot, which lasted for several days, so she ended up going to the doctor. She didn't have a clue as to what she was in store for next. This physician informed her that she was about to become a mother, bearing a love child. She told Ted, but he did nothing at all to help her. He actually ran in the opposite direction and that was the end of their relationship.

Marilyn had the baby, and he was a beautiful child, with dark curly hair and gorgeous dark eyes. Her other children were all blond with blue eyes. If she wanted to, which was not the case, she could have tried to convince her estranged husband that it was his child. She contacted her husband and decided to reconcile with him. He was elated and welcomed her and the child back home with open arms. She was very blessed to have such an understanding and loving husband. It seemed that no matter what Marilyn did, things always worked out for her. Too bad that some of her luck didn't rub off on me.

I need to add that Marilyn became a highly successful designer, receiving numerous awards for her talents over the years. She and I had not stayed in touch for many years, as she was busy raising a family of five children and pursuing her career. Only recently have we reunited along with another good friend, Cheryl. The three of us get together for lunches, doing a lot of catching up. Marilyn is still the same fun loving person with an unbelievable amount of vibrant energy. My good friend Cheryl is also the daughter of one of my favorite bosses I was fortunate to have. One of the sergeants at work became highly enamored of Cheryl. He fell madly in love with her and after a short courting period they were married.

They now live around the corner and across the street where her wonderful mom Annie resides. Joe and I are very blessed to have them as our close friends.

With Marilyn reconciling with her husband, she turned the one year lease over to me. I felt very sad about her departure, as she had a great sense of humor and always had an entertaining tale to tell. I also found myself suffering financially. I didn't know how I was going to pay the rent. I was bound to a year's lease, and even if I broke the lease, I had no idea where I would go. I didn't want to impose on my mom again, although I knew that she would have put up with me if I asked. I was also working swing shift from 4pm to 12am and didn't want to be making the drive between Balboa and Huntington Beach. I knew that I would have to find another roommate, but in the meantime I started working as much overtime as I possibly could.

I would start my shift at 4pm as the day shift was leaving, and I would still be there to greet them when they returned the next morning! I was doing this about three times a week and it was exhausting. I also came in for matron transportation to Orange County Jail whenever they needed me, regardless of my disdain for the assignment. My whole life seemed to revolve around working, there was no time for a personal life, but I was paying my rent.

My crazy schedule finally caught up to me one night. I just fell apart, hyperventilating and feeling like I was going to die. I ended up in the emergency room where they gave me even more medication and warned me to slow down on my work schedule. All work and no play was apparently more than what my delicate system could handle! I had the will, but the body wasn't cooperating.

I went home that night and jumped into my cozy bed, snuggling with my cat Gussie, who always had such a calming effect on me. With all the medications in my system, I fell into a deep sleep for 7 or 8 hours. What a blessing to get a normal night's sleep! After a week of recuperation, I was ready and eager to get back to work.

I truly loved my job. The anticipation of what was going to happen each night was always so exciting. I did everything in my power to never miss a day because I was afraid I would miss something. Every night was different, nothing predictable or mundane about this job!

One of the lieutenants I adored because he was always so thoughtful and kind to me, called me at home shortly after my trip to the emergency room, and asked if he could come by and visit. I was thrilled that he cared so much about my well-being and invited him over. He arrived carrying a small bouquet of flowers with a card with a really nice get well message. I loved the attention, especially coming from someone I really liked.   At the end of his visit, he invited me to a party that evening at another officer's house. I told him that it was my first night back at work, and I didn't think that I should take time off. But he talked me into it, telling me that it would be good for me, and no one would mind. I told him that I would think about it.

Of course it didn't take much arm twisting to convince me, and I could hardly wait to get there, hoping that Tim, my lieutenant friend, would be there, anticipating my arrival. I was not disappointed. As soon as I entered, Tim was by my side. He went out of his way to find me a comfy chair and get me a drink. I could see the eyebrows lifting as people began to notice how much attention I was getting from him. I totally enjoyed their reaction; after all, he was a popular lieutenant, and he was paying attention to me. And he definitely wasn't hard on the eyes, either! I had an insatiable appetite to be noticed; enough attention was never enough for me.

Tim and I eventually ended up in his car, making out for most of the night. I finally got around to asking if he was still married and he said yes. I think I knew in my heart of hearts that he was married, but I could pretend that he wasn't, as long as I didn't ask the question. But once I did ask the question, our make-out session came to an abrupt end. I was ashamed of myself, I let his kindness and charm cloud my judgment. After our display, I knew, I would be the talk of the Department. Again, I wasn't disappointed. I really didn't want the reputation of an easy mark, especially with a married man, but news travels fast within the police ranks! People think women are gossips? The officers I worked with could out-gossip any woman I ever met!

It made me sad that there would be no relationship between Tim and me. I thought he would have been the perfect guy for me. He was so kind and thoughtful, something I longed for in a relationship after being with such an abusive husband. But as life went on, I would find myself saying the very same thing about many other men.

I got lucky and was able to convince one of the co-workers, Evelyn, to share the townhouse I was renting. She really wanted a place of her own, but I convinced her that with her working the graveyard shift, and me on swing shift, we would be like ships passing in the night. I was so relieved to find someone who would be reliable in making the monthly rent. You couldn't be a flake if you wanted to keep your job at the PD.

Evelyn was a redhead and fit the stereotype to a tee. It didn't take much to provoke her, or make her fly off the handle.

When I got promoted and ended up being her supervisor, she was not happy. I had my work cut out for me, trying to keep her temper under control, especially because there was another employee, constantly criticizing her work.

One evening at work she flamed out and started waving a pair of scissors around in a very threatening manner. I had to forcibly remove the scissors from her clutch, because I wasn't sure if she intended to use them on someone. This incident led to the deterioration of our relationship. She said I was showing favoritism to the other employee, which was not the case. I was actually trying to protect her from doing something she would regret. I didn't want to see her lose control and hurt someone and end up losing her job, or even worse, end up in jail.

I thought I could smooth things over by taking her out for a drink at the local pub, which was known as a notorious cop hangout. In the past, I got in trouble at this pub for spending the night at the bar. I was having a fling with the bartender who poured a killer drink. I loved the song "Lay Lady Lay" by Bob Dillon and he would play it for me on the juke box for hours on end, while we were engaged in amorous activities. Let's just say there was no need to turn on the heat, we generated plenty of our own!

Unfortunately, my car had been spotted by my supervisor in the wee hours of the morning. He read me the riot act, accusing me of being unprofessional and telling me that my behavior was totally unacceptable as an employee and supervisor of the PD. He was pretty scary. Needless to say, that ended my overnighters at the bar!

I still frequented the place, and thought Evelyn might lighten up, once she discovered that there were cops present, and that she could dance and let her hair down, for a change. On this particular night, one of the officers asked me out for dinner for the following night, and of course, I accepted. Once again, Evelyn was not happy with me, she had not been approached by anyone for a date, and the green eyed monster reared its ugly head.

She got even with me, though. It turned out, that the officer who asked me out had a reputation for being a womanizer, and made the rounds of the female employees. Unfortunately, I didn't know about his bad reputation when I accepted the date. That night I had fun with this guy, and we ended up being intimate. After having such a wonderful night, I thought that we might become a steady twosome. I told Evelyn about our date, and this is when she laid it on me, that he had called her and asked her out, and worse yet, she had accepted, and was going to dinner with him that night. I told her I could not understand why she would go out with him after we had just been intimate the night before. She showed no reaction to my comments, only stating that she planned on keeping their date. I was very upset, and told her that I felt more betrayed by her than by him. I let her know that hooking up with a friend's romantic interest was a sin in my book, and particularly under these circumstances. I let her know that I could not forgive what she was about to do, but it did not phase her. I told her that if she was trying to get even with me for the problems at work, this was not the way to handle it. No matter what I said, she stated that she was going out with Mike. I even recruited a couple of my friends to talk some sense in to her, but it fell on deaf ears.

I heard the doorbell ring, and before I could exit the front room, Evelyn opened the door and there was the low life. He said hello to me, and then asked Evelyn if she was ready to go. I was somewhat stunned at the complacent attitudes coming from the two of them. Here was a guy I had been intimate with just a few short hours ago, and his reaction towards me was that of greeting a stranger on the street. I was blown away. Anger and hurt were seething from my pores.

After this episode, it was obvious that I would have to ask Evelyn to find other living conditions. And when the opportunity presented itself, I would have to kick this guy in the area he so casually used to inflict pain on unsuspecting victims like me! After some time passed, I cooled down and realized that Evelyn did not grasp the seriousness of the situation. I felt that it was her neediness for male attention, even worse than mine, which drove her to do what she did. Still, I was pleased to learn that she was only asked out the one time by that jerk. She never brought up the subject again, nor did I.

Shortly after this incident, Evelyn had a breakdown, and had to medically retire. She had a lengthy stay at the mental health unit at one of the local hospitals. My friends and I reached out to her, and did all we could to help her, but it wasn't enough to pull her out of the deep abyss she had fallen into. It was very heartbreaking to watch her physical and mental downward spiral. I forgave her for our past problems, and to this day she and I remained good friends. We communicate by mail and an occasional phone call, since she moved to Northern California.

11 BILL

My supervisor started paying an unusual amount of attention to me, which caused me some stress. I didn't know what to think of it in the beginning, and ignored him as much as I could politely get away with. I heard that he and his wife were having problems and were splitting up. I wasn't sure how I felt about his advances at first, but he started winning me over with his exuberant personality. I did not find him to be particularly attractive, which was always a major must on my list. What was appealing, was his ability to take charge. He was a protector type, which was important to me, given all my problems and insecurities. He also possessed a keen sense of humor and could get us laughing until we cried. He started looking better and better to me as time went by.

Alas, we started a hot and heavy relationship, and I started becoming extremely attached to him. At work he would bring me wonderful lunches and treats and he had fun hiding them in the evidence lockers downstairs, making me guess which drawer he had hidden them in. It was a bit juvenile, but it made us laugh. He and I were pretty clandestine about our relationship as neither he nor his wife had filed for divorce, so playing our little hide and seek game under the noses of our co-workers, who didn't have a clue, added a little excitement to our relationship.

Eventually he moved in with me. Having Bill move in came at the best time as his financial assistance was greatly needed, even though I was hesitant about us living together, due to his marital status.

Bill maintained an apartment downtown as a front, so his soon to be ex-wife and bosses at the PD would not become alerted to our personal arrangement. At the time, it was very much frowned upon to engage in our type of romantic cohabitation. Even though Bill was separated, he was still married in the eyes of the PD as well as God!

We had a great time together. He would take me on trips and to special events and concerts. One of the most memorable was Neil Diamond at the Greek Theater. It was so romantic sitting outside under the stars. It was a magical evening, and I think I really fell in love with him that night. Or was it that I was in love with love at that moment, like so many other times in my life?

Bill was always thinking of fun activities for the two of us to enjoy. We had another memorable outing to the deer park in Anaheim, CA. The signs cautioned people upon entering the pens, where the deer were waiting with baited breath to chew up whatever you might be carrying or wearing. Of course, being the animal lover that I am, I completely ignored those warnings. Several deer converged on us, starting to tear my straw purse to shreds in a feeding frenzy. At the same time, Bill was under attack, too, with deer standing on his shoes so he could not move or get away. He was making some strange sounds as I was hysterically cracking up. The most important lesson we learned that day is that you really don't want to run out of deer food, unless you're standing really close to an escape route! We were both trapped, and I was laughing so hard that I actually wet my pants a little. Finally a couple of groundskeepers came to our rescue. They had to bribe the rascals with treats, long enough to divert their attention away from us, so we could escape. The imprints of deer hooves on Bill's leather shoes made me get even more hysterical. I couldn't even speak, I was laughing so hard! Every now and then we would remember this incident and get almost as hysterical as we did when it first happened.

We had a wonderful trip to Northern California, with many stops along the way. Our accommodations in most of the inns and hotels were beautiful, my favorites being the ones with awesome views of the Pacific Ocean. The one negative to the trip was travelling down Highway One, the rugged two lane road, carved into the mountain side with sheer drop to the seashore. Not realizing that once you take this highway stretch of 73 miles, there was no turning around or getting off until you completed the entire 73 miles of sheer terror, I hyperventilated the entire way. Of course, it drove him crazy and wore me to exhaustion. My fear of height and claustrophobia was not a good prerequisite for this scenic trip on the road to hell. Even the maximum dose of feel-good pills was failing. There were no pubs along the way either, where we could stop for cocktails and relax for a little while. I lost several pounds that day from so much hyperventilating.

Relief finally came, when we arrived at Carmel, and checked into a beautiful hotel, most importantly, on level ground. We skipped the scenic route going home, opting for the freeway. No way will I ever travel on that road again in my lifetime. It was really sad that all that beauty was wasted on me.

We truly enjoyed one another's company during our first few months together. I know, putting up with me and my phobias, was not an easy task for any man. In the beginning, like so many other relationships, beginnings are the time for deception.

Bill was extremely generous and was always spoiling me with gifts, which I accepted graciously, of course! The best and most amazing was one birthday morning. Upon awakening, I discovered that the bedroom was packed with so many gifts that I couldn't even get out of bed. There were practical items as well as personal, everything from a beautiful brown coat with faux trim, a gorgeous dress and boots with matching jewelry to an ironing board and iron. New pots and pans, which were badly needed, were wrapped to perfection, several towel sets, sheets; and the list goes on. Was he trying to tell me something? Maybe domesticate me just a little? He had stayed up most of the night wrapping, and could hardly hold his head up; he was exhausted. The icing on the cake, so to speak, was the beautifully decorated cake and ice cream, which we shared for breakfast, while taking a break from opening all the presents. It was spectacular, a perfect birthday. I think he was as overjoyed at being able to spoil me, as I was at being spoiled! I realized that I could get used to this treatment; I had to make this relationship work!

One Christmas together at Big Bear was not such a happy time. Bill had presented me with just a single gift, a feminine pearl handled gun. This was not Bill's' usual gift giving. He always lavished me with many packages and wonderful surprises. What a shock that was! The gun was not loaded, according to him, but upon checking it out, there was one little bullet in the chamber. I couldn't help wondering how that lone bullet got there. Bill laughed off the entire thing, blaming it on the guy who sold him the gun. Wouldn't a cop, of all people, check the chamber just in case? Or do cops become lax about this type of thing, because they are around guns all the time? Bill did try to make it up to me by slipping a $100.00 bill in a very mushy card after my insinuations of trying to do me in, making me feel guilty for having such thoughts about someone whom I was supposed to love.

We had another disastrous trip to Wrightwood on a very cold and snowy day. We had played in the snow for several hours, not wearing proper attire. I became frozen like a Popsicle, and lost the sensation of being able to feel very much of my body. Before frostbite set in, we decided to call it a day. Shaking from the cold and never warming up, even with the car heater blasting away, was not a good sign. I ended up with a case of pneumonia which knocked me out for almost a month. Several trips to the hospital traumatized me, which brought on the panic attacks. Then extreme agoraphobia set in. I was unable to drive the two miles to work, and relied on Bill to play chauffeur. There were no new pills on the market that relieved symptoms better than Valium, even though they were losing their effectiveness. Tears and fears were flowing daily. I wondered if ever there would be an end to it; if life would ever return to normal. We truly enjoyed one another's company during our first few months together. I know putting up with me and my phobias was not an easy task for any man.

After several months of recuperation, I was able to attend a Christmas holiday party for all the employees of the Police Department. Finally I could wear the gorgeous dress and jacket Bill had given me on my birthday. It was a great time for all... until the end of the evening. Until that night, I never realized that Bill had a drinking problem. He won a fifth of vodka at the party, and proceeded to down the whole bottle! His personality took a startling 180 degree turn. After falling off the bar stool, he started hurling insults and accusations at me, for all to hear. He even accused me of rendezvousing with one of the waiters that night. An ugly and embarrassing scene was unfolding, so I left, heading for the car. Bill followed and jumped in the car, pushing me into the passenger's side, and took off. He was driving on the wrong side of the road, swerving like a maniac, while still hurling ugly accusations and insults at me.

My guardian angel, no doubt working overtime, sent a patrol car after us. They were able to pull us over by pulling in front of us and stopping. It was a new officer and he was visibly shaking. He had just found himself in the middle of a mess, not knowing what type of action he should take. After all, this was a senior sergeant, highly regarded by his peers. He had the presence of mind to radio in for assistance, and within minutes another patrol unit pulled up with a lieutenant behind the wheel. The lieutenant grabbed Bill by the arm, pulled him out of the car, and put him in the front seat of his unit. He instructed me to drive the car home. Instead, I decided to follow them to see where he was going to drop Bill off. They headed towards the station which was just a couple of blocks away from the hotel where he had the room, which he used as a front.

As he was walking toward the hotel, I approached him and told him to get in the car. Not the smartest thing I've ever done, considering his drunken state and confrontational state of mind. Instead, he reached inside the car and snatched up my new coat and threw it in the gutter. I was so confused by his hateful attitude towards me, since I had done nothing wrong, that I started crying and pleading with him to straighten up. Somehow in all the confusion, he again ended up behind the wheel of the car, heading toward our condo.

Upon arriving at our place, he started grabbing all the Christmas presents he had so carefully positioned under the tree earlier that day. He would take them out and throw them in his car and I would follow him and take them back out of the car. I took them back in the house and placed them in another room, out of his sight. My cat Gussie was watching as we passed each other with our hands full, him taking stuff out and me bringing it right back in. I swear she knew exactly what was going on, or if nothing else, she seemed to find it very entertaining! Bill finally wore down and literally passed out on the couch. This was not a good start to the holiday season.

When he finally came around late the next day, he asked why he had slept on the couch. I asked him if he recalled last night's party and how the night ended. He shook his head and said, the only thing he recalled was winning a fifth of vodka. He said, "I didn't drink that, did I?" with a very remorseful look on his face, knowing all the while, that was exactly what had happened. Bill had a reputation for being able to put away his fair share of booze, but I had never seen anything to this extent. Years of working for the Alcohol, Tobacco, and Firearms Department had definitely taken its toll on him. Witnessing him drinking himself to near death, and the resulting anger and hatefulness aimed at me, was an eye opener and a real disillusionment. Still, the holidays turned out well after all, as all the packages were neatly placed back under the tree.

Loren always talked about going to the mountains for the holidays, and talked Bill and me into going with her and her fiancé to Big Bear over the Christmas holiday. One more trip to the mountains over the holidays with them just might be fun. I really had to work my charms on Bill to convince him that it would be good for us to get away, and it worked. Before we left, Loren and I decided that a spin on the lake, wearing ice skates, would be an adventure. We were even able to talk the guys into it. There were many warning signs about the thin ice, but stupidly we ignored them. By the grace of God, none of us fell victim to the icy waters, although there were far too many close calls. The day of fun ended when the close call became reality and Loren's skate cracked the ice and her foot went into the chilly water. Thankfully it was not her entire body! After this incident, we all decided we would pursue a little safer sort of fun and opted for skis and inner-tubes instead.

My medications were getting the better of me and I was constantly closing my eyes or falling asleep at the most inopportune times. I had high hopes that this getaway might put some spark back into our relationship. Unfortunately, I just couldn't get my act together. His wall came up and at the time I was just too tired to care or do much of anything about it, except to explain to him what was happening to me. His demeanor told me he wasn't buying my excuses. Once this trip was over and we arrived home, I knew the blush was off the rose, so to speak, and our relationship became strained and uncomfortable. I didn't know how to salvage what little was left. I didn't want to face another breakup; I wanted this to work.

Upon returning to work shortly after the holiday bash, one of the sergeants approached me and asked if Bill had assaulted me in any way that night, as word had traveled throughout the department about his drunken episode. Of course nothing physical had occurred, and I assured the sergeant that it was just too much booze, that all was well with us. The sergeant went on, saying that I should not protect Bill if he had touched me in a combative manner. They were making a big deal out of this, and my thoughts were that they were trying to get some dirt on him. But that wasn't going to happen, as the only damage was to my coat, not my body, fortunately. Bill had never raised a hand to me. Had he done so, he would be saying his prayers behind bars. I might have been susceptible to emotional abuse at times, but I would never allow someone to physically abuse me.

My agoraphobic problems were not getting any better, and the more drugs the doctors prescribed, the more of a zombie I became. Lovemaking and physical contact was one of the furthest thoughts from my mind. Sleep was what I craved. This state of indifference, and lack of attention to Bill, was definitely the beginning of the end for us. It didn't mean that my feelings for him had changed; it was just that my emotions and feelings were being stifled by so many drugs, but the drugs were the only thing keeping my agoraphobia at bay.

My reality was thrown completely out of balance, when I learned through several sources that Bill had finally filed for divorce, and was seeing another woman. Apparently this woman resembled me in many ways, except that she had a dog, while I had a cat. This was news much too difficult to accept or process. Right after learning this, I came home one night finding that all his belongings were gone. With all that we had been through, I still thought the love was there, and that we would never break up. I never imagined that I would be thrown into this nightmare, and that he would leave me in such a callous manner, with no explanation or goodbye.

How does it turn out this way when someone professes undying love to you? With all the trauma and stress of the break up, my illness consumed me. There was no climbing out of the depression pit that swallowed me, at least not for a very long time, no matter what the doctor gave me.

Trying to escape from the pain for just a little while, one night I started drinking, hoping to just pass out into oblivion. But instead, I just got more and more drunk. Soon I wasn't even aware of what I was doing. I ended up calling a dispatcher friend of mine, telling her that I would like to shoot that good-for-nothing. Unfortunately she took my drunken theatrics as a real threat; she knew that there were at least two guns in my possession. She feared that my threats could become reality, and sent the cops to my house. By the time they got there, I had gratefully passed out in bed. I was startled awake by someone speaking in a loud voice, telling me to wake up. Present was one of my least favorite supervisors, hovering over me. There were also several other cops in my room looking through my belongings. The sergeant asked me where my guns were and of course I told him, thinking in my stupor that they were overreacting; too many cop shows for these guys. I was astounded when I realized that my drunken threat had been taken so seriously. No matter what a man does to break your heart, they are not worth going to jail for, or committing a sin that God may not forgive you.

The cops took my guns and booked them into evidence. The next day I was at work and was called into the captain's office. He smiled and said he had no qualms about releasing the guns to me, and had no fear that I would be using them. I assured him that nothing like this would ever happen again.

Running into Bill at work was so awkward and painful. He would pass me by in the hallway and never acknowledge my presence. I just could not understand how he could turn so cold and almost hateful at times.

A very short time after our breakup the word was out. Bill had married a girl much younger than myself; almost twenty years his junior. It was not the lady with the dog, for whom he had left me, but someone new who worked in law enforcement. This was a hard blow to my ego and to my heart. I struggled with it for what seemed an eternity, but at length, I faced reality and got on with my life.

After several years, I got some satisfaction when my phone rang one day, and Bill asked if we could get together and talk; this, after divorcing his child bride. It pleasured me beyond description to tell him no. No longer was I addicted to this relationship; hooking up once more was not an option. The love was gone, not to return, not ever.

12 Mr. Gucci Boots

Months had passed and it was time to join the land of the living again. My dispatcher friend Janice turned out to be a good partner to hit the clubs with. We both loved dancing and good music, and above all the men, even after being burned so many times! If men could play the game of indifference and date several people at the same time, so could I. This way there were no attachments or obligations, even though deep down that's what I longed for. Meeting guys at clubs is not advisable, as everyone pretty much knows, but these short term dalliances helped to relieve the emptiness and emotional pain I was feeling. One night at our favorite spot in Newport Beach, my eyes zeroed in on one dark haired flashy dude, who was captivating the ladies as he swirled around the dance floor.

Before too long, he noticed me looking at him and asked me for a dance. Without any hesitation, we were out on the dance floor, where he proceeded to spin me around and dip me as if I was a contortionist. Laughter was the first thing out of my mouth as trying to keep my balance was a feat in itself. This was a lot of fun! After a few more spins with the dark and mysterious stranger, he sat down at our table and introduced himself as Tony Arnsareti. He was dressed in the finest of disco attire, which was popular at that time, Gucci boots, white pants, and a very large ostentatious opal ring. We went through the usual customary questions and answers, where we worked and what we did for a living. Tony said he was a businessman and dealt in imports. Once I told him where I worked, he became very interested and started asking a lot of questions. It didn't seem too unusual at the time, but later I understood why.

We set up a date for the next weekend for another night of clubbing and dancing. After a very enjoyable time that evening, he wanted to introduce me to his sister and her family who lived in Laguna Beach. It was getting late and I thought it was a bad time to pop in on one's family, but he insisted. I didn't really know Tony so I was apprehensive about going to a stranger's house. He said he had business to discuss with his sister and since we were in the area, he might as well take advantage of the opportunity. Tony lived in the Los Angeles area, so he said.

Meeting his sister put me somewhat at ease as she appeared to be normal and was quite friendly. After a few moments, Tony said they needed to go to the office to discuss the last deal they had just negotiated and would not be long. It was almost forty-five minutes later when they re-appeared, apologizing for leaving me for so long. During the wait I visualized what horrible fate might be in store for me. Why were they taking so long, leaving me sitting alone on the couch with not even a cup of coffee? Were they planning my demise? Were they mass murderers deciding what methods they would use to kill me? I was getting ready to go knock on the door before I totally freaked out when they re-appeared. I told him I was tired and not feeling well and asked him if he would take me home. On the drive back I calmed down as he started telling jokes, entertaining me with his great sense of humor.

Once home, he wanted to come in for a few minutes. He stayed for more than an hour, managing to bedazzle my roommate with his wit and charm, but it was time to call it a night. I sensed that there was something slightly dangerous about Tony, which I found exciting. Hard to believe that this would appeal to a coward like me, but I was enthralled.

We went out several more times. It was thrilling to be with such a free spirited guy who seemed to enjoy the finer things in life. But suddenly, without any warning, he disappeared, no more phone calls, no more anything. It was difficult to understand, because things seemed to be heating up between us.

Shortly after his disappearance, I received a call from the Los Angeles Sheriff's Jail facility, where he was incarcerated. He said, he had done nothing wrong, claiming that the cops had pinned a crime on him, which he did not commit. I asked what the charges were; he said it was narcotic sales. He asked me if I had ever seen him high on drugs, or if he acted suspiciously when talking about his business, or if I had seen him behave in any way that would've sounded an alarm in my head. I told him no, to my knowledge he was always straight and drugs would never have entered my mind. I truly believed what he told me, I was becoming very enamored with him, and having too much fun to give him up. He proceeded to tell me that he was falling in love with me, and missed me a lot. He begged me to visit him at the jail facility. The thought of going to a jail almost paralyzed me, particularly in Los Angeles. His pleas got the better of me, and I told him that I would try to make arrangements to get there.

My dispatcher friend thought it would be an adventure, and that we should go. We picked a day and I loaded up on my meds and away we went. It was an experience that I would not forget in a big hurry. Seeing such a facility on TV and actually being there, were two very different things. Huntington Beach's jail was bad enough, but this was gruesome. Hearing the inmates' wolf whistles and foul language made me uncomfortable enough, but hearing those big doors lock behind us really freaked me out.

After meeting with Tony for a few minutes, I told him that we had to go. I explained that the atmosphere was getting to me. Tony promised to call and send letters. He said with his connections he would not be there much longer. The idea of him having "connections" caused me some consternation. I watched cop shows and when a criminal had "connections", it usually wasn't the good kind. I was afraid I might have put myself in a compromising position. I had a responsible job as a supervisor at HBPD and I did not want to jeopardize that.

What a relief to walk out those jail doors! Whatever possessed me to go there in the first place? Tony did not look so appealing or exciting in his jailhouse dungarees. The nerves kicked in and the pills came out.

The next evening at work, still not sure what to think about the jail visit, I was checking out a suspect's alias in the "hot files", provided by our Vice Detail. Curiosity got the better of me and I decided to check out the nickname Tony sometimes used. His moniker came up, but it indicated a different name than what Tony had given me. There were numerous aliases listed, but no Tony Arnsareti. Just to put my mind at ease, I pulled the mug shot that corresponded to the file. My heart came to a standstill and I went into pure shock. It was he! There were pages and pages of CIA and FBI records on this guy! He had been arrested recently for an attempted hit on a male subject in another city. We were one of the assisting agencies at the time of his apprehension in that case.

Immediately after discovering this information, I pulled one of my co-workers aside, who was a good friend of mine. She knew that I had been dating this flashy guy, and she had met him once in the parking lot when he picked me up after work. She looked at the mug shot and confirmed that it was definitely Mr. Gucci boots. Simultaneously we both looked at one another and let out a piercing shriek that brought the front desk officer running in, ready to draw his gun! He thought someone from the public had come in and was giving us a bad time. We weren't ready to spill the beans about what had brought on the shrill screams so we stammered out some lame excuse that left the officer scratching his head, but he left us alone.

I realized that I had to contact the Chief, and set up an appointment as soon as possible. He needed to know whom I had been going out with, and maybe offer some advice as to how to end it gracefully without Tony becoming suspicious. I met with the Chief the following day and shamefully explained the predicament I had gotten myself in to. He smiled at me, turned around in his seat, and pulled what looked like a novel from the desk behind him. He said that this was an FBI dossier on the person I knew as Tony. He told me that he was aware of my relationship with Tony, and the Feds were quite interested to know if there was any information I could furnish on his activities. I told him I knew nothing about his business, only that he had mentioned he was in the import business, but he had never elaborated on any of the details. He said the Feds, as well as the Los Angeles Vice Detail, might be interested in interviewing me. He asked if I would have any objections to speaking with either of these agencies. My heart was pounding so hard, I could barely hear what he was saying. He repeated the question again and I told him I would cooperate in any way I could. I ran down the stairs, cornered my friend, and let out another deafening cry. She tried to console me, saying everything would work out, but the thought of spying on a dangerous criminal had me trembling with fright.

Tony called me and said he would be out of jail in a couple of days. He said it didn't take long for the law to figure out that he was clean; the whole mess was a setup. I tried to stay cool and collected while talking with him, when all I really wanted to do was tell him that it was over and hang up! He said within a few days we would be together again and that was keeping him going. He went on to say some cops were corrupt and could be bought for a dime, and he gave me the names of two of our vice cops who fit the profile. He told me I should be cautious around these guys as they were bad news. Hearing this spun my head in a million different directions. This planted seeds of confusion and distrust for both sides. Tony named some incidents involving these cops, and some of what he said I knew to be true. I knew, I should immediately tell the Chief about what Tony had said, and I would also ask him how he wanted me to handle it when Tony got released and came knocking on my door. Tony also mentioned that he had sent me a couple of letters and some cartoons he had drawn. I didn't let him know that they ended up in the trash can. Terror was setting in again; sleeping and eating was out of the question. I was living on pills and nervous adrenaline.

The day after I first talked to the Chief, I was called back to his office. His suggestion was to string Tony along, and see what he had on his mind, basically spy on him. He asked if I had any objections. I told him, I would do whatever he wanted me to do. Right after our meeting, I was directed to the Vice Unit where our detectives, investigators from LAPD Vice Squad, and FBI officers were waiting to interview me. It was just like a scene out of a movie, all these serious official looking guys strategically positioned around the room with me in the middle being drilled as if I were the one under suspicion. Needless to say, I was stressed and scared out of my mind, and just wanted to get out of there as fast as I could!

The first question thrown at me was from the LA cops, asking me if I had seen his "piece". I hadn't a clue what they were talking about, when one of our guys said, "I think they are referring to a gun, Norma" in a condescending manner like I was a real dumb blond! In my defense I had never heard the term before, so how should I know! I had never seen him with a weapon and if I had, I would have run in the opposite direction.

Questions were fired at me in rapid succession, and as I was trying to answer them, I took note of the reactions of our two alleged crooked vice cops. I spoke right up and told everyone what Tony had said about them. Their response was difficult to interpret. I did notice that they kept shooting looks at one another and I thought they appeared somewhat uncomfortable. I answered all of their questions truthfully, stating I just didn't know what his business was outside of being involved in the import industry as he had told me when we first met. I was told by the LA investigators that there was word out that Tony might be involved in an illegal gambling scam. They said it was going to take place aboard a bus that would be heading towards New York, and asked if I had heard anything about it, to which my answer was no. After this harrowing interview, I was instructed to make a tape recording detailing everything I knew about him and my involvement with him. Later that day, one of the Vice Detectives told me that I should consider going with Tony on this bus trip. I told him he was crazy, and there was not a chance in the world that this would happen. Assisting our department was one thing, but putting myself in the line of fire of dangerous criminals was quite another! I was loyal, but not crazy!

A short time later, I was leaving work around midnight and spotted Tony's car in the parking lot. He exited the car and said "Didn't I tell you I had connections?" I was not happy to be surprised like this, but I did my best to remain cool and collected, telling him it was great to see him. He told me to get in his car so we could talk for a minute, and then he would follow me home. Once inside the car, I reached down as something was hitting my foot. There was the "piece" the Vice cops were referring to. My heart took off and it was hard to catch my breath. I was afraid, I was going to start hyperventilating any minute! What gall and stupidity this guy had to sit in the police parking lot with a gun under the seat. I played the stupid blond routine and went on asking him all kinds of questions about his stay at the jailhouse and completely ignored the fact that there was a gun under my seat. I just wanted him to disappear, and deeply regretted the day I had laid eyes on him. Now I wonder if he didn't purposely place that gun there, just to scare me and keep me in line. I was afraid it was not going to be an easy thing to get rid of this guy.

Any excuse I could conjure up not to get together, I used. But he was very insistent, so my excuses only worked a few times. When we did get together, he was always asking me what was wrong and my excuse was fatigue and work. I could not figure out why he was still interested in spending time with me, and the only logical thing that came to mind were my contacts and ability to obtain information from work. This guy was dead wrong if he thought I would ever break the law for him or betray my department. Not a chance in hell.

Our vice guys told me that the word was out that Tony's wife had gotten wind of her husband's involvement with me. They said she was far more dangerous than Tony and violence was part of her everyday life style. She threatened, she would get me, and I had better start looking over my shoulder. I had no inkling that Tony was married. He appeared to come and go whenever he chose, and when I had asked him if he had ever been married, he told me "no way." This was another shocker on the list of many.

When I returned to work the next day, I was called to the Vice Unit again. I was told again that I should be very careful because no one knew what they might have in store for me, or when they might strike. I told them I hoped they were going to be there to help me if something did happen. I let them know, my nerves were so shot that medication was the only thing keeping me going, aiding in controlling the anxiety attacks which were now becoming an almost daily occurrence. This was all I needed to hear to put me even closer to the precipice, where I already was! One small push and it would be all over! There were only so many Valiums I could swallow in a day. I couldn't stop shaking and visualizing how she was "going to get me." One of the vice guys told me that I should move to Texas, where I had relatives, and get lost. I was also told that if something should go down while I was with Tony, I would be as guilty as he was. On one hand, the cops were encouraging me to work with them and spy on Tony, and even hop on the gambling bus they suspected was going to be involved in a crime. Then on the other hand they were telling me I would be as guilty as Tony if anything happened! I didn't know if I was coming or going. My mind was in a constant state of upheaval; concentrating on work was almost impossible.

A couple of the girls and I went back to the infamous club where I had first met Tony. We had made friends with the band, and I needed a little release from all the tension, and of course there was a musician who was one of the nicest guys in town; I wanted to tell him my story. During his break that night, I started telling him my saga and he was so supportive, yet also terrified of the mess that I had gotten myself into. This was the kind of guy I should have been looking for. He was a gentle and understanding soul and I had always cared for him deeply, but alas, he had been involved with a lady for some time, and wasn't about to change his relationship with her. I respected him greatly for his faithfulness and honesty. He had told me, if he were not involved, I would be the lady of his choice, adding, he saw no harm in being friends. He insisted on driving me home and said we could make arrangements to pick up my car the next day.

I had not heard from Tony for about a week, and was beginning to think that his wife had put her foot down and I had escaped the nightmare somewhat unscathed. But upon arriving at my complex, we saw Tony's car parked in front of my building. It was now about 3:00AM. My friend Jack and I sat in the car for a few minutes, both of us shaking visibly, trying to decide what to do. We drove off and circled the complex several times in hopes that Tony would give up and leave. No such luck. We decided to go get a cup of coffee and collect our thoughts. We sat there weighing all the options, how I should handle it if Tony did confront me. We decided he would drop me off in the back of the unit and I could slip in the back door if Tony was still in the front.

When we returned, Tony was not in sight and I breathed a big sigh of relief, convincing Jack I would be all right and that he should head home. Once I opened the back gate, there was Tony standing in the open doorway of the garage. He started yelling at me, asking me what I was doing, how could I treat him like this after he had gone through so much being unjustly locked up. I could hardly utter a sound. All I could think about was how long had he been waiting for me to return, and worse yet, what will be his reaction. Finally I gathered my nerve and explained that I had been a nervous wreck, and my friend Jean and some of the other girls from work and I needed to get out for a while, and try to relax. I don't think he bought the story, but at least he did not become violent, which was my biggest fear. He spent what was the rest of the night with me, which I hated.

In the morning he started talking about us going into business together; something he had casually mentioned before his jail time. He said he had a deal going with some other investors to purchase a night club in L.A. or Orange County. I told him I had no money, my job at the PD was very important to me, and I had no desire to venture into any business deals. He was very irritated at my response and told me after he had the papers drawn up and the plans on course, I would change my mind. Sheer terror was now surging through my entire body. I just wanted this nightmare to end! I certainly didn't want to go into business with this gangster! I didn't know how I was going to put an end to this. I just wanted to curl up with my sweet cat and go to sleep, and when I woke up have my old normal life back. I vowed when my life did get back to normal, I would never again complain about it being too dull!

Within the week I had taken out a loan and handed it over to him. He had checked different locations where we might be able to get in on the ground floor and possibly partner with other investors. I wasn't sure if this was the right approach to get rid of him or if I was just getting in deeper and deeper. I thought it was worth a try, since I hadn't been able to come up with an alternative plan.

Once I handed over the cash, I instantly regretted my decision. I called Tony and said I did not want to be involved any further and I wanted my investment back. He said he could not return my money; he was already working with some people to partner with them in a club in L.A. Anger set in and I threw caution to the wind, insisting he find a way to get my money back. It wasn't that it was a huge amount of money, but still I had to take out a loan to get it. I was totally disgusted with myself for getting into this situation. I felt, I had to do something to right my bad decision making.

As time went on and I didn't hear from him, my anger became overwhelming and whatever good sense I had flew out the window. You would think I would have just counted my blessings that he might finally be out of my life, but no, not me, that made way too much sense! My roommate agreed to help me find him so I could get my money back. I had a phone number for him and knew approximately where he lived, which was all I needed to go in pursuit.

As I am writing this, what I did that day still sends shock waves through my body. We drove to L.A. with me packing a loaded gun concealed in my purse. My intention was to confront him and wave it in his face to scare him into giving me back my money. I had to have been temporarily insane. There is no other rational explanation for me doing something so stupid and so dangerous! I called his number from a pay phone and a female answered, most likely his wife. I demanded that she put Tony on the phone. When I heard his voice I went on a vocal rampage. I told him I was right around the corner from where he lived and that I had a gun and would not hesitate using it; that I wanted my money back. His response was that he had invested it and I needed to be patient. I threatened him, stating I had a gun and if he didn't return my money, there could be big consequences. Again he said it was tied up with some investors at a club in L.A. He gave me the name of the club, but I was so freaked out I couldn't hear what he was saying. I told him I expected him to work something out and get the money back, with an implied "or else" at the end of my demand. In the background I could hear a female screaming profanity at the top of her lungs. Tony tried giving me other excuses and I told him I did not want to hear it, I just wanted my money back. This was the last time I ever had a conversation with Tony.

What a crazy lady I was to threaten a bad guy like Tony. Within a few minutes I settled down and said we should go home. There was no way I was going to go knocking on his door. What was I thinking? I should say the brain was not operating at all.

It was nothing short of a miracle that I didn't have a stroke. Only a crazy delusional person would pull something so outrageous. It's especially hard to believe my roommate went along with the whole thing, and even drove the "getaway car"! She was in law enforcement, too, and not considering what damage I could have done to her and her career because of my recklessness was unforgivable. But she told me, it was the most excitement she had ever had, and I should not feel badly. Maybe she was just as crazy as I was! She even said, it was too bad that we weren't able to confront him and wave the gun in his face. Thank God in heaven, we never made it happen that day.

I phoned my brother in Texas who was a dentist in the army and serving at Walter Scott Hospital. Jerry had experienced a lot of trauma in his life, the worst being Vietnam. Normally I would not have burdened him with my problems, but I knew he would do everything in his power to help me get out of the mess I'd gotten myself into, plus I had no one else to turn to. He told me to sit tight because he was coming to California within the week.

When he arrived, I felt as though a huge weight had been lifted off my shoulders, as though the troops had come to rescue me! Jerry peppered me with questions about Tony and wanted to know where he lived. I gave him the little bit of information I had and he told me not to worry, he would take care of the problem.

The next day Jerry introduced me to Eddie, my bodyguard for the next few weeks. Jerry told me in an ominous tone that his acquaintances had taken care of the matter and I would never be bothered by Tony again. He did caution me about Tony's wife though, saying he felt it would be in my best interest to have Eddie stay with me until things were under control. Of course, I started drilling him for details. I wanted to know how and what he found out and what Tony's reaction was when whoever it was showed up at his front door. He refused to share the details with me, which was torture for someone like me, and told me to just concentrate on relaxing and getting on with my life.

Jerry was aware of my health problems stemming from my anorexia, and suggested that I visit with another psychiatrist and try some other medications. The meds I was taking were not working as well as they did in the beginning, my system was probably becoming immune to them. I promised him that I would.

Eddie the bodyguard was a great guy and a lot of fun. I thoroughly enjoyed his company and loved that he would take me to work and pick me up at day's end. He spent the nights with me, and handled his business affairs, whatever they were, while I was at work. He was very clandestine about his personal and business life and, considering what he may have been involved in, I didn't push him for details, as hard as that was, being the curious (or nosy) person that I was. I felt well protected in his presence, and the .45 he carried most certainly helped my feelings of security.

I could not wrap my head around everything that had happened. This stuff just doesn't happen to a person like me, except maybe in the movies. Part of me loved the adrenaline rush and the drama, but the other part of me shook me in my boots when I faced the reality of the dangerous situation I had gotten myself into. I continued to drill Jerry about who his friends were, confronting Tony and his wife. He would only say very mysteriously, that they were people who owed him a favor.

A month went by, and the dust had settled. I no longer heard from Tony, and was sorry that Eddie would be leaving soon. Eddie said he was attracted to me, but that we lived in conflicting worlds. As much as I hated to agree, I knew he was right. Right before he left, he held me close and kissed me for the last time. Yes, I must admit we had begun a romantic relationship the first week he came to stay with me. Kissing him for the last time left me feeling sad and alone.

Interestingly enough, the two vice guys Tony had named as "bad cops" put in for retirement shortly afterwards. I was no longer in the hot seat at work, and life began to get back to normal, or as normal as my life ever was. I could focus on my job without my brain going in a million directions, there were no more distractions. I took the letters and the cartoons Tony had sent me from jail and tore them up into microscopic pieces. Getting rid of this last tie to Tony gave me closure. I felt this chapter of my life was finally over and I could move forward.

After a couple of days of recuperation, I couldn't keep from thinking what will happen next? I felt like a junkie coming down from a high, thinking only about my next fix. Only for me it wasn't drugs I was addicted to; it was excitement. It didn't make much sense that a coward like me would crave the kind of excitement that could lead to danger, but that's how it was. At times I could visualize being peppered with a spray of bullets and my friends standing graveside eulogizing, their main mantra being: All she ever wanted was to find a good man. They would have that phrase engraved on my head stone.

During all the chaos, I never mentioned what really happened the night Tony surprised me at my condo. It was far more terrifying than I revealed at the time. Tony was consumed with rage when he saw me coming home at 3 AM, I'm sure just assuming that I had been out with another man. He grabbed me roughly by the arm and dragged me upstairs to my bedroom, where he proceeded to rape me. There is no other way to describe it. I was by no means a willing participant. By this time I knew that he was a dangerous criminal, so I was in fear for my life. I couldn't let him know what I was really thinking, so while I was not a willing participant, I also did not resist, and tried as much as was humanly possible to act normally in the midst of a brutal act, just lying there willing it to end quickly.

Taking my brother's advice, I sought out a new psychiatrist. I agreed to allow him to try a new drug on me. The side effects made me delusional and zombie-like. This was supposedly a new wonder drug, but it made me worse than I was before. It was very discouraging. I so longed to be a normal, functioning human being. Always making excuses about why I could not do everyday things that most people take for granted, was exhausting and embarrassing. I knew that cops just don't understand the types of psychological and physical ailments that plagued me, their favorite phrase being, "It's all in your head". Every time I heard that, it was like a knife in my heart. Even though realistically I could understand where they were coming from, I still became very defensive, as though I was being attacked. I dreamed daily of just being "normal". How sad is that? No one knows or understands how inadequate and insecure these illnesses make you feel, until they've walked in those shoes; they truly devastate your life.

The dust started settling at work and I was starting to get my nerves under control, which allowed me to relax and sleep at night, well, most of the time, anyway. My brother had apparently taken care of the Tony matter, and I finally stopped looking over my shoulder every time I left home. Now I just had to deal with the extreme embarrassment I felt around my co-workers, particularly the Vice guys. My stupidity in becoming involved with such a sleazy character was humiliating, to say the least. Sometimes I couldn't even believe it was really me.

There was plenty of trouble brewing at the PD. One officer had gone over to his ex-girlfriend's house and it was not clear if they argued or what, but tragically his service revolver went off, striking her in the head and killing her. The department put him under arrest at our facility while an investigation by the sheriff's office was taking place. He was later found not guilty of manslaughter and released from the holding jail. He later married one of our dispatchers and has remained so for well over thirty years. Only the officer will ever know the true story.

We had a lieutenant, who, while working the vice detail, one night detected a hole drilled in the men's divider of the stall in a public men's restroom. It was a well- known fact that the public men's restrooms were frequented by some unsavory types. On this particular night, while stationed in this particular stall on surveillance, a penis appeared through the opening, almost touching him in the face. Even though the lieutenant should have suspected this would happen, he reacted violently. He took out his heavy night stick, and whacked the guy's penis, inflicting a great deal of pain and permanent damage to his private parts. I'm told, the man's screams could be heard over the entire city, surely an exaggeration, but it must have been pretty bad. The vice lieutenant was placed on administrative leave for a short time, but was absolved of any wrong doing and was back to work in a very short time. It was never quite clear what the victim's final prognosis was, but we all knew it wasn't good.

Parties, prostitutes, bimbos, and one can fill in the blanks, were out of control at the officers' shooting range. The building boasted comfy couches, stashed booze, and a stereo system, to name a few of the amenities. It was a hangout where the officers could let out their hostilities and act like maniacs, without the prying eyes of the brass. One night one of the "ladies of the evening" blew the whistle on them when one of the guys got out of hand with her. It was not clear exactly what happened, but it was enough to open a full-fledged Internal Affairs investigation. Officers were banned from the range after hours for a short time, but when the dust settled, they were back in full swing, although without the hookers. Most of the women who attended their shindigs were referred to by the officers as "bimbos", although I'm sure they had no idea. Most of the poor girls probably thought they were invited there because the officer was interested in a relationship with them. Unbeknownst to them, they were usually interested in one thing only. Only once did one of my female co-workers and I make an appearance, just to check it out. We felt out of place and unwelcome. The cops thought we were there to possibly spy on them and rat them out.

One of my friends at the PD, who was aware of the trauma that I had recently suffered with Tony, was insistent that I meet her dad. He was a little older than me, in his mid-forties, but she said he was a wonderful guy, and she believed that we would really hit it off. Gary was a pilot for a private firm and made a good living. Finally, a guy that sounded normal. She set up a meeting and she was right. We hit it off from the moment we met. We had dinner together, and so began the "getting-to-know-you" phase. Conversation flowed so easily between us, and he just had a way of putting me at ease and making me feel most protected. We were so engrossed in our conversation that we didn't realize how much we were drinking, and before we knew it, we were headed to his house. Not my plan at all. This was my friend's dad! You know the old adage, one thing leads to another; well, it did. We ended up bouncing the night away on his waterbed. The getting-to-know-you phase obviously didn't last very long! The next day I could have kicked myself for letting this happen, not only because he was my friend's dad, but I thought that this was probably the beginning and end of what could have been a very nice relationship.

The next week, much to my surprise, Gary phoned me at work. I was working the 4PM to midnight shift. He asked if I had any plans for the next couple of days. He wanted to pick me up after work, and take me home, so I could pack a few things for a trip to Las Vegas in a private jet. Immediately, I went in to "uh oh" mode, just thinking about flying at night with only one pilot started me trembling all over. I immediately downed a Valium, maybe it was two. I wanted to go, it sounded like a once in a lifetime experience, but my nervous system was going haywire just contemplating it. I promised him I would think about it and get back to him within the hour. All the girls at work ganged up on me, pressuring me to go, insisting that I would be an idiot to pass up such a wonderful opportunity. They were amazed that I even had to think about it. Most of them wished they were in my shoes. They finally convinced me. Reluctantly, I called Gary back, and told him that this coward, who was scared to death of having her feet off the ground, was going to join him... well, I left out the part about being a coward, hoping that the valium would do its thing, and he would never know what a basket case he was traveling with.

I grabbed a few things from home, and off we went to Long Beach Airport. I had never packed so fast, it would be a miracle if I wasn't missing something really important, like underwear or even worse, my make-up!

Once we arrived, the fog was so thick, you couldn't see the runway. Just what I needed to calm my frazzled nerves! Gary ushered me into the plane, where he fixed me a powerful cocktail and said there would be no problem taking off. Trying to quell my rising fear, I gulped it down so fast, it made my head spin. He said, the instruments would do the navigating and we could sit back and enjoy the flight. I knew there wasn't a chance in hell that I was going to enjoy this, one bit, but I kept that information to myself. I stopped looking out the window as you could not see the nose of the plane due to the dense fog. I figured if I didn't look out, I wouldn't know, and what I didn't know wouldn't put me in a full-fledged panic attack, although I felt like I was on the precipice already. Another stiff drink and a prayer to the good Lord above got me through the takeoff. I knew that I should relax and take in the moment, but whom was I kidding? Once we got above the fog layer, Gary seemed calmer and not so intent on reading all the gauges and dials. He said, the plane was now on automatic pilot and we could sit back and enjoy our drinks.

Unfortunately, it wasn't long before I saw him tense up and he again took over the navigation of the plane. Of course, I had to know what was going on, and he said that the auto pilot was not functioning properly. I became a little manic at this news, and immediately started asking him questions as to how I could fly this thing if something went wrong. I thought this guy is in his mid- forties which sounded old to me at the time, the prime age range for a heart attack or stroke. My mind and heart were both racing as he attempted to point out a few survival tactics if something should go amiss. After taking two Valiums and washing them down with two cocktails, not much he was saying was sticking in my head for long, basically just going in one ear and out the other. There was nothing to do but sit back, be quiet, and pray. He handled the problem very well and did not show much emotion as he flew the twin engine Cessna. I think he sensed that I was on the verge of coming unglued, and was doing everything in his power to exude calmness. Feet on the ground, it was pretty cool being greeted at Vegas Airport. The red carpet was rolled out, I felt like royalty! We were escorted from the field in an enclosed carriage type vehicle and taken to the main airport where Gary had to fill out some forms. Then they hailed a taxi to take us to our hotel, which was the International; today it is known as the Hilton. I must say this whole red carpet treatment really impressed me, I thought I could get used to this quite easily, except maybe for the flying part. If only I could beam myself there, life would be perfect!

We checked into our room which was a suite with a sitting room, full bar, and all the amenities. Gary was a class act, and he continued to impress me. He asked if I would like to go downstairs for an early breakfast or late dinner, but I opted for room service and a shower, and he obliged without complaint.

We enjoyed our evening together and before I could get my wits about me, it was morning and I was awakened by the intoxicating smell of coffee. Gary had ordered a continental breakfast and also presented me with a card for the beauty spa in the hotel. He had set up an appointment for me to have my hair done and a manicure and pedicure. This was a guy who was in charge, and knew what a lady liked. He told me, we would be going to a dinner show that evening, if this was agreeable with me. You bet! I hadn't been treated like this, ever, and I was going to revel in every moment of it!

After my beauty treatments, which were terrific, I felt so special and thought I looked pretty darn good, too. The stylists in these hotels are first rate, and know what they are doing. I was so exhilarated by this whole experience; then the hammer dropped. That afternoon Gary received a phone call. His boss needed him to fly to Denver and pick him up. He was terribly upset and felt very badly that this was to end our stay together in Vegas. He said that he would book me on a flight whenever I wanted to leave town. He said I should stay and at least catch the show. I had no desire to attend the show on my own, or to stay in Vegas by myself. I felt pretty devastated that our getaway had to end so abruptly and worse yet, that I had to fly back alone. I don't think he realized just how traumatic flying was for me, and I didn't say anything, I knew he felt badly enough already about having to cut the trip short. I told him to get me a flight as soon as possible and I took off later that afternoon with a cocktail in hand.

A few days later, Gary called and apologized again for having to leave me in the lurch. I told him I understood, but I really didn't, even as I was saying the words. He said, we could try another time, and hoped that we could get together for dinner soon. I thought for sure Gary and I had connected and would be together again, but that was not to be the case. I did not hear from him again until several years had passed. I learned from his daughter earlier that he was going through an on-again-off-again relationship that had apparently been off when we got together but now it was back on again.

When he called back, which was about five years later, he tried to explain to me what was going on in his life at the time we met, and how badly he felt that I had gotten caught in the middle. He said he had feelings for me now as he had from the beginning, and would like to get together. I told him I was involved in a relationship and was very happy. He said he was glad for me, then went on to say he has been diagnosed with cancer a year ago, and did not have a lot of time left. He felt he needed to square things with me. Of course I felt devastated for him, but seeing one another again would not have changed anything. His daughter told me when he passed away, also telling me he had very strong feelings for me and felt very badly about how things had turned out between us. This was the second man in my life who wanted to see me before they left this earth. While so very tragic, I guess it's a compliment that they thought enough of me after so many years had passed to want to see me and make things right.

13 DONNY

I decided I needed a change of scenery after all the chaos of the past months so my friend and I decided a weekend in Palm Springs was just the ticket. Hitting all the disco clubs was a sure cure for the blues. Stocking up on my old reliable medications, we hit the road. It was the disco era and we loved it. After watching John Travolta gyrate his incredible body in Saturday Night Fever, we were ready to hit the dance floor and find some Travolta clones of our own!

We ended up at The Canyon Club; a very exclusive establishment in town which backed up to one of the mountain ranges in Palm Springs. The place was packed, as it was a weekend night, and everyone was partying the night away. My radar was trying to track that Travolta look-alike, but instead sighted in on a brown eyed rascal with some good dance moves. We hit it off immediately, spending the night discoing away. He even had some original steps of his own that were quite impressive.

Towards the end of the evening, he told me most of his life's history. Donny was into real estate, specifically buying fixer-uppers, refurbishing them, and then selling them at a substantial profit. He had lived most of his life in the desert and enjoyed four wheeling in the most remote areas he could find. He wanted to take me on one of his excursions the next time I visited Palm Springs. I reluctantly agreed; I was not a lover of the desert or the desert heat. But I thought joining him on one of his excursions might be exhilarating and it is always good to experience new things some of the time. This could be accomplished by Valium and a few Brandy Alexanders, the drink of my choice at the time.

Phone numbers were exchanged and I extended an invitation to Donny to come and visit the beach if he was ever in need of a change of scenery, not really thinking he would take me up on my offer any time soon. I wasn't quite ready to jump into another relationship, so I decided I would keep it platonic at first, and see where it led. I know most men have no interest in doing the whole "let's just be friends" thing when they are interested in a woman, but I thought I would at least give it a try.

By the time I arrived home the next day, Donny had already phoned and left a message. He said he really enjoyed the evening with me, and would most definitely like to connect again. Donny said if my invitation was still open, he would like to accept and visit the following week. My first thought was: Here we go again! I knew if I invited him to stay with me, I would be sending a message that I wasn't quite ready to send. I returned his call and explained that I would be more comfortable visiting the desert with my friend a few more times, giving us the opportunity to become better acquainted before he came to stay with me. Donny handled the news like a gentleman, saying that he understood, and looked forward to my next visit.

A month passed and during that time Donny called numerous times. I looked forward to our talks and learned a lot about him and his family background during these conversations. Maybe, just maybe, this might turn into a meaningful relationship after all. Donny was an attractive guy; not as tall as I usually lean towards, but at least he was taller than me. His hair was dark brown and his eyes almost black and twinkly. He had the little boy look going on, and a cute smile to match. Much as I hate to admit it, I was a shallow female; looks were always an issue for me. A person's character and personality are what's most important of course, but if I wasn't physically attracted to them, I generally wouldn't invest the time to get to know them. Lord knows I probably missed out on some really great men because of my obsession with good looks.

As the months passed, we started spending more and more time together, either at his place or mine. His house was comfortable with overstuffed furniture and a retro vibe. My favorite spot was the pool, where I would spend most of my time when we weren't out on the town. We enjoyed dining out and taking excursions into parts of the desert that most people probably didn't know existed.

Donny was father to five children. The two eldest boys lived with him and his two daughters and youngest son lived with their mother. I liked the idea of a ready- made family. His kids were polite and could be a lot of fun to hang out with. Both his sons were teenagers, so it wasn't like I had to do diaper duty.

The younger of his two boys was my favorite. He and I hit it off from the get go. He would constantly tell me that he wanted me to move in with his dad and eventually get married. It might have been his influence that persuaded me to quit my job and make the move. It was difficult leaving the PD, as I had several good friends who would be sorely missed. Because of my illness and insecurities, my friends were my safety net; part of my very survival, so not having them close by made me nervous and sad. But I knew that eventually I would make new friends and adjust to my new life, and my friends were still just a phone call away if I really needed them.

The Department put together a goodbye luncheon for me at a local restaurant, and so many people signed up to attend, that they had to have two luncheons back to back. Sitting through two luncheons, I managed to imbibe a bit too much scotch, and could not remember half of the festivities. From what I was told, I had a great time, and the party was a hit! I was very touched that there was such a large turnout, and being told by many that I would be missed.

One of my friends from the PD, Lisa, was going to sublet the townhouse I had been renting for several years. This was a smart move for both of us as she needed a place, and if things didn't work out with Donny, I could move back and rent a room from her. For once I was using my head and not just my heart and preparing a plan "B", just in case. I kept trying to convince myself that this was a good move, particularly after the Bill and Tony fiascos. I was mortified by what had happened, and it was hard to look some of my co-workers in the eyes, knowing that some of them sat in judgment of me. This would be a positive and uplifting life change, or so I kept telling myself.

I had worked at the PD for seven and a half years, and had acquired a small pension. Regretfully, instead of using the brain God had gifted me with, I decided to pull the funds from the retirement system and ended up blowing it all, without even being able to account for where it all went. It just went so fast.

Moving is a nightmare, and this one was no exception. I had an antique piano and there was no way I would give it up. It had cost me $250.00 and on a city employee's salary this was a big purchase. Donny was not pleased, but he finally accepted that the piano and I were a package deal. After many days of packing and throwing out and loading the U-Haul, we were Palm Springs bound.

Rearranging Donny's house was a nightmare, and trying to fit in all my belongings and the piano made for tight quarters, but we made it work. All was going fairly well the first month. Then the bumps in the road became sink holes. Donny would wake up in the middle of the night, and want to have a conversation among other things. Anyone disturbing my deep slumber experiences the wrath of Norma Jeanne. No matter how much I explained to him that I had a terrible time getting back to sleep, and that it would ruin my next day, as I could only function at half speed, made no difference to him; not to mention the horrific headaches that accompanied the lack of rest. His thinking was: if it didn't affect him the same way, it shouldn't bother me, either. Also his constant use of marijuana was a big turn off to me. None of this was present in the beginning of our time together. As mentioned before, beginnings are the time of deception in a relationship, and I should have had my eyes open wider to see the warning signs as they were present. But, alas, I chose to look the other way, as I so badly wanted to have a partner in life.

After just five months, and my giving all I could, to have this arrangement work, I couldn't take it any longer. He had worn me down, and I knew for my health's sake, I had to move out. I kept thanking God for putting these road blocks up to marriage, because divorce court would have been right around the corner.

I found a bachelor apartment in town and moved what I could find room for, leaving most of my furniture at Donny's for the time being. I had also brought my precious cat Pritchess with me on this journey. Donny had a cat that stayed out most of the time in the wretched heat. I do not know how the poor baby survived the sweltering sun, but he was a true survivor and ended up as my beloved Caddy Boy later on. My cat was a real trooper and seemed to adjust to wherever I landed, which had been a few motels before locating the apartment. It was quite a feat to hide her in and out of the local establishments, but it worked out. Having a wonderful pet by your side made the world a much better place to be, no matter how screwed up things get. Eventually she ended up as my Mom's baby. My Mother convinced me that it was unfair to subject the cat to so many environments and that it would eliminate some of the stress placed on me.

Having settled in, a week or so later, one night I was relaxing peacefully in my little apartment and just happened to look out the window. I was horrified to see what looked like a huge swarm of date roaches buzzing around the palm trees! I went for a closer look, because I hoped my eyes were just playing tricks on me. Unfortunately they were not. All I could think of, was that I'm not setting my foot outside, and those disgusting creepy crawlers better not even think of coming inside! I tried to put it out of my mind, but a short time later, I was lying on my couch relaxing when I happened to look up at the ceiling and see one of these big ugly roaches rapidly falling in my direction. It landed on my chest and as loud as I screamed, I was surprised that no one came bursting through my door, thinking someone was being murdered in my apartment! I bolted straight up, headed for the phone, and called Ray, a sergeant at Palm Springs PD, whom I had met earlier in the week. Oh yes, we did not let any opportunities escape to become acquainted with someone that might just help out in the future. All I could think of, was that he has a gun; he can blow the sucker away with one shot! Ray only lived a couple of doors down the hall from me, and came to my rescue in record time. He said, he heard someone screaming, but hadn't realized that it was coming from me. He seemed to be quite impressed with the strength of my vocal cords. He was able to locate the big bad roach, and mashed him with one large stomp of his foot. The after-effect was almost as scary as the live bug, but Ray was a gentleman. After slaying the beast, he even cleaned up the remnants.

This incident did work to my advantage. Ray took this opportunity to invite me to dinner at one of the upscale restaurants in town. We started going out a few times a week, and he was always surprising me, taking me to new places. He was a class act, and enjoyed the finer things in life. I was feeling very spoiled. During this time, Donny and I were still talking about the possibility of working out our differences, but having Ray in my life kept me from jumping back in with both feet.

Even though I was dating a wonderful man, I still had a hard time reconciling myself to the fact that Donny and I were through, after all we had shared. He was having difficulty accepting it, too. He called frequently, always wanting to get together to see if we could work things out. There were times I did miss him and all his crazy antics. I won't lie, life with him was never dull. I do believe I had some sort of crazy addiction to this man, because I just couldn't seem to let go entirely, either. I could've ended it once and for all, simply by not taking his calls, ending all contact with him. But I just couldn't bring myself to do that.

One night after Ray and I had been out, we went back to my apartment, where we snuggled on the couch, watching T.V. All of a sudden, there was a loud noise coming from the window just above our heads where we were lying. Donny had popped the window out of the frame, hoisted himself up, and was proceeding to step right on us as we lay on the couch! Ray came close to decking him, but I begged him not to, so he backed off. Donny was shouting at me, asking how I could be seeing someone else so soon after he and I had only temporarily split. He accused me of fooling around on him with Ray, which was not the case. Ray asked if I wanted him arrested for breaking and entering but no way could I do that to Donny. Ray felt I was defending Donny, and he became somewhat angry with me. As far as he was concerned, Donny should have been thrown in jail. Ray finally decided, he was going to leave and let me fend for myself. I actually let him go. The message I sent to Ray was that I was choosing Donny over him, and I suppose that is what I did, whether that was my intention at the time or not. Donny eventually calmed down and we decided to try dating again, to see if we could salvage our relationship.

After a few weeks of seeing each other, Donny began trying to convince me that I should move back in with him, and leave my cockroach infested apartment behind. Before I had a chance to decide, late one evening, I received a phone call from a past love, Jason, whom I had met at a popular club in Newport.

My relationship with Jason had been short lived, but I was crazy about him. We had an off-and-on affair as he was living in the San Francisco area, only coming into town on occasional business trips. After several months of a scorching romance, the phone calls ceased, and the surprise visits at the front door ended. I again had my heart broken. Months later he appeared at my old condo in Huntington Beach. One of my friends was subleasing it, and recognized him immediately. Knowing how I had felt about him, she felt confident that it would be okay to give him my address and phone number in Palm Springs. My friend called me, and told me what had happened, and warned me to be prepared for Jason to show up on my doorstep once again. He had told her that he would be driving to the desert that night, in hopes of seeing me.

When I got the call, my heart just about jumped out of my chest. Even though I was expecting it, I was still just so ecstatic to hear from him again. I'll never forget, about 11PM he phoned me and said, he was at my apartment building and needed to see me. The complex was a secured building, and the only means of entry was for me to hit a buzzer to let him in. I froze when I heard his voice. He explained how much I meant to him, and seeing me again was all he could think about the past months. I was so surprised that my response was to simply say I had to think about it. After making this unbelievable statement, I asked him if he would be staying in town for the night. Jason said he had seen a Best Western Motel down the street and would check in. What was wrong with me? I had dreams of this moment, of being with him once again, and all I could say, was that I would think about it? This guy was almost the complete package. He was tall, handsome, and the most unbelievably sexy man I had ever known. Jason was very intelligent and talented, and wrote beautiful poetry. What was I thinking? I lay in bed the remainder of the night wrestling with my thoughts. As soon as it was daylight, I headed out for the motel, only to find that he had already checked out. I thought that I was going to hyperventilate from utter disappointment. My vacillating over the pros and cons of possibly getting involved with Jason had driven me to the edge. My seeing him could have put my longing for him to rest, or we could have discovered our relationship was meant to be; now I was afraid that I would never know.

Later that day I was able to locate a phone number for Jason and when I called, a woman answered the phone. I asked for Jason and she identified herself as his wife. I was thrown off guard by this announcement; he had never mentioned a wife! My reluctance to open my door to him turned out to be the right decision, after all. I never did learn why he drove all that way to see me, and that nagged at me for a very long time. I told myself, I had to let it go, even though to this day, I wish I had hit that buzzer and had that evening with him, just so I wouldn't have to wonder what might have been.

As a result of Donny's relentless pursuit of me, I did end up moving back into his house. I knew, it probably wasn't the smart thing to do, but to be honest, I simply couldn't take living with roaches anymore. I realize, that sounds like a crazy reason to move in with a man, and in hindsight I have to admit, it probably was, but at the time, all I could think about was getting away from those bugs and being able to live in peace, without fear of some creepy crawly appearing out of nowhere. The final straw was one morning after my shower when I felt something on my leg. One of the largest and ugliest roach beasts was crawling up my leg almost to my thigh. It was a horrific experience, and my screams brought no response from my friend, Ray, nor anyone else in the building. I was sure someone would have called 911, but it was not the case. The choice to move back in with him seemed like the lesser of two evils at the time; so I relented and agreed to try it one more time.

I looked around for employment, and ended up being hired by a local hospital. My job was to do medical transcribing in the lab. I had no clue about the specialized terminology and was totally lost. I was told that I would catch on, but I knew better, right from the get go I didn't think this was going to be the ideal job for me. The odor and sight of body parts and formaldehyde were enough to turn my stomach, but I kept telling myself to toughen up! I made it through one day, and decided to give it one more chance. I showed up the next morning, and was told to take notes for Dr. Jones in the morgue, as he was cutting today. This news threw me off balance; in the morgue? Cutting? I convinced myself to be strong, that this would build character and be a new learning experience. I took the elevator down to the bottom floor and stood in front of the door only to find myself being helped off the floor as I had temporarily lost consciousness. It was pretty obvious that being in a room with dead bodies wasn't going to work for me. I immediately handed in my resignation after this experience and headed for the unemployment office.

Donny and I were barely breaking bread together, and I knew in my heart of hearts, that the demise of our relationship was only a matter of time. But, once again, I didn't listen to my heart or pay attention to what was staring me in the face. I have always thought that one should exhaust every possible opportunity to salvage a relationship, to the point of exhaustion. I know better today, after many years of trial and error.

In order to maintain my wavering sanity, and to escape Donny's constant presence, I hit the employment pavement once again. One of the first on the list was a brokerage firm, needing someone to answer the phone and take messages. What a piece of cake this would be, I thought, until I met the woman in charge. One hour into the job and she was already telling me how I should write the messages down and criticizing my handwriting as too fancy. I always thought my handwriting simply reflected my artistic nature. She continued hanging over my shoulder, blasting demands in my ear to the point where I couldn't even hear the people speaking on the other end of the phone. I finally put my pen down. I stared her straight in the eyes and told her, she was welcome to take the messages herself as I didn't need to put up with her crap. Most of the other girls in the office were grinning from ear to ear and I even got a thumbs up from one of them. I may have told her to take it and put it where the sun don't shine, she had my blood boiling so badly that I don't really remember what I said to her, only that it definitely wasn't complimentary. So, yet another job bit the dust.

After a few days of recuperating from this unpleasant experience, I contacted a very nice doctor who needed a front office girl to take messages and call in prescriptions. Little did I know that this would be one of the toughest jobs I ever signed up for. This man saw a minimum of sixty patients a day. There was no time to even go to the bathroom, let alone step outside for a cigarette! Yes, I admit I smoked for many years. It helped to keep my weight down. I was an anorexic and nicotine was part of my diet, something to do to keep me from eating, plus I really enjoyed the taste of tobacco.

The nurse in the office did not understand that I had no command of medical terminology. She would shout out prescriptions for me to call in and I had to repeatedly ask her to spell it out, which was an extreme irritant to her. To say that I was beyond nervous, is an understatement. It was such a huge responsibility to phone in the prescriptions correctly. So even though she wasn't shy about showing her irritation, I continued questioning everything she blurted out. I not only had to organize the office, but also occasionally assisted the doctor with patients, handing him his tools while he stitched someone up or put a cast on a leg. I did not have the stomach for this type of work, but managed to hang in there for several months, until I left the desert life behind, forever.

One weekend Donny was smoking his wacky grass, and insisted that I try a puff or two. After all this time together, he said, I should experience what he enjoyed so much. Why my common sense evaded me on this particular occasion, as well as my values, I don't know, but I learned to regret my decision to listen to him. After a few puffs, I became giddy and then came the lapses of memory. One minute I was out in the desert and the next second inside the car and then in the house and then back to the desert. There were total lapses of time and place. I was freaking out, almost like having a near death experience. I could not get control of myself, and the blackouts were beyond frightening. I recall Donny's son raising his fists to his dad and yelling at him, "What did you do to her?" All I knew for a certainty, was that I was going to die. After many hours and with God's grace, I started regaining my sanity. I woke up and found myself lying on the couch at Donny's, with absolutely no memory of how I got there. His son was sitting next to me and told me the grass had been laced with Angel Dust. He said his father should have known that, and never should have urged me to try it. I finally began to feel somewhat human. Having David nearby reassured me that all would be O.K.

This harrowing experience was the proverbial straw that broke the camel's back. I started making my plans to move back to Orange County. I expressed to Donny my extreme disappointment and anger at him for urging me to try such a dangerous drug, causing me a trip to hell and back. I told him that I could never trust him again. He repeatedly assured me that nothing like this would ever happen again. I told him, he was right, it won't happen again, because I was leaving. Believe it or not, he became very upset and just couldn't understand why I wouldn't give him another chance. I won't lie, in spite of everything, I did feel melancholy and sad at times, I truly had wished for a happily ever after with him. Deep down I knew, I was not entirely through with this relationship; I still had feelings for him. I told him, we could remain friends, he could come visit me, and we could call one another. It would be another adventure for us, I told him.

Breaking up is one of the most difficult things for me personally to go through. No matter how bad the situation, no matter how sure I am I'm doing the right thing; it still tears me apart mentally and physically every time. So it surprised me that I was able to move on in spite of his pleading for me to stay. Being eternally optimistic, I thought maybe things would change for us in the future, but for now I knew what I had to do. The desert life was not for me. I grew to hate everything about it. I needed the Pacific Ocean in order to smile again.

I wasn't sure if I could land my old job back, but I sure was going to try. Some of my friends came to my aid with a small U-Haul, and helped me load up most of my belongings. We couldn't load the piano though, and I told Donny I would return for it. He said he felt the piano should remain with him after all I put him through. After all I put HIM through? This statement not only mystified me but also served to reinforce that I was definitely doing the right thing!

We headed out, and I immediately went into full blown panic attack as we drove through the small mountain ranges. I never stopped hyperventilating the whole trip. To make matters worse, the friend I was with did not drive, so it was up to me. Poor girl, she had to be terrified riding with someone who was clearly terrified herself, hyperventilating, crying, and violently shaking the whole way! I remember finally ingesting a handful of valiums and saying prayers to get us safely to our destination. The drugs helped, but I still could not stop the hyperventilation. Sometimes I wonder why I never had a heart attack or stroke. If you have ever hyperventilated or know someone who has, you know what I mean; it takes a terrible toll on your body.

I finally decided to get off the freeway and take surface roads, and promptly proceeded to get lost at every turn. I just couldn't handle all the twists and dips the mountains offered, but I couldn't handle the mad rush of the freeway either. Normally it would take two hours to get to Orange County, but it took us well over four. This was the last time in my life I ever drove on a freeway. This experience had ingrained in me a sheer terror of freeway driving, and nothing was ever going to change it. The relief I felt at hitting town in one piece was so intense, I could have easily gotten out of the car and kissed the ground! Thank God for guiding me through, and also for letting mankind invent valium!

It was great to be back in the Big O.C. (Orange County) I hadn't realized just how much I missed my friends and the aroma of the salt air from the ocean, until I was back. I pledged to myself that I would never leave it again.

Moving back to my mom's house in Balboa was really going back home. Being raised in such a fabulous environment was never so much appreciated as it was now. I knew this would not be a permanent arrangement, as Mom's beach house that she had been renting for over thirty years was the typical beach rental, with small rooms, one bathroom, and no storage. Definitely, there was no privacy for either of us. But staying with her helped me to get my life and my sanity back again.

I contacted the HB Police Department and learned that they had a temporary opening in the Records Division and I was welcomed to test for it. This also required a background check that would take a few weeks to complete, but I was ready for whatever they wanted me to do. I just wanted back in, and never appreciated my former employer as much as I did right then. After working at the PD part-time for several months, a full time position finally opened. Unfortunately it was on the graveyard shift, in transcribing, where reports are dictated by the officers. And I detested typing. But it would get my foot in the door, so I accepted the position.

My friend, who was subleasing the condo, offered me a room to rent temporarily. Working this vampire shift, I needed to be closer to the station. It was an adjustment moving back into the tiny guest room after having full range of the place in the past, but it was better than driving to Balboa with the strange hours I was working.

I did not adjust well at all to the midnight shift. After three months, I was losing it mentally. It's just not normal to be up all night long, while the rest of the world is sound asleep, and especially hard to adjust after sleeping like a normal person on the weekends. I can recall hallucinating at one point, and seeing images on the wall, which I knew were not real, but they managed to scare the life out of me anyway! I hung in there as long as I could, because the supervisor on nights was a real trip and I loved working with her. She believed in the Ouija board, and we would all play on a nightly basis. It was creepy watching that little arrow point out answers that were pretty right on at times. I believed one of the girls, who originated from Boston, was part witch. It was uncanny how well the Ouija board worked for her and how much influence she had over our supervisor. Our supervisor believed so strongly in it, that she insisted her new spouse quit his job as a police officer at Huntington Beach and go to work for the D.A.'s office. The board said he would get killed on duty and she was convinced beyond a shadow of a doubt that the spirits who guided that board were sending them a warning! As it turned out, it really was a great move for him; he became a very well respected Superior Court judge. As for her, she ended up leaving her husband and children, became a lawyer, and disappeared.

Even after I was able to change to a more normal shift, I still struggled with my demons. My agoraphobia seemed to be escalating. I got to the point where I couldn't drive. I parked my car in the apartment stall and left it there until it was towed away. I swore I would never get behind the wheel again. One of the ladies from work started picking me up in the morning and arranged to have someone take me home at night. There were times when I literally could not make myself walk out the front door and was afraid I would lose my job after calling in sick so many times. I yearned to get out of the house, but couldn't do it alone. The pool of our complex was only two blocks away, but I couldn't make it, unless one of my friends came over and went with me. I needed that security blanket just to go two blocks! Swimming really helped so much to alleviate some of my stress. The Valiums were no longer effective and I had to turn to other medications, which turned out to be worse in the long run. The Valium was recreating the original problems I had, and I became a guinea pig for my doctor, using me to experiment with new treatments. It zapped every ounce of energy I had, just trying to keep it together enough to hide my condition from my co-workers. This malady was not something our macho cops would understand. I knew they would see it as a mental deficiency.

The transcribing supervisor I worked for on my new shift also seemed to have witch-like powers, but in a different way. She was not someone I could share my problems with. She was a real slave driver, and just cold and callous most of the time. She didn't have much of a life, so the job was her whole identity. She thought being a tyrannical dictator was the only way to keep her subordinates in line. This woman put me on eleven different shifts over an eleven month period. I felt she was punishing me for escaping the graveyard shift sooner than she thought I should. Apparently I hadn't paid whatever dues she felt I owed. Unfortunately, there were quite a few in the department at that time with her mind set.

But we still managed to have some fun, probably much to the chagrin of our dictators. One Christmas we had a party at work and exchanged gifts with our peers. I happened to get one of those one-piece PJ sets with the feet and the drop seat in the back, apparently so you could use the facilities without having to strip down naked. My co-workers were becoming hysterical picturing me wearing this bunny suit, encouraging me to try it on. I foolishly took the bait. I put it on and started prancing around like Jessica Rabbit, attracting quite an audience. Before I knew it, a bunch of people were behind me, pushing me forward. One sergeant was shoving me the hardest down the halls, and seemed to be enjoying shoving me a bit more than he should have. All of a sudden I was crashing through a closed door, only to find myself right in the middle of a press conference the chief was giving regarding a very serious hostage situation! I thought for sure this was curtains for me, as I slunk out of that room, all of those people hurling daggers with their eyes at my retreating back! But as luck would have it, we had a great chief at the time. He actually got a chuckle out of it, although he did request not to do it again. I later found out that all the time I was being shoved around the building, my back flap was open and all that was visible was my very sheer panties and a good shot of my behind! The people who instigated this whole thing were laughing hysterically, and their hysteria was contagious. I started laughing so hard and couldn't stop, to the point where I could not contain my bladder. Lucky for me only a few splatters slipped out! But really, could this day have gotten any more embarrassing? Even though the Chief wasn't angry with me, my supervisor reamed me up one side and down the other, and wrote me up for disorderly conduct. I'm sure she was disappointed that I was never formally reprimanded. Most everyone enjoyed my tale of the drop drawers and the laughs that ensued, something you need once in a while to counter-balance the seriousness of the environment we worked in. As this story was told and retold, it was embellished upon more with each telling, until ultimately I was almost totally naked running around the department exposing most of my private parts.

14 DETECTIVE BUREAU

No matter how hard I tried to adapt, the ever changing shifts were doing a number on me, both mentally and physically. I managed to get a medical release from my doctor to get off the late shift. I expected that I would have normal hours, but my supervisor from hell was not about to let that happen. She made sure, I would stay on rotating shifts. But I got lucky once again. I landed an opening in the Detective Bureau, working days, with weekends off; you can't get much better than that! It was in the Economic Crimes Division, as an assistant to the detective investigating bad checks and forgery. What a completely different atmosphere it turned out to be! The detectives treated me as if I had a brain, and were respectful, most of the time. It was a much more relaxed environment, and fun and games were not only allowed but encouraged! The mentality was you could do your job and still have fun, happy employees are productive employees. After where I'd been, I thought I had landed in paradise.

Once in my new job, I discovered my immediate boss happened to be my past lover, who had been instrumental in my getting hired, and with whom I had had a tumultuous relationship. He was the one, whom I had threatened to shoot while in a drunken state, only to wake up to find several cops in my bedroom removing a couple of my guns from the premises. In today's world, I would have lost my job, and possibly had criminal charges filed against me. Thankfully times were different then and people were far more forgiving.

I had several partners during my first year in detectives. In 1981 I got a new partner, Debbie, and we became best friends, in spite of our 20 year age difference. I don't know if I was immature or she was an old soul, probably a little of both, but our friendship just worked. She and I have a long history of getting into mischief and today enjoy reliving the tales of our wild past. Our immediate boss was a detective by the name of Ryan. I thought Ryan was a hunk, with a terrific personality. He was a big macho guy, but the things that would come out of his mouth could unintentionally send you into hysterics.

My affair with Ryan started out slowly, with the passing of notes to one another, just like kids in junior high school. He was always so flattering and I ate it up like a kid in a candy store. Ryan was the type who inspired confidence in him no matter what he did. He was in control and I always admired a man in control. Not only was he good looking, but in my fairy tale world, he was going to be the hero who would rescue me from myself.

After becoming better acquainted over a few months, we both came to the same conclusion, we were soul mates who were destined to be together. But.., yes, there always seems to be a "but," when it comes to my love life, did I mention he was married? Ryan assured me he was going to leave his wife, and he eventually did. He left her approximately eleven times, only to slink back each time with his tail between his legs. His wife welcomed him back every time, after some requisite begging and pleading. I never understood how she handled the knowledge of his repeated indiscretions.

I was absolutely obsessed with Ryan, I literally felt I couldn't breathe without him. With all my psychological issues brought on by my agoraphobia, he was the one person I felt safe and secure with. I was falling apart without him. I believed with all my heart and every ounce of my being that he was the love of my life, and we would somehow end up together.

It took all my focus to stay on track at work. I was so obsessed with Ryan that I couldn't think of anything else. I confessed to Debbie about Ryan, although she knew from the get go what was going on. I constantly bent her ear asking her opinion about how I should handle everything in this illicit relationship. For her young years she was very wise, and without her input I would have made worse choices than I did. What a great friend to put up with my incessant chatter. I was always telling her that she was an excellent counsellor and to send the bill at the end of the month.

What a cast of characters behind the walls of the HBPD. They ran the gamut, from mildly entertaining to downright scandalous.

One of our happier stories is of the scientific forensic man and wife team, who were both so gifted and talented in their field. Ken was a genius and moved on to much bigger and better things after life at Huntington Beach Police Department. He wrote several books and one in particular, Bale Fire, was a huge success. He sold the movie rights to a studio and soon his story will be hitting the big screen. I know envy is an ugly trait, but envious I was. How I would love to have that kind of talent!

One of our more scandalous tales is of a very handsome, charming officer, who caused women of all ages to swoon at the sight of him. His blond hair, blue eyes, and gentle manner were irresistible. He always sported a tan, which only enhanced his well-developed physique. He dated almost every woman in the Department, his only prerequisite being that they were at least mildly attractive. He asked me out once, and, hold on to your seats, I actually turned him down! I know you're thinking, this was not my usual M.O., this was not the Norma you've become accustomed to. With such a handsome hunk, I would normally have said yes before he was even finished asking, but his reputation as a ladies man, and personally knowing all the women he had scored with, was a big turn off for me. This turned out to be a wise decision, and believe me, I didn't make many of those in my younger years. His sexual prowess worked well for him in the Vice Unit, where he was assigned as a Lieutenant. He could throw the line out, and the hookers were hooked and later cuffed and booked. Rumor had it, that he wasn't above having sexual liaisons with these hookers, and considering his reputation, likely they were more than just rumors. Later it came to light that his wandering eye wasn't limited to females, he also enjoyed the occasional sexual dalliance with a man. He once told a story about a Hollywood party he attended, boasting that he would suck whatever landed in his mouth. A totally disgusting remark, one he should have kept to himself. Once his boasting made the rounds of the PD rumor mill, he became somewhat of a piranha with the women, who were totally turned off by his alternative lifestyle and his crude description of it.

Harry also developed a taste for drugs. It wasn't too difficult back in those days to raid the evidence lockers and help yourself to the confiscated stash. Being the lieutenant in the Vice Unit, he had free access to whatever was in the evidence lockers. He was finally caught, which lead to him being asked to resign in lieu of the department possibly filing criminal charges with the D.A's office. Being a fairly bright guy, he chose to resign. A couple of years later he died under mysterious circumstances, found dead of a gunshot wound out in the middle of nowhere. To this day, no one is sure what led to his demise, besides a 38 to the head. There has always been a cloud of suspicion of foul play surrounding his death. There was a lot of speculation after it happened, that maybe he became involved with the wrong people, maybe drug dealers or gangsters. We will probably never know what really happened to him, but he obviously made some very bad choices in his life. What a fall from grace, from achieving the rank of Lieutenant and getting the much sought after Vice Unit assignment, to trysts with hookers and drug addiction, to a tragic and lonely death in the middle of nowhere.

We had another officer who exhibited scandalous behavior. My good friend Cheryl told me a story about how she and her sergeant husband were peacefully asleep late one night when the phone rang. When she answered, the caller said "I want to f--- you". She knew immediately who the caller was and handed the phone over to her husband who happened to be a sergeant at the PD. She told the caller he would have to check with her husband first. He had heard rumors about Saul Whitker having a dark sexual side to him, and this was not the only time Saul had been accused of making this type of call to a fellow officer's home. Rumor was, he had sexual liaisons with some of the women he arrested, and the kinkier the better. He was the good looking wholesome boy next door type, someone you would never suspect of doing the things he was accused of. Saul was a sergeant in the Helicopter Detail, and had so much to lose if news of his sexual escapades spread to the powers that be, but it didn't stop him. My friend's husband did confront him after the telephone call and of course he totally denied he ever made the call to him or to anyone else. Just like the cops that couldn't resist the evidence drugs, he put himself in the line of fire, jeopardizing his career. After being confronted, the calls ceased, but he later got into some other kind of trouble and he too was asked to resign from the Department. It was all very hush-hush, so I can only assume it was something pretty bad.

While all this melodrama was occurring, I was consumed with Ryan and with trying to keep my sanity. He would come over to my apartment and spend several hours at least once or twice a week while he was still living part-time with his wife. Hard to know what lies he told her in order to get away for those few hours. As weird as it sounds, I truly felt very badly for her. It had to be a nightmare every time he packed his bags and went out the door. I tried many times to end our relationship when it became obvious to me that he was unable to cut the ties with her. I fooled myself each time I broke up with him, thinking that maybe this time his fear of losing me would be the catalyst he needed to leave her once and for all, and start a new life with me. I knew he was unhappy at home, but he still clung to Sharon like a security blanket. Another obstacle to divorce for Ryan was money. He was very money conscious and was always bragging about being worth a million plus, due to the wise investments he had made. That was a lot of cash in the seventies. I know he didn't want to lose any of it, and a divorce would be saying adios to at least half.

There is no excuse for what I did, and to this day, I am deeply ashamed that I ever had anything to do with him while he was a married man. At the time though, he was like a drug to me, and I was an addict.

Several times I noticed his wife walking in front of my apartment. One night I opened the door and asked her to come in, telling her we needed to talk. I explained to her my addiction problems, my agoraphobic agonies, and how Ryan was the only person I felt safe with. I told her I knew he really did love her and there were times I literally begged him not to leave her because I knew he wouldn't be happy if he did. I told her I thought he was going through some type of hormonal changes, what most would probably refer to as mid-life crisis I suppose, and I believed that was at the root of his problems, not being able to decide what it was, or whom he wanted.

As we sat there sharing a bottle of wine, I proceed to get smashed, and I ended up spilling my guts about my weakness for her husband, how I just couldn't say no to him. She sat there quietly listening to me go on and on about my feelings for her husband. I actually liked her and admired her composure, had it been me on that side of the fence, I probably would have leapt over and pulled out her hair! I found my heart literally aching for both of us. His behavior was totally selfish, with no real regard for what he was putting us through, and he did not deserve her loyalty and understanding. At that moment I knew I did not want to do anything further to hurt her, but unfortunately these feelings went by the wayside the next time he left her and showed up on my doorstep. Ryan told me later that his wife would never forgive me, and had a deep hatred towards me. I didn't blame her. If the shoe had been on the other foot, I can't say I would've shown as much grace as she did. To this day this is one of my biggest regrets, I wish I had the opportunity to convince her how truly sorry I am.

As Ryan and I continued our tumultuous up and down relationship, life at the PD continued to be exciting with rarely a dull moment. I remember one incident that left us looking like the Keystone Cops. A red Porsche was travelling at a dangerously high speed through the city and several patrol cars went in pursuit, after the Porsche blew through a red light. The driver of the Porsche turned out to be a formidable opponent for our patrol officers. He knew how to handle that Porsche, and was able to lose the officers when they lost control of their police units and ended up on the beach off Pacific Coast Highway, much to their embarrassment. Before this, the suspect had driven right through a golf course, startling several golfers who were used to errant golf balls, not cars hurtling by at a hundred miles an hour! Once the patrol officers were out of commission, stuck on the beach, motorcycle officers took off after the suspect and nearly caught up with him until both officers lost control of their bikes and went down. This guy had single-handedly managed to put two patrol cars and two motorcycles out of commission, seemingly with little effort, humiliating and embarrassing the officers; an assault to their massive egos. At that point it was probably a good thing that they hadn't caught up with him!

It just so happened, there was an off duty LAPD officer who had his radio on while he was watering his front lawn, and heard the whole broadcast of the pursuit. He grabbed his service revolver and fired off a couple of rounds when the red Porsche flew by him in a blur. None of the shots were successful in slowing the guy down, but it was a valiant attempt.

As the guy continued travelling at speeds well over 100 miles an hour, LAPD units joined in the pursuit as he entered L.A. County. With numerous units in pursuit, they finally were able to stop him when he lost control of his shiny red Porsche. Unfortunately when he lost control, he smashed into one of their police units which created a chain reaction, causing several other police cars to collide. The suspect was not injured during the crash but his beautiful car was totaled. Oddly, later he was found to be extremely battered and bruised when being booked into the jail. One can only surmise how he got those injuries.

While we had our fair share of entertaining stories, we also had heartbreaking ones. A twelve year old girl who was last seen in Huntington Beach went missing, and was later found dead in the Los Angeles National Forest. Forensics determined that she had been sexually assaulted and severely beaten. After a long and exhausting investigation, our homicide detectives were able to identify her killer as Rodney Alcala. He had been posing as a photographer and had approached several young girls at the beach, promising them if they allowed him to take pictures of them in their bathing suits, he could land them a modeling job in Hollywood. This particular little girl may have been swayed by his promise of a modeling career, or he may have simply abducted her, forcing her into his vehicle. Since she is not here to tell the story, and he has never admitted his guilt, we will never know what really happened that fateful day.

It was so heart wrenching, watching her family come into the Department day after day, for several months, to discuss the case with the investigators. The expressions of sorrow and loss worn so openly on their faces just tore at your heartstrings. Everyone in the Detective Bureau was impacted by the investigation and this family's intense grief. One sergeant in particular became so emotionally involved with the family and the investigation, that he began having emotional problems of his own. There were days you could smell the alcohol emitting from his body. He had always been a very caring person and this tragedy took its toll on him. How very difficult it has to be to try and restrain your own personal feelings, so you can maintain the appearance of being in control when such a horrific crime has been committed. Cops have to be able to handle all kinds of horrible things; that's the nature of the job, but when it comes to crimes against children, they are just as human as the rest of us. At the time, Huntington Beach was a small peaceful community, so we weren't accustomed to dealing with crimes of such a horrific nature.

After they identified the suspect, one day they brought him in, to the Detective Bureau conference room. I happened to be passing by when he brushed up slightly against my arm. I know it sounds hokey but I kid you not, I immediately sensed evil emitting from this monster, it was the oddest sensation. And when he looked at me with his dark hate filled eyes, I got the cold shivers throughout my whole body. The strangest thing was, that I didn't even know at the time that this was the suspect in the murder. It's hard to comprehend that evil monsters like Rodney Alcala were once precious innocent babies. Alcala was proven guilty and has been incarcerated for many years. He became quite famous when he chose to defend himself in his last court trial. Fortunately he wasn't a very good lawyer and was convicted of several murders. Ironically, it was later discovered that Alcala was a contestant on television's The Dating Game, and almost won the date with the young hopeful girl looking for love. God was definitely looking out for that girl that day.

To ease all the tension from work, my friend Debbie and I decided to visit a popular club that was owned by the Righteous Brothers and dance the stress away. Debbie had just married when she started her job at the bureau. Fortunately for me, her husband at the time did not appear to object to her accompanying me to the clubs. He enjoyed his own time out with the boys so he wasn't in a position to object too much.

It's an understatement to say that we met some very interesting characters. Debbie, being a beautiful girl with long natural red hair and a figure to kill for, attracted guys like flies to honey, as my grandma used to say. She had everything going for her, brains and looks. Debbie was totally unassuming, and was and is one of the nicest and most caring people you would ever want in a human being or in a friend. And her work ethic was beyond reproach, the bosses definitely knew they had a gem in her.

When we went out on the town, we definitely attracted plenty of male attention. I was tall and thin with long blond hair, and Debbie was a beautiful thin red hair siren. We were both attractive in different ways, which proved to be a good combination, because we never attracted the same men, nor were we ever attracted to the same man, something that can end a friendship. Often I would take on the mom role and make sure that none of the men got out of line with her. But there were many times she took on the motherly role with me, probably more than I did. She always watched my back and did her best to keep me out of hot water. Believe me, I wish I would have listened to her on many occasions; I would not have made some of the very bad choices I made with the guys I encountered at the clubs.

While my relationship with Ryan was up and down, mostly down, I was out enjoying the single life. Debbie was not only my partner in crime at work, but also my after-hours partner. Our favorite hangout was a club called The Hop. On one occasion there was a charity event and the Righteous Brothers and other entertainers were appearing. They had an auction with the proceeds going to aid homeless children in Orange County. When they brought out a large cardboard copy of a record that Bill Medley and Jennifer Warren had recorded, The Time of My Life, Debbie insisted that I should bid on it. This was my favorite song at the time, and after consuming far too many vodka tonics and being prodded by Debbie, I started bidding on it. Debbie had had her fair share of vodka tonics, too, and she was practically pulling me out of my seat and raising my hand for me each time a number was called. The amount was climbing, but she seemed oblivious and kept on insisting that I raise my hand and bid, reminding me that, after all, it was for a good cause. I was somewhat confused at the time, thanks to Absolut and the frenzied bidding process, and did not realize that I had won the final bid of $400.00! I didn't have a lot of money, and this was definitely not something I had budgeted for, but it was too late, and at the time I was feeling very charitable, and tipsy. I thought, what the heck; I do have one credit card I don't owe anything on. When I went up on stage to collect my prize, I told Bill Medley that at the least, I deserved a kiss for what I paid for his cardboard record. He accommodated me rather reluctantly, and planted a smooch on my cheek. He was still a very attractive man, and I was still feeling the effects of the Absolut, so I was hoping for more than a peck on the cheek, but it was better than nothing, and the crowd seemed to enjoy it.

We had one very major problem. We had driven Debbie's car, and it wasn't big enough to accommodate the huge record. We had no idea how we were going to get my new treasure home. While we were standing by the car pondering what to do, two guys who had overheard us, came to our rescue. Both of the guys were musicians and quite attractive I might add; not to mention very nice. They had a van and said they would be happy to drop it off at my place. We stood around chatting with them for a while before we agreed to accept the offer from these two chivalrous guys. The older one was quite attracted to Debbie and wanted us to hear him play at a club in Long Beach the following week. The younger of the two, Dave, seemed to like me and I was attracted to him too. I loved his long dark hair, and it smelled so good! Usually I didn't look twice at guys whose hair was even shoulder length, but on a musician, particularly him, it was totally sexy.

After dropping off my cardboard treasure, I gave Dave my phone number. He told me, he wanted me to come to his gig at a club in Long Beach. I told him I would really enjoy seeing him perform and to call me whenever he wanted to get together. There was a considerable age difference between him and me, and my impression was that he was just being polite, not looking for any connection other than friendship between the two of us. That was okay with me, as Ryan was still my number one heartthrob, and no one was going to take his place, even though I wished someone could.

The next morning when I woke up sober, my first thought was: What have I done? I was in no financial position to be charging $400.00 on a credit card! I immediately phoned Debbie and asked her if she thought I could cancel the charge and return my treasure, which in the light of day was really just a flimsy cardboard replica of a record. She laughed hysterically, reminding me that it was for charity, and how tacky it would be to ask for a refund of my charitable donation to the poor homeless children. I knew, she was right, but I was panicking, wondering how I was going to pay for it. I knew I was stuck, but I was consoled by constantly reminding myself that I had done a good thing for the kids on the street.

The following week Debbie and I went to see her friend play at a club called Bogart's. It was an upscale establishment located in Long Beach, with numerous pictures of stars, and of course, Humphrey Bogart's photos adorning the walls of the club. At this time, Debbie was separated from her husband, so she thought there would be no harm in hearing her new acquaintance play and sing in his band. She felt comfortable as long as I tagged along. This guy, whose name is long forgotten, was totally enamored of Debbie, and wanted to take her to dinner and become better acquainted. As it turned out, she did see him a couple of times, and although he was a very nice man, there was just no love connection for her.

Dave called me several times and we would talk for hours. He was a very interesting person as he had travelled extensively with different musical groups and had some fascinating tales to tell. He wondered if I was ever going to come and hear him play, and I always told him that I would try, but never did. To this day I am sorry that I never accepted his invitation. In spite of the age difference, I will always wonder where things might have gone with us. Plus I always try to be a person of my word and it wasn't nice to continually tell him that I would try, and then never show up, especially when he was such a nice person. I think what really held me back was Ryan, even during our off times; he was first and foremost in my mind.

So whatever happened to my $400 cardboard record? Once I saw it in the sober light of day, I realized how ugly it was, so it was relegated to hanging in the garage, until years later, during a move, a boyfriend attempted to toss it, but I readily retrieved it and it now is displayed resting on the rafters in the garage.

As mentioned several times, life was never dull at the PD. The cops hung out at their shooting range, which was really a shooting range by day and a party den at night. It was a decaying shack with couches and pool tables and a make shift bar, where they entertained some unique female locals. Some of these women were local prostitutes who had been arrested by our officers, but were still welcomed by them with open arms, when they were off duty. One of their frequent guests was a cop stalker who would follow police units around town until they stopped and gave her the opportunity to make them an offer they couldn't refuse. She drove a hot red sports convertible and while most of the officers knew her reputation and steered clear of her, there were still several who fell prey to her persistent advances, and became sexually involved with her. There were two officers who eventually jeopardized their positions on the force. While a sane person would think that they would have enough brains not to jeopardize their career for a one night stand, those raging male hormones have been known to destroy many a career and many relationships.

When the Detective Bureau would become thick with tension, I felt it was my duty to lighten things up. One day I decided to come in wearing pump-up boobs, with a dark red wig and my new set of bright blue contact lenses. I also put on my tightest fitting dress with a long slit up the side. I couldn't believe it, but no one even seemed to notice! That probably should have told me something, like maybe they were so used to my strange shenanigans, that they didn't even pay attention anymore! Not one to be ignored, I started using the pump to pump up my boobs as I walked around the room, full of men sitting at their desks. I stood right smack in front of one of the detectives' desks, working that pump as fast as I could, with my boobs growing by the second, only to have him look at me blankly and ask if I needed something.

This didn't slow me down. I went into my sergeant's office, on the excuse of discussing one of my cases with him. As I worked that pump, I could see his eyes grow big as saucers and his mouth open wide, as if he wanted to say something, but didn't quite know what to say. By now I was pumped up enough to put Dolly Parton to shame. All the while I was able to keep a straight face and continued talking about my case as though nothing was happening. He finally said "you changed your hair color, didn't you?" I told him that I had, and thanked him for noticing, batting my eyelashes as hard as I could, in hopes that he would notice my new aqua blue eyes, too. At the same time I was still pumping away, to the point, where I was afraid they were going to get so big they would explode! His face turned beet red as he suggested that I sit down before I topple over. I just smiled, and calmly strolled out of his office. As I made another round through the room, everyone finally started to notice, and I could feel 20 pairs of eyes staring in my direction. It took one brave soul to make the first comment... then the room erupted with laughter and the comments started coming from every direction. The best one was from one of the girls who said, I looked like a hard drunk broad who belonged on a barstool, not in the police department's detective bureau. Unfortunately, she was serious; she definitely did not see my prank as humorous. But attitudes like hers never stopped me from trying to lighten up the mood and give people a few laughs. I loved being the center of attention as long as it was all in good fun!

Any time one of us had a birthday, we celebrated it with a cake and a gathering in the Detective Bureau conference room, better known as the "war room". I was the designated happy birthday songstress. My voice leaves a lot to be desired, it may have even caused some ears to bleed, but the guys loved it. They would unsnap their holsters and pretend they were going to shoot me, howling like coyotes whose ears hurt when they hear a siren. This birthday ritual continued for many years but since my retirement several years ago, they have not been able to find a replacement. I'm sure there are some equally bad singers in the bureau; they're just smart enough to keep it to themselves. Several people made a recording of my singing and it is played in lieu of my presence, but I've been told it's just not the same as the real thing. I've also been told that they could send that recording into war zones and scare away all the bad guys, just as long as our troops were armed with ear plugs first. I have been asked many times to come back to sing for someone's birthday, but stepping back into that building is something I just don't want to do. Once out of there, there was no going back for me, I no longer feel as though I "belong".

It is remarkable that after working at the Long Beach Police Department for 37 years, I accumulated very few close friends. It's OK with me. Though few in number, above all, my dear friends Debbie and Cheryl more than make up in quality for the sparse numbers.

Cheryl was a character, to say the least. Over the years she held many different positions in the PD, the chief's secretary, the auto theft secretary, and in the Bad Check Detail, chasing down paper dead beats. Cheryl terms herself a "fluffy girl" and being overweight has never been a concern for her. She always had a "love me as I am" attitude, and most people did. With her infectious laugh and gregarious personality, no one really notices the few extra pounds.

In Cheryl's younger years, she was without a doubt one of the best loved drunks you would ever want to encounter. You could always count on her to be more entertaining than going to a comedy club. She topped the list of my fun loving party friends. And talk about hooking up with losers! she topped that list, too. I should note, that she has given up the demon booze, and married a devout Christian. She is one of the most spiritual people I know. She and her husband are very involved in their church, and they do ministry at the prisons, and in senior citizen homes. What a transformation from her earlier years! She was always religious, but in her earlier years she embraced both her religion and her party girl lifestyle, now her religion is the mainstay of her life, and the party girl lifestyle has gone by the wayside.

But let's get back to her past. Cheryl was dating a guy who decided to steal her car and dump it out in the boonies, and then disappear. Thankfully her car was eventually discovered by the police. She tracked the guy down and he had absolutely no explanation or excuse for stealing her car and disappearing. He just did it. Another one of her boyfriends would be sitting in a group, and suddenly pull up his shirt (he definitely didn't have a six pack to show off) and jab himself with a needle, giving himself insulin injections for his diabetes. Some of us were squeamish around needles, so, if we saw it coming in time, we had to avert our eyes.

Cheryl and another coworker, who was Cheryl's best friend at the time, would take off for a weekend, ending up with what they thought were the loves of their lives, only to realize at the break of dawn that they just might not have been thinking too clearly the night before. I guess this sort of revelation happens to a lot of people one time or another, but it seemed to be a pattern for her. I think she was seeking love, just like I was, in all the wrong places.

One of my most memorable Cheryl stories was celebrating my mother's 90th birthday at The Spaghetti Factory. Cheryl was going to meet us there in the upstairs bar. When I reached the top of the stairs, the only person at the bar was Cheryl. She was sitting in a slanted position, this big woman on this tiny little barstool, with what looked like a plant with a little brown bear holding a balloon. On the other side was an empty wine carafe. Right away I thought this was going to be a night we wouldn't forget. And I never have.

As I approached her, at first it seemed like she didn't recognize me. I asked if she could make it down the stairs. She assured me, "No problem". She managed to make it down the stairs alright, but graceful she wasn't. She would miss a few steps, but always managed to stay in an upright position, slipping and sliding as she went. She was definitely drawing attention as she stumbled drunkenly down the long staircase. But she didn't even notice, and probably wouldn't have cared if she did. She reveled in being in the spotlight, especially when she was drinking. Once she made it safely to the bottom of the stairs, she spotted my mom, comfortably seated in her wheelchair, and ran over, grabbed the wheelchair, and started shoving her all over the restaurant. She was announcing in her most robust voice that everyone had to wish this 90 year old lady a happy birthday. Cheryl is a big girl with a big voice, and soon it became infectious, and most of the patrons started singing happy birthday to my mom. At first, my mom looked terror stricken; the look on her face said "why is this madwoman screaming frantically and pushing me around the room?" But once everyone started joining in, she loved being in the limelight.

She finally returned with my mom and handed the wheelchair over to me, and promptly stumbled, landing on a very old frail gentleman, who was part of our birthday gathering. She ended up toppling to the floor, and the old gentleman was left scratching his head, trying to figure out what just crashed into him. Fortunately there were no injuries to the man, and happily for Cheryl, she had enough padding when she flopped to the floor to avoid any broken bones, maybe just a few bruises. She popped right up off the floor, as only a drunk can do, acting as though nothing had happened, and looking puzzled as to what everyone was looking at. The whole night was a total success, with all of us leaving weary from laughing hysterically at Cheryl's antics. My mom said this was the best birthday she had ever had.

There were a lot of fun people working at the PD years ago. We would plan outings together, something no one really does anymore. Some of the most enjoyable were a couple of trips to Catalina Island. It was standard procedure to have as many Bloody Marys as we could gulp while sailing to the island. It was amazing, how many of the girls got sea sick, despite wearing patches. Could it have had anything to do with the Bloody Marys? I did everything I could, to avoid the sick ones like the plague. Just the sound of someone heaving would make me heave too. I never got sea sick as long as I avoided them. Not that I didn't feel empathy for them, I truly did. One girl amazed me as she stood and watched someone throwing up. She kept saying it didn't bother her, but she got a nasty surprise when all of a sudden she barfed up her drinks all over herself! I kept warning her not to look, but instead of heeding my advice, she just kept bragging about how it didn't bother her. She was bragging right up to the moment when she started spewing Bloody Marys. I know it sounds mean, but I just couldn't contain my laughter. During the boat ride over, some of the quiet girls turned out to be the rowdiest. We were sitting on opposite sides of an aisle and as male passengers would come down the aisle, some of the girls would slap their butts and then roar with laughter, while the rest of us cringed with embarrassment. Fortunately all of the men except one took it good-naturedly, and even he didn't do anything but kind of glare at them.

Once we hit the island, it was more drinks before the groups went their separate ways, depending on what they wanted to do. Some of them went parasailing. No matter how many drinks I had, I couldn't muster up the courage to get into one of those flimsy looking contraptions. Anything over two stories was not in my comfort zone. Others went shopping, or rented little carts and toured the island. At the end of the day, we would all meet and raid some of the local pubs. We could always count on Cheryl to be there, egging us on and entertaining us.

Despite my craziness over Ryan, I managed to have fun without him. Our togetherness was so on and off, half the time I couldn't keep track of where we stood in our relationship. I wasn't about to sit home and be miserable, like I had done in the beginning. I guess I was becoming immune to the situation.

Several of my friends and I enjoyed the brunch cruises through Balboa Harbor. The brunch consisted of endless Champagne and laughter, with the food being the least of our interests. For Debbie's birthday we went on one of these brunch cruises. We thought we would put together an outrageous display of sex toys to embarrass her. The best one was a small wind-up replica of a penis. We wound up a bunch of them and sent them wobbling down the main corridor of the boat. None of the other patrons enjoyed our sense of humor. Before long we had the whole floor to ourselves, as they escaped to the outside deck or to the lower level. It was hysterical watching those little penises grinding away down the corridor, and even more comical watching the horrified faces of the stuffy patrons. We also had a penis gun that shot out sparks. Anyone, brave enough to walk by, got zapped. We were fortunate that we didn't end up getting tossed overboard by the crew, or by other patrons. No doubt, the thought crossed their minds.

On another sea venture, we all had dates, and tried to clean up our act; no naughty toys. Again, this was an all-you-can-eat-and-drink champagne affair. While the men were more interested in chowing down, the girls were busily partaking of the free flowing champagne cocktails. Cheryl's boyfriend at the time was a really big jovial teddy bear of a guy, whom we called Big Mack. On this occasion, Big Mack had imbibed his fair share of champagne, plus probably a fair share of three other kinds of libations, to the point, where the waiter just started leaving the whole bottle, to save some trips! Big Mack stumbled when trying to get up from his chair, and landed on the drummer. The musician was very good natured about the incident as long as none of his drums were damaged. A short while later Big Mack tripped once again and just about crushed a tiny elderly man, sitting across from us, who could not have weighed more than 90 pounds. The guardian angels were working overtime for both, as the little man was miraculously not injured, and Big Mack popped right up, seemingly oblivious to the commotion. Sounds like a partnership for Cheryl, made in heaven, as stumbling and landing on elderly men was something they most definitely had in common.

The entertainment was a live trio; the guitar player started flirting with me. This upset the guy I was with, to the point where I thought a fight would ensue, but reassurance from me that I was not interested, seemed to appease him. Of course I really was interested in this young handsome musician and was sorry to be stuck with this unreasonable and jealous drunkard. On this particular brunch cruise, my older brother and mother, both teetotalers, had joined us. Both were totally humiliated by all of our drunken antics. My mother handled it better than my staunch opinionated brother who was totally shocked and appalled at our behavior. You never saw two people so happy to see a boat landing!

Our Detective Bureau gang would often have get-togethers after hours, and it was common for retired officers to show up. During one of these gatherings at a local Sheraton Inn, a retired officer, whom I hadn't seen in many years, came onto me like gangbusters. He was extremely attentive and stuck to me like glue and I actually had a difficult time getting rid of him. He was a big guy, not attractive, but he had a way of making you feel extremely special and protected. Before I left the party, he practically begged me to go out with him the next time he was in the area. He lived in Northern California, but said he was in the process of moving to this area in the near future. I told him to give me a call when he got settled and maybe we could get together for a cup of coffee.

15 MR. ROGERS

I was extremely busy, as I had taken on another job that my friend Jessie had arranged for me. It was working for a multi-millionaire who lived in one of the most desirable areas in Corona del Mar. His home was situated on the bluffs in Cameo Shores with the most fantastic view of the Pacific Ocean. The pristine beach below was a sanctuary, where no marine life or shells could be disturbed. It was incredible. There were times, when it was tempting to stroll down there and collect a few mementos from the white sand, but knowing that getting caught meant paying up to $500 in fines, was quite the deterrent. The beaches were private, and difficult for the public to enter. Access to the gateway required a key, which was only issued to residents. There was a long stairway to reach the beach, as all the homes facing the ocean were situated high up on the bluffs. I was awestruck that people actually lived like this.

Meeting Mr. Rogers for the first time was definitely memorable, just the first of many memorable and unique encounters we would experience. We all met at a great restaurant in town. He was a nice looking older man, in his seventies, with a great head of silver hair and a nice smile. He wasn't able to get around on his own and had caretakers on hand 24 hours a day, with Jessie being his main caretaker. As he entered the restaurant, he was speaking some unrecognizable language in a very loud booming voice. The only word I even remotely could make out was "balderdash". I was a little taken aback, as were other patrons in the restaurant, but Jessie didn't seem to pay the least bit of attention to his bizarre behavior, apparently she was used to it. As they sat down, I wasn't sure what to expect or what might come out of his mouth, but he proceeded to ask in the most normal voice if I was his new bookkeeper, which I acknowledged, indeed I was. This part-time job was a financial Godsend, and it didn't sound as though it was going to be difficult.

I found out later that the job would also require me to take care of him on occasion, and he was quite a handful. Mr. Rogers did not walk well without assistance. If his nurses weren't available, it was up to me to get him up, keep him balanced, not an easy task since he was definitely no lightweight.

One of Mr. Rogers' biggest joys was going out every day for lunch and we would dine in the best restaurants in town. I had no objection to this; I was getting to enjoy all of this fine dining and getting paid to do it! There were times I felt guilty for getting paid but then there were times it was quite demanding, not to mention embarrassing, and I more than earned my money on these latter occasions.

Because Mr. Rogers required someone to be with him 24 hours a day, it soon became my job to spend the weekend nights at his home. The guest room faced the ocean front. The sound of the waves would lull me to sleep. I was even getting an hourly salary for sleeping!

There was a sound alarm in my room, in case Mr. Rogers needed assistance. One morning, around 3:00AM, out of a sound sleep I was awakened by the sound of him shouting very loudly. He had slipped out of bed and was on the floor. It took every bit of my strength trying to lift him up, but he was just too heavy for me. After many unsuccessful attempts, I came up with a solution. I wrapped my legs around him like a crab, and told him to push while I bounced up and down with my feet. No doubt we looked ridiculous, but thankfully no one was watching, and it worked! In hindsight, I should have called the Fire Department. But it made for a good story and gave us a laugh later on.

Mr. Rogers had few joys in life: dining out, smoking his cigarettes, and enjoying his cocktails. But Jessie was a tyrant, and was always phoning or showing up, drilling us about how many cigarettes he was given that day, or how many Manhattans he drank. Before Jessie made him quit smoking cold turkey, he was allowed fifteen a day. He would always announce "cigarette" in a loud booming voice when he wanted to light up, no matter where we were. Of course, this was back in the days when you could still light up inside a restaurant. He definitely was not a soft spoken man, nor was he shy. He paid absolutely no attention to the other patrons who would oftentimes stare at us and whisper.

Later I learned that when she wanted something, Jessie would manipulate Mr. Rogers by slipping him a few extra smokes or drinks. She was very greedy, and really knew how to work him. I heard many stories from the other two nurses, like Jessie telling him that her daughter or son needed new clothes, or, on a bigger scale, new cars and two new condos for each of them. Mr. Rogers was very generous, and anything she asked for, she pretty much got. He adored Jessie, and if you said anything negative about her, he didn't want to hear it. His attorneys, who were out of state, handled most of his financial affairs, including bonuses for us girls. It was later learned that Jessie would send the nurses, and even me on one occasion, to his bank to pull petty cash, which amounted to over $1,000.00 each time. She explained that this money was needed for household expenses, although we always charged his accounts when dining out, grocery shopping, gassing up the car, for just about everything that I could think of. It was later learned that this money was being withdrawn on a weekly basis from his savings account at a local bank, and used for her personal expenses. Again, there was no telling Mr. Rogers what Jessie was up to, she had him completely fooled, and he idolized her. He had all his faculties, and nothing ever escaped him. Jessie was the exception; she was his "darling girl", as he called her, and could do no wrong.

During a luncheon outing with Mr. Rogers, we encountered an unexpected surprise. Mr. Rogers, one who enjoyed the finer things that life had to offer, and could afford to do so, wanted to dine at a five star restaurant located in one of Fashion Island's classy hotels. The nurses, including myself, had never experienced the pleasure of even setting foot inside the hotel, so we were eagerly looking forward to our first visit. We spruced up Mr. Rogers in one of his finer attires and took extra pains putting ourselves together as well.

When we arrived, there was a host of excited hotel personnel; moreover, men dressed in suit and tie were running around with wires attached to their jackets and holding hand-held communication sets. We asked one of the clerks at the front desk what all the excitement was about. She said that a candidate for the presidency was checking in at their facility. She did not yet know who exactly, but said it was creating quite a stir.

We found our way to the dining room, only to be greeted by numerous Secret Service Agents asking us what we were doing at the hotel. We explained to them that we were not staying at the hotel, but were here only to have lunch. Two agents guided us to a booth toward the rear of the dining room, saying that this was our designated area and that we would not be allowed to sit anywhere else at this time, due to security precautions. Of course our interest heightened as to who this special person or celebrity was, and it was getting the better of us.

As one of the agents passed in our direction, Mr. Rogers belted out loudly: "Sir, who is this person getting all this attention?" No one could refuse or pretend not to hear Mr. Rogers when he spoke, which was more like a loud command from a megaphone. The man bowed down and whispered, "it is George H. Bush, and he is about to enter the room and have lunch with his wife". Mr. Rogers responded, just as loudly as before, surely it could be heard throughout the hotel: "Bush is my man, and I give a lot of money to the Republican Party, so he better win this election". As he was making this announcement, the Bush family was being seated in a booth across the room. Mr. Bush heard the loud remark, raised his hand, waved in our direction saying, "Good man, over there". Mr. Rogers was overwhelmed by the notoriety and beamed with pride.

We had a wonderful lunch, and felt very special, as we were the only ones in the restaurant with the Bush family, and the bus load of Secret Service Agents. This just doesn't happen every day to most folks. The girls and I were most relieved that Mr. Rogers was on his good behavior, and had no stomach upsets or upchucks and above all no embarrassing "balderdash (fart)" remarks, which he used quite frequently while navigating about. It was a good day, enjoyed by all.

There were so many memorable times spent with Mr. Rogers, some good memories, some not so good. Another unforgettable episode was after he had just recovered from a bout of the flu. He and I had ventured out for lunch at an upscale seaside resort restaurant in Newport Beach. He was still on antibiotics and I advised him to order something bland and skip his ritual Manhattans. But as it was often the case, he wanted what he wanted, and there was no reasoning with him, so he ordered his clams on the half shell and his Manhattans. As nice and generous as he could be, he was also the typical rich man, very spoiled and used to getting his way. After making it through lunch with no incidents, I headed to the ladies room with a sigh of relief. But my feeling of well-being was short lived. Upon returning to the dining room, I stared in horror and disbelief at a pile of poop by Mr. Rogers's feet! I noticed the other customers were staring at him wide-eyed, and they seemed to be holding their breath. Apparently, during my brief sojourn to the ladies' room, Mr. Rogers had a blow-out like Mt. Vesuvius! I can't even describe the full extent of my horror and embarrassment, it was like an out-of-body experience, as if I were someplace else, watching myself go through the motions of extricating ourselves from there. Surprisingly, Mr. Rogers seemed very calm and quiet, unaffected by the whole thing. I told him to sit tight and I would get the valet to bring up the car. I paid the bill, which of course seemed to take an eternity. When I helped him out of the chair, I saw that his entire suit was saturated with his feces. It was rolling off him and onto his shoes. It was much worse than what I had anticipated. I had foolishly convinced myself that it was just a little pile of poop on the floor. The valet had come back with me to help me get him into the car and I must say it was one of the longest walks of my life. I never said a word to the valet or to Mr. Rogers until we were inside the car, I was rendered speechless by the whole thing. In truth, what could I say? I don't think "sorry" would have made that poor valet feel any better. But I tipped him very generously, and then stomped on the gas and got out of there as fast as I could.

We started driving after I had rolled down all the windows, to help with the terrible stench. Mr. Rogers then told me in a very pitiful voice, that he was very embarrassed. I asked him, why? He said, he had a terrible accident. I asked him what had happened. All the while I had my head turned and was laughing hysterically, out of his view, as I did not want him to feel any worse than he already did. I just couldn't contain my laughter. I'm sure it was nothing but pure hysteria after what had just happened. I told him the drinks and the rich food, while on medicine, must not have agreed with his stomach. He said, I was right.

Once home, I had him walk into the shower with all his clothes on, which I later disposed of. After all, he was a multi-millionaire; he could afford to throw away the poopy clothes. What an unbelievable mess he was! It was by no means a pleasant task cleaning up everything. No guilt about being paid, this time!

In my mind, the incident lingered on for a long time. I couldn't get the look on the faces of the other customers and servers out of my mind. All I could think of was to thank the good Lord that I wasn't there to witness it happening. It had to be His divine intervention compelling me to visit the ladies' room right at that moment! I don't know how I would have reacted, if I had been there at the fatal moment when he blew. It was two years before I had the nerve to return to that establishment.

Because Mr. Rogers required someone to be with him 24 hours a day, it soon became my job to spend the weekend nights at his home. The guest room faced the ocean front and the sound of the waves would lull me to sleep. I was even getting an hourly salary for sleeping!

There was a sound alarm in my room in case Mr. Rogers needed assistance. One morning around 3:00AM, I was awakened out of a sound sleep by the sound of him shouting very loudly. He had slipped out of bed and was on the floor. It took every bit of my strength to try and lift him up, but he was just too heavy for me. After many unsuccessful attempts, I came up with a solution. Like a crab, I wrapped my legs around him, and told him to push while I bounced up and

226

down with my feet. No doubt we looked ridiculous, but thankfully no one was watching, and it worked! In hindsight, I should have called the Fire Department. But it made for a good story and gave us a laugh later on.

Jessie thought it would be a treat for Mr. Rogers to see a live production of a play with Mary Martin and Carol Channing that was playing at the Ahmanson Theater in L.A. She made reservations for a suite at the Beverly Wilshire Hotel for Debbie, me, and Mr. Rogers, reserving a separate suite for herself and her friend Sandy. Her plan was to have her married, Newport Beach PD detective friend also join her later in a private room, which she had arranged solely for this illicit rendezvous. This woman never stopped scheming at the expense of Mr. Rogers. All of these rooms were on his dime, and they weren't cheap. Debbie and I were not aware of her plans until we were cautioned not to contact her under any circumstances, once she checked into Room 221. She and Sandy had a suite adjoining room 221, so this made it convenient for her to engage in her private activities. Debbie drove Mr. Rogers and me to the Beverly Wilshire.

I had not been in the L.A. area for quite some time. I wasn't excited about the prospect, but I hoped that once we hit ritzy Beverly Hills, I wouldn't mind so much. I had never been in the Beverly Wilshire Hotel. Upon entering, I noticed a heavy musty odor of old carpet and walls that surely had mildew under them. There was remodeling in progress, and from all outward appearances, the building was in dire need of a facelift. Still, I felt a special surge of nostalgia for this place, as it had housed many famous celebrities and dignitaries from all over the world. I hoped that, out of respect for its famous past, the developers wouldn't modernize it too much.

After checking into our room, which was very antiquated and not nearly as opulent as one would expect, we dressed for dinner in the main dining room. Mr. Rogers, Debbie and I were the first to make an appearance, and were escorted to our dining area. Within minutes Jessie and Sandy joined us, and our jaws almost fell to the floor. Jessie was wearing a light colored see-through top, with no bra underneath. She had really pushed to the limit showing off her new boob job. Her friend Sandy also had a provocative outfit on, leaving very little to the imagination, but nothing like Jessie's. Jessie could easily have been mistaken for a downtown hooker with her size 44 E's in plain view for all to see. The only one that did not look embarrassed was Mr. Rogers. He had a major grin from ear to ear. It doesn't matter how old they are, men will be men. The waiter took one glance, and he, too, wore a big smile, although I don't think his was an admiring one.

During dinner, we just missed being hit by a plate being hurled through the air by one lone male patron. We heard him yelling that he had never eaten such garbage and that the hotel had a nerve to serve and charge so much for such crap. It was quite evident that this guy was just trying to get out of paying for his meal, as he had pretty much finished everything before he began making a scene. We later found out that the restaurant did not charge the guy. We surmised that maybe this was the guy's scam, going from restaurant to restaurant, making scenes to get out of paying his bill.

The next day we toured Rodeo Drive, window shopping. That's all we regular humans can afford to do on Rodeo Drive. Mr. Rogers enjoyed this outing, while Debbie and I wearied of pushing the wheelchair block after block. Jessie and Sandy were off on their own, and when we crossed paths with them and saw all their shopping bags, we wondered just whose credit cards had paid for all their expensive treasures. That night was the play at the Ahmanson, so we had a good excuse to cut the sightseeing short. Only Mr. Rogers, Debbie and I were to attend the play and have dinner out in one of the high end restaurants. Jessie and Sandy had their own plans, which did not include spending any time with Mr. Rogers or with us.

We headed out for an evening of entertainment and looked forward to an epicurean dinner and an enjoyable musical. I can't recall what Debbie and Mr. Rogers ordered that evening, but I will never forget what I had. In this first class restaurant, I thought the salmon would be an outstanding choice, and this was confirmed by the waiter. I do not recall the dish as being outstanding, but for the price we paid, I thought I should eat it all. I did recall having a slight stale aftertaste upon finishing, but didn't give it much thought.

Jessie had purchased front row seats for the three of us, which made it easy to situate Mr. Rogers comfortably. Being that close, every little line, every wrinkle, even the beads of sweat on the actors' forehead, was pronounced. The first half of the play was very enjoyable. Those two ladies were without question superstars! Once the curtain rose for the second half of the play, I started getting severe pains in my stomach, and nausea like I had never experienced before. I abruptly excused myself and ran to the nearest restroom. There I spent the entire last half of the play exploding from both ends. I didn't know which end to aim at the toilet, and found myself missing it altogether a couple of times. I was a mess, besides the puking and diarrhea, I was sweating profusely, my makeup was running down my face, and my clothes were in disarray. If anyone had come in at that moment, I could easily have been mistaken for a crazy lady! I felt like it was never going to end, and there was even a moment or two, when I thought I might black out, but I did not want to be found lying in a pool of puke, so I summoned every ounce of willpower I had, to stay conscious. I kept thinking poor Debbie and Mr. Rogers were probably wondering what in the world had happened to me, but I did not dare to wander away from the toilet.

After about two hours, I found the strength to stand on my two feet. I grabbed a handful of paper towels and headed out to the theater, barely able to keep my balance. The room felt as if it was spinning. Upon entering the theater, the only two people left in the entire theater were Mr. Rogers and Debbie, both still in their front row seats, just sitting there and staring ahead. Even in my sick state, I was amused to see just the two of them sitting in that great big theater all by themselves, not speaking, just sitting there staring straight ahead as though they were still watching the play. Out of nowhere, an usher appeared and asked if I was all right. I told him that I was having a near death experience, and asked him if he had any plastic bags I could use. He was very helpful and retrieved several bags for me. I explained to Debbie what had happened, and told her, we better get out of there while I was able, plus it was getting late and catching a cab might be challenging.

As we left the theater, I started gagging again, but I was determined that I would not throw up here on the street. We got lucky, or so we thought, and spotted one cab in front of the theater. From the outset, for some unknown reason, the driver had a really hostile attitude, plus he was a pretty scary looking guy. He grumbled and cursed under his breath the whole time he was helping me put the wheel chair in the trunk of his cab. Once we were seated in the cab, I felt that it was only fair to warn him about my food poisoning, but when I did, he turned around, glared hatefully at me, pointed his finger in my face, and said "You will not get sick in my cab, because if you do, I will lose business and this is not going to happen". Mr. Rogers came to my defense and said "Sir, this lady cannot control it if she has to puke". I very firmly told Mr. Rogers it was okay and to be still. It was obvious that this cabbie was not someone you wanted to piss off. Mr. Rogers sensed the seriousness of my warning and never uttered another peep for the rest of the ride. After the cabbie shot us another hateful glance, we sped off.

On the way to the theater, the driver had taken us on a scenic route with no noticeable ghettos. Not this guy. He ended up driving through East L.A. or at least what I guessed was East L.A., definitely the scary part of town. Plus his driving skills left a lot to be desired. He had a heavy foot and every time he stepped on the brake, we thought we might go flying right over the seat and through the front window. Needless to say, the three of us were very nervous, and sat in stone cold silence, wondering just what this maniac might have in mind for us, since we were trapped, at his mercy. If he wanted to intimidate us, he was succeeding. On top of being scared of this crazy cabbie, I was struggling not to puke. If you've ever had to suppress this bodily function, you know it's not an easy task.

By the grace of God, we made it back to the hotel. When the driver pulled up to what appeared to be the main door, he was told he would have to unload us around the block at the other entrance. Our cabbie from hell commenced screaming at the door man and within a few seconds he was pushing this poor man against the side of the building with a closed fist. We all sat in the cab, too scared to move, thinking surely there was going to be bloodshed. Back in those days, we didn't have cell phones; otherwise a 911 call would have been in order. After another minute of shouting obscenities, he approached the car and let us out. Once we were allowed to exit the vehicle, we practically threw the money at him and then we ran for it. What a wretched experience the whole night was! Having to endure the cab ride from hell on top of it all, had stressed out all of us. All I could think of was visiting the bathroom. I knew, I wasn't going to be able to control Mother Nature's revenge much longer.

Once in Mr. Rogers's room, I helped him into the bathroom, where I proceeded to vomit all over the place, splattering that nasty salmon in the commode as well as on the floor and walls. It was impossible to believe that the human body could expel what seemed like tons of waste. How could all of that be inside my skinny body? I had held back during the interminable cab ride, so now it was like Mt. Vesuvius erupting again. Just when I thought things couldn't get any worse, Mr. Rogers suddenly fell ill and started vomiting himself. He was apparently one of those people who just can't witness someone else getting sick without getting sick himself, as was Debbie who wisely made herself scarce. We were two pretty pathetic souls, puking in disgusting harmony all over that bathroom. All I know is that I have never in my life been that sick to my stomach. Even in a four star restaurant with outrageous prices, you are not exempt from food poisoning!

Once my poor body was drained after many hours, I managed to get Mr. Rogers settled in for the night. I immediately collapsed into bed and asked Debbie to order several cokes from room service. This seemed to be the only remedy for nausea that worked for me. Then I passed out and awoke the next morning feeling like I'd been hit by a truck. Our Beverly Hills trip had finally come to an end, and I was so looking forward to getting home.

On the way back to Mr. Rogers's house where his other nurses were awaiting his arrival, we had one more weird experience. While driving on the freeway, some freak in a pickup truck pulled up alongside of us and lifted up his butt. We could clearly see that his pants were pulled down. He was grasping his penis in his hand and going to town with it. We rolled down the window and Debbie and I both laughed out loud, and then made some derogatory comments about not being very impressed. What a way to conclude a trip that was intended to be a classy, memorable experience. Instead, it turned out to be one of those trips from hell. I mean, who would have thought that staying at the Beverly Wilshire, touring Rodeo Drive, dinners at 5-star restaurants, and front row seats at the Ahmanson could possibly turn out badly? I learned later that Jessie and Sandy had a great time. Jessie's latest heartthrob, even though she had been married for many years, had been able to join her for a sleepover, while Sandy enjoyed her adjoining suite. She also had a friend of hers come and stay and keep her company for the night, all at Mr. Rogers's expense, of course. Who said life was fair?

16 CHASON

Between my full-time job at the PD and working part-time for Mr. Rogers, I didn't have a lot of time for myself. In a way it was a blessing, because I didn't have so much time to dwell on my relationship with Ryan. He was still playing his games, going back and forth between me and his wife. As much as I didn't want to face it, I think I knew in my heart of hearts that he would never leave his wife permanently. And if I was truly honest with myself, I knew that leaving his wife was the wrong thing to do, even though it would surely break my heart if he didn't.

One evening I received a call from Chason who said he had temporarily rented an apartment in the area, and would like to see me. I was not the least bit interested, but I wasn't doing anything, so I thought, why not? At least I would be getting out, and doing something besides working. We went on several dates, and he appeared to be enthralled with me, so enthralled that he actually annoyed me. Truth be told, if I had been attracted to him, I probably would have been thrilled at all of the attention! He talked about buying me an expensive home on Spyglass Hill in Newport. He even took me to look at a couple of repos. Back then you could have picked up a gorgeous four bedroom home with a pool and a view of Newport Harbor for $295,000.00. In today's market it would be more like a few million plus. He said he was determined to find a beautiful home and move me in. He even bragged to my friends that he was looking for a five carat diamond ring for me. He was good at waving the proverbial carrot under my nose!

On the rare occasions, when I could get a little extra time off, we did manage to have some fun adventures. We spent a weekend in Julian, (an hour east of San Diego) which is famous for their apple pies. We stayed in a charming bed and breakfast inn up in the hills, with a wonderful view. We rode in a horse drawn carriage through town, and did some wine tasting. There were some wonderful restaurants in town, and we hit them all. Even though I still wasn't physically attracted to him, being treated like a queen was growing on me. But even as we grew closer, I knew there was a lot I wanted to change about him. For one, I hated his outdated wardrobe, so, once back in town, I made sure that he bought new clothes. I also convinced him to see my dentist and get his front teeth straightened. In the end, it really didn't matter what he did to please me, I still was not attracted to him. But I hung in there, those proverbial carrots dangling in front of my face.

My friend Debbie and her husband at the time joined us for some of our adventures. We spent a day at Wild Animal Park and went out partying that night. We saw a spectacular band and even though it was fun and a memorable evening, I couldn't help wishing that I was enjoying it with someone else.

Chason did come up with some wonderful ideas for fun though. He arranged for me and some of my friends, a trip to the American River for white water river-rafting. He got us a beautiful motor home that slept six comfortably. He said a friend owed him a favor or two, and the use of the motor home was repayment. He actually boasted that quite a few people owed him favors, and I often wondered why. He never seemed to work, or talk about a job, just about favors that were owed to him, and he always seemed to have money, from some unknown source. But I didn't ask too many questions. No sense looking a gift horse in the mouth, I thought.

I was able to talk Jessie into giving me another weekend off. She was such a control freak, and hated to see anyone have more fun, or more anything, than she did, so I was shocked when she said that I could take the time off. I'm sure there was something in it for her, because she definitely was not the generous type. One of the many perks of my job at the PD was the ability to accumulate vacation time, and it was rare, that any request for time off was denied. So with all my bases covered, it was time for our road trip.

My other friends, Cheryl and Jerry, her husband at the time, as well as Debbie and her soon to be ex-husband Tim, loaded up the motor home, and the six of us were off. Chason enjoyed driving, so no one argued with him about being the chauffeur. The motor home was very comfortable, and while Chason whistled merrily as he drove the rig down the freeway and through some pretty winding roads, the rest of us were playing cards and having a great time in the back.

I was feeling a bit queasy and light headed as the day progressed, but decided nothing was going to spoil our trip. Before long, my nose was running, my eyes were watering, and I felt feverish, so I decided that a toddy or two might help. It did help, but only temporarily.

Once we arrived at our destination, we met up with our crew who would guide us through the rapids. Part of the package deal was that the guides would provide dinner both nights, which sounded great to us after the long drive. They really put on a great spread, even making brownies in a pot over the fire, that smelled out of this world, and, from what everyone said, tasted as good as they smelled. Unfortunately I had also lost my appetite. After spending a restless night, I dragged my sick self out of bed the next morning, determined that nothing was going to keep me from joining my friends. I was so excited about our adventure that my flu-like symptoms would just have to take a back seat. I loaded up on Kleenex and after a brief orientation, off we went.

Our guides were very professional, and cautioned us that people have drowned in this river. It was imperative that we listen to all their instructions and follow them closely. They had suddenly become so serious and stern and I remember looking at Debbie, saying: "We could drown?" It had never occurred to me that we could be in danger; I just wanted a fun-filled boat ride!

We started out slowly, stopping along the shore several times, enjoying a few snacks and listening to a few war stories from our guides. I was really not feeling well at all, but there was no way that I was going to miss out on any of our adventure, and so far it had been very relaxing and peaceful. But as the day progressed, the size of the waves did too. Paddling the boat through the rapids was a lot of work, and it turned out that we weren't very good at it. It was a real rush dodging all the rocks while the waves would come splashing over the boat, enveloping us in white water, I couldn't stop laughing. The guides, however, did not find it humorous. The poor guys were paddling like fiends, screaming as loud as they could over the sound of the rapids: "Paddle! Paddle!." As soon as we would hit a rapid, all of us except Tim and Chason just simply stopped paddling and sat there, stiff as boards, too scared to move. This didn't happen just once, it happened every single time we hit a rapid! In between rapids, the guides would practically beg us to please make sure not to stop paddling when we hit the next rapid, and then the next rapid would come, and down went the paddles! I don't think those poor guys ever worked so hard to keep the boat afloat! They definitely earned their money that day! We probably became one of their "what not to do" war stories, told to other groups for years to come.

As the sun was getting ready to set, we hit the final rapid, rated a three plus. What a thrill ride this was, at least for me, not so much for the poor guides who once again were doing all the work. All their lecturing and begging for naught, they got very little help from us! We all got totally drenched and swallowed a lot of river water as we flew over the rushing waters. I totally loved this, probably more than anyone except maybe Tim, despite the fact that I was feeling rather green. There was a professional cameraman at this fast rapid, who took many shots of us screaming as we rounded the bend in the stream. I still have my pictures displayed, although it is hard to recognize any of us, as we were engulfed in water. But you can't fail to notice that almost no one is paddling.

As we approached the campsite, part of the crew was preparing our dinner. We were also being instructed as to what we should expect on our last day on the river. I was praying that I would feel better the next day. That night after dinner, we sat around the campfire for a while and Chason could see how sick I was, and was doing his usual fawning over me. He even removed my soggy tennis shoes and socks, and placed them by the fire to warm them up. Unfortunately he put them just a little too close to the fire, which was apparent when we started smelling burning rubber. At least that gave us all a good laugh.

After our big day on the river, we were all exhausted and went to bed early, because the plan was to hit the river again at daybreak. But I only got worse as the night wore on, and ended up spending most of the night throwing up. I tried to make it to the outdoor restrooms, but a few times only made it as far as the motor home bathroom. Needless to say, no one got a good night's sleep that night. Instead, they were subjected to listening to me either throwing up or running back and forth from the motor home to the restrooms. I felt so badly for them; the last thing I wanted to do was ruin the rest of their trip. By morning, I was in bad shape and knew I couldn't take another day out on the river. I was so disappointed; no doubt this would be the only time I would ever get to do something like this with my friends. After our first day, it became obvious that none of them, except Debbie's husband, Tim, would ever care to go river rafting again. I think most of them enjoyed the food more than the river rafting.

I tried to convince everyone else to go on without me. I knew that I had no choice but to stay at the campsite, close to the restroom. It killed me to stay behind, but I had a high fever, and felt sick as a dog. Cheryl and Jerry decided that they didn't care to do another day out on the river. This was very disappointing to Tim who was looking forward to another day of rafting. He didn't feel that it was right to go with just him and Debbie, leaving everyone else just hanging out at camp. So, sadly, we packed up and headed back home. If it hadn't been for Jerry, who was pretty adamant about leaving, I'm sure the rest of them would have gone rafting on the last day. The fees had already been paid, and were non-refundable. I think he was secretly happy that he had an excuse not to go again.

I know Tim was very disappointed, and I felt somewhat responsible. If only I could have gone, I think everyone else, including Jerry, would have gone too. And it really didn't sit well with Tim when, during the drive home, Jerry suggested making a detour to hit a gambling casino. He had been in such a hurry to get home, and now he wanted to go gambling. Obviously it wasn't eagerness to get home, but more eagerness to get out of another day of river rafting. But Tim wasn't going along with the program, he said no way; if I don't get to go river rafting, then he doesn't get to go gambling! Although the rest of them wouldn't have minded going to the casino, that was the end of that idea, and home we headed. Regardless, it was one of the more thrilling experiences of my life, quite an adventure for this cowardly girl, and I feel so fortunate to have done something so far out of my comfort zone. If my body would allow it today, I would do it again!

After such a wonderful experience on the American River, and feeling as if I had been in a different world, it was difficult at best to settle back into the routine at work. But, as always, there was something interesting going on at the PD. Unfortunately, this time it involved a young officer who was very spiritual and was out to save the world. But instead, he ended up going over the edge. He spent every free moment reading his bible and preaching to anyone he could get to listen. He was always on the prowl for a captive audience. When he got off work, he would head out to a special section of Harbor Blvd known for prostitution. He would approach the women and preach to them about going to hell if they didn't change their ways, trying to scare them straight by describing just how bad an eternity in hell would be. No one knows if he ever actually convinced any of them to heed his advice, but he certainly threw his heart and soul into it.

Not only would he spend time on Harbor Blvd., but he branched out and started preaching on Hollywood Blvd. Many of his co-workers were becoming quite concerned with his obvious obsession with these prostitutes and his efforts to help them; it got to the point where he wouldn't talk about anything else. No one ever mentioned how he was handling his job as a police officer, but apparently he was managing to stay under the radar.

It turned out that he was just too young and inexperienced to deal with the burden he took upon his shoulders to save these women. He ended up committing suicide by shooting himself in the head. Everyone was devastated, his family, his friends, and his co-workers, because he was a good man, just trying to do something good in the world. He often told people that it was his calling to save people like the prostitutes he sought out, but apparently he got to a point where he felt his attempts were futile, and he just couldn't handle what he perceived as his own failure. In retrospect, many felt responsible for not intervening and attempting to get him the professional help he so badly needed. I only pray that God forgave him for how he ended his life. I'm sure the good Lord takes into account the mental stability of people when they end their lives in such a way.

But life goes on, especially in a police department, where crime never takes a day off. One day when all the brass were Code 7, at lunch and out of the office, and there was no one with any supervisory authority around, a crisis arose. I was assigned a bad check case, where the victim was Governor Deukmejian's sister. She owned a travel agency and had sold a ticket to an individual for a flight up north. The check was written on an account that had been closed. I was only halfway through working the case, and had not yet had a handwriting comparison completed to positively identify the account holder as the person who wrote the check.

I received a phone call from the governor's sister stating that the suspect was now boarding the flight out of Long Beach Airport, and she wanted him removed from the plane and arrested. I needed to act right away on this, but I did not have the authority to contact Long Beach PD and ask them to arrest the suspect. I looked all over for someone to help me, but it was lunch time, and the bureau looked like a ghost town.

There was no choice but to make a decision and take the responsibility, as reluctant as I was to make that call. Under normal circumstances, I would have told the victim to wait until I could complete my investigation and obtain an arrest warrant, but this was the governor's sister and all I could think of was the headline "Police refuse to arrest suspect who ripped off Governor's sister!" splashed across the front page of every newspaper in California. At the same time, I was aware that if I screwed up and made the wrong decision, there would be stiff repercussions, especially because my supervisor and I did not get along at all.

I decided to make the call, figuring I had a 50/50 chance of it being the right decision. I explained the circumstances to Long Beach PD and they said they would respond to the airport and attempt to contact the suspect, whom I had described to them. As it turned out, the suspect I had listed was not the same guy who had boarded the plane using the stolen ticket. It was his twin brother who had stolen his ID, and then had written the check for the ticket. Their handwriting was almost identical to the untrained eye. Only a forensic investigator specializing in handwriting examination would be able to determine whose signature was on the check.

The plane was held up for almost an hour while Long Beach PD was doing their investigation. They called me, stating that they needed a detective out there to assist them with the arrest, or I could come and help with the processing. Just about this time, two of our detectives returned from their lunch break. I quickly explained to them what was happening and that they had to go to Long Beach Airport and help with the arrest. They were both laughing as they went out the door, saying I probably cost the airlines a lot more money then what the check was worth. And indeed I did. I was told that due to the flight being delayed for an hour, the loss was over ten thousand dollars to the airlines. Although the airline wasn't very happy, much to my surprise, my supervisor actually commended me for taking such swift action. After all, this was the governor's sister, and I'm sure, he could imagine the headlines too. If this had been a regular citizen, and not someone with such political clout, the outcome would probably have been much different for me.

My job with Mr. Rogers was taking up all my free time. I was working all three of my days off from the PD, which left me very little time for myself. But I couldn't say no, because I knew that if I did, I would be replaced in the blink of an eye. As far as part time jobs go, it was a cushy one with lots of perks, and I also needed the extra money. Even though my free time was very limited, I tried to help my Mom out whenever I could, making sure that she was eating right and taking care of herself. She was getting quite fragile and somewhat forgetful at times, but at 90 years old she was still living on her own. She loved her independence and being at the beach, and the rent on her Balboa beach cottage was unheard of. The owners really liked her and had barely raised her rent in 40 years. For what they were charging her, she wouldn't have been able to live anywhere, especially so close to the beach.

With almost all my time spent working, I was excited when Jessie asked me to accompany Mr. Rogers on a trip. The plan was to go to Palm Springs; my friend Debbie would come along to help me out. This was just the first of many times when she would accompany me on trips to lend a helping hand with Mr. Rogers. Debbie couldn't join us until she got off work, so I had given Chason some money to drive Debbie down after she got off. I didn't want Mr. Rogers to know that Chason was there, because even though my relationship with Mr. Rogers was obviously platonic, he still felt possessive of me, so we never discussed my dating life. Chason and Debbie arrived earlier than expected, so I asked them to wait while I got Mr. Rogers settled in his room. They went into the bar and ordered drinks while they waited. I later learned from Debbie that she thought that he had paid the tab with the money I had given him, but as they were leaving, they were chased down by the waitress who told them that they needed to pay their bill. Debbie was embarrassed beyond belief. This was a very upscale hotel, and being chased down for not paying your bill was probably something people would be gossiping about for days to come. Chason didn't seem fazed by it at all and just stood idly by while Debbie paid the bill. This was my first inkling that Chason was not all he pretended to be.

I told Chason that Debbie and I had to take Mr. Rogers to dinner, and there was no way for me to spend time with him, which I had explained to him when I asked him to drive Debbie down. It had been our agreement all along for him to drive Debbie down and then head back to Orange County. But now he had decided to just hang out until we put Mr. Rogers to bed. I told him that this situation put me in an awkward position, because I couldn't just leave Mr. Rogers to spend time with him. He said that he would just stop by for a minute, and then be on his way. I should have known better. Once inside the room, there was no getting rid of him. We were in one of the first class suites. The rooms were spacious, and Mr. Rogers' room was on the other side of the suite from mine.

It seemed that once Chason saw how big the suite was, he figured that there was room for him, too. He knew that I was upset with him, but that didn't deter him from doing what he wanted. He was a chain smoker, and I told him that he would have to go outside to smoke. He convinced me that a couple would do no harm, and then the overbearing jerk proceeded to cloud up my room with so much smoke that I almost had to cut

244

my way through it. Worse yet, it appeared that I wouldn't be able to get rid of him until morning. He claimed to be just too tired to make the drive home. I bit my tongue and agreed to let him stay; only because we had just entered a business partnership with one of my friends and we needed him to help us out, otherwise that would have been the end of Chason.

During the night, opening my eyes to glance over at the other bed, I discovered him openly picking his nose! I was totally disgusted and I nastily told him to get up and get a Kleenex. Again, he didn't seem fazed at all by his slovenliness, or by being caught doing something so despicable. The next day Debbie and I packed up Mr. Rogers and his belongings, and, along with one of his nurses, we hit the road, bound for home. I was so relieved when that trip was over.

17 THE CALENDAR

My friend Lisa and I had come up with an idea to make some extra money. We wanted to show that women over fifty could still be sexy and attractive by marketing a pin-up calendar. If I had only known the stress and expense this little brainchild would lead to, I would never have started. I had to be out of my mind at the time, to even consider such a venture, when I was already working two jobs, taking care of my mom, and trying to maintain my relationship with Chason, such as it was.

Chason offered to help recruit the women for the calendar, and also offered to accept responsibility for most of the expenses of the project. I figured that his offer was to be shelling out some money for expenses, but as it turned out, his only contribution was to do the accounting and keep a set of books. He didn't even follow through with that. It soon became apparent that his only real interest was interviewing the women, and as I learned later, trying to score with a few. Chason did have a good camera and tried his hand at being our photographer. Unfortunately he might have had a good camera, but being good at using it was another thing. None of his photos were of sufficiently high quality to be used in a calendar; we never considered using them. We advertised for women in the local newspaper and received numerous responses. We met with the ladies who were interested in participating as pinups in the calendar at a local restaurant. Several were selected and told they would be notified in the near future as to what photographer they would be meeting with.

Jessie caught wind of our project, and insisted that she had to be one of the pinups. She told us that Mr. Rogers would financially back her, and she wanted the best photographer in town to do her photos. Jessie did have a beautiful face, but the rest of her was, to put it nicely, disproportionate. The only way a photographer could do her any justice was to film only her upper half, including her new set of silicon breasts, of which she was most proud. One day shortly after her procedure, she greeted Debbie and me at Mr. Rogers' door and immediately ripped off her top to expose her 44 D's. Talk about no class, I have no clue what possessed her to think that we would want to see her implants!

It was difficult to find a photographer whom we could afford, so Debbie said that she would talk to her soon to be ex-husband, who was a very good photographer, although not a professional. Tim agreed, and we set up times for some of the ladies to meet us in a park, where we could use Mother Nature as a backdrop. Some of the photos were good, but not the professional caliber we needed for a calendar. Still, we were not discouraged to the point of giving up on our project. Jessie wanted to be in the calendar so badly, that she even gave me a day off now and then, so we could work on it. I still believe, the calendar was a good idea, but like everything on earth, it takes money to make it happen.

One of the models who responded, happened to have been a stand-in for a famous movie actress who died at a young age in a tragic accident. She said that she would be more comfortable if we came to her home, which was located in a very exclusive section of Newport Beach. Tim and I knocked on the door and were greeted by a young girl who was wrapped completely in small chains and keys around her waist. One look at her, and you knew, this girl was not dealing with a full deck. She led us into a living room that took our breath away, and I don't mean this in a good way, and then she left to get her mother. We hesitated to even sit down, because the sofas were so filthy. We couldn't even tell what color they were supposed to be. The coffee tables and shelves were covered with filth, and the floors appeared as if they hadn't been cleaned in years, if ever. The stench was just awful, making it difficult to breathe.

We looked out toward the pool area and saw the entire cement walkway to be covered in feces. There stood what appeared to be a white husky. I say appeared to be white because, like the house, it was so dirty and matted it was hard to tell. However, the poor dog was not neglected physically; at least it had a large dish of food and water nearby.

Our model soon appeared, dressed in something that would have been popular in the 50's. She walked us back to her dressing area, so we could give her our opinion on what coat she should wear. I explained to her that this was a pinup calendar, so a coat would not be appropriate, for what we were doing, less was more. She was quite disappointed, as she was itching to show off one of her furs. She cautioned us about her husband, who sometimes walked around with his gun, she said. She said, he was harmless, but thought that she should warn us, so we wouldn't be alarmed if he should appear. Tim and I were looking at one another wondering if we should cut and run, now? This whole scenario was one of the most bizarre experiences of my life. We were looking around thinking, where are the cameras? We must be on Candid Camera or something, this just could not be real! After looking around the house, we managed to convince her that what we needed was an outdoor photo shoot. There wasn't a single area, inside the home or outside, where you could do a photo shoot that wouldn't include filth and trash in the background. Just before leaving, the daughter came up to us and asked if we wanted to see her room, which she opened with one of many keys that were tied around her waist. You couldn't help feeling empathy for this girl, and I often wondered what her fate was. At least we were spared a tour of the whole house when her mother said that she was on a tight schedule and didn't have time.

Once outside, we located a small park down the road and asked if this would be comfortable for her. Rather abruptly she informed us that she did not want to be part of the calendar after all, and off she went. We were puzzled by what had happened to change her mind so abruptly. At the same time, we were relieved. Dealing with such an eccentric individual would probably have been more trouble than what it was worth. There were many other ladies interested in participating, who would hopefully have fewer demands for us to contend with.

Between working full-time at the PD, working weekends at Mr. Rogers, and working on my calendar project, my poor nervous system was screaming for relief. But once I committed myself to the calendar project, I felt I had to give it my all. I wasn't able to devote as much time to selecting the candidates and lining up a professional photographer as I would have liked. Tim took excellent pictures, but did not have the commercial grade cameras needed to produce professional results.

Before Tim hung it up, we had one more notable experience with one of the girls, when she was posing on a boat, cruising the harbor. She was changing into her outfit, not realizing that she was exposed to passers-by, when shouts of "take it all off baby" came from a group of guys paddling by in their canoes. She was practically stark naked and in full view of these guys, and we could see a couple of them grabbing for their cameras to snap photos of the poor woman. They were hooting and hollering, but she didn't really see the humor in the situation, so Tim and I did our best to hide from her our amusement.

We were fortunate to locate a professional photographer who was willing to work with us at a fair price, so we arranged for some of the girls to meet with him. His work was first quality and some of the photos were outstanding. Jessie, always the queen bee, insisted on going to a photographer that would do a lot of air brushing, which cost a small fortune. I thought that my partners would help with expenses, but it seemed, whenever a bill came up, they conveniently happened to be someplace else. Jessie threw in a couple of bucks, but I still had to dole out several hundred dollars. I couldn't say no to Jessie, since my job with Mr. Rogers depended on her.

I found myself becoming more and more upset with Lisa and Chason for not holding up their end of the bargain. I found a photographer on my own, who took some decent pictures of me, and I paid for the entire session, as I pretty much was paying all the expenses related to the calendar. I knew better than to ask my partners to dip into their pockets for any assistance, for I knew what the answer would be. About this time, Lisa decided to leave our partnership, and wanted nothing further to do with the calendar. She could not stand Chason, and felt that he was ruining the project.

Interestingly enough, Chason eventually rented a room from Lisa, but there was never any love lost between them. She constantly complained about him. My advice was to throw him out, but she wanted the extra income, so she put up with him. It was a bad decision to even start such an expensive, time consuming project when the players did not see eye to eye; I think it was doomed from the beginning.

It was really sad to see the calendar project get shelved after all the hard work, stress and expense that we had put into it. And there really were some outstanding pictures. Most of the girls were so excited to think that their snapshots could end up in a pinup calendar. I felt we really let them down, and ourselves also. I still believe it was a good idea, and would have been a huge success if only everyone had been able to work together, and complete the project. We had it all put together, except for having the calendar printed, but I just did not have the funds to do it all myself. As it was, I got stuck with most of the miscellaneous expenses and felt rather bitter towards these two who had flaked out on me, who didn't understand the meaning of "partner". As a last resort, I contacted several magazines in hopes that they might be interested in publishing for us. It was to no avail. But at least, I tried.

About six months after the calendar disaster, on nationwide TV there was an entrepreneur who had the same idea, and put together a calendar of ladies over fifty. I must say his photos were not nearly as good as the ones we had. I do not know if he made much money off the deal, but at least he had his fifteen minutes of fame. I had also hoped to donate some of the proceeds from the calendar to a battered women's organization or to another worthwhile charity.

Chason, instead of reaching in his pocket and doing something worthwhile with what little money he did have, he wasted it on flowers. Every week I would get a delivery at the PD of a dozen long stem red roses in a gold box. The first two times it was exciting, and I enjoyed the oohs and aahs of my co-workers, but as the weeks dragged on, the novelty wore off, and I was simply annoyed at the waste of money, when I could have used it to help with the calendar. It got to the point where I dreaded seeing that gold box, and would have liked nothing more than to just toss them over the balcony in protest. There were weeks when three boxes of roses would be delivered, and I would just groan each time. This went on for several months, and when I questioned Chason about why he was so obsessed with sending me roses, he told me that a guy owed him a favor and this was part of the payback. I told him, it was enough; he should try to think of something else that might benefit society, instead of just me. To this day, I am not fond of red roses; any other color is great, but forget the red, they bring back bad memories.

Not only did Chason overwhelm and satiate me with the bombardment of those red roses, he had another friend who apparently owed him a favor. Fortunately this one owned a limo business, which sounded much more appealing than flowers. One night the girls and I went to the Performing Arts Center to enjoy the Spanish National Ballet. Lo and behold, there was a limo waiting in the driveway to escort us to the theater, with champagne and hors d'oeuvres. I would take this over red roses, any day! One morning he even sent a limo to the house to take me to work, orange juice included! This was something I could get used to, but unfortunately the rides ended much sooner than the blasted red roses.

I could not stay upset with Lisa, as she learned that she had developed pancreatic cancer and the prognosis was not favorable. After learning about her condition, I felt terrible, that I had ever been upset with her. All of her friends and family were at her side, supporting her through all her grueling treatments. It was a very sad and draining time to watch her transform into a skeletal version of her former self. She blamed Chason's presence in her home as part of her physical breakdown. She was positive that the stress of living with him was a contributing factor in her health problems. Lisa did not survive very long; within six months had passed away. Many of us from the PD were heartbroken for the loss of such a good friend and co-worker.

Prior to Lisa's passing, Chason had moved out, heading up to Northern California, where he was reportedly working in car sales. He called me and wanted me to take a trip up north, and invited my friends Debbie and Tim to join us. Chason said he was doing well at the car dealership, and that he could possibly help me out with some of the expenses from the calendar fiasco. I agreed, but told him that I would have to bring Gizmo, my treasured Shih Tzu. He was my baby, and I tried to take him with me wherever I could.

Oddly enough, a while back in time, as we were just strolling around, window shopping at Fashion Island one day, Chason was the one who had spotted Gizmo at a pet store. I had no intention of buying a dog, but after one look at this little guy, I just had to have him. Some other people in the store with three screaming rug rats were grabbing at him and yelling to their father that he had to buy the dog for them. One of the girls in the store came up to me, begging me to take him. She said, he was a delicate little puppy, and this family would not be a good fit for him; she had a feeling about me, that I would be the perfect mom for him. I just couldn't resist, and pulled out one of my credit cards that didn't have any charges on it, and bought this wonderful God-given gift of a creature. I was so blessed to have my little guy for almost fourteen years. As my friend Debbie said, he was a gentle little soul, one who brought me more happiness than I can ever express.

Chason drove down and picked up Gizmo and me, and off we went to Paso Robles. Debbie and Tim could not join us the same day, but would head up the following afternoon. We checked into a beautiful inn that overlooked the ocean, with access to the beach. This establishment accepted pets, so I was relieved to know that none of the hotel staff would be walking in and spooking him; or worse yet let him out. Chason was acting more nervous than usual, continuously leaving the room to make calls, which he said were work related, but I had my suspicions. Knowing him, I was sure, he had another female victim all lined up, and was trying to convince her that he would be purchasing a 5 karat diamond ring in the near future for her, and maybe a house with a multi-million dollar view. When I asked him where he lived, and suggested that he show me his place, he said that it was too far out of the way, as he was living in Atascadero. All he'd really told me was where he was working, but I wasn't even so sure that he was telling the truth. I just wanted him to hold up his end of the deal and dish out some much needed funds he owed on the calendar, and I would be satisfied.

Debbie and Tim arrived in the early evening, and once settled, we all went out to dinner. Everything was much better once they were around. Chason, who had been a chain smoker, had done the cold turkey routine, which was very surprising, as he was a true addict if ever there was one. I suspected that someone important to him had influenced his quitting, although he did cheat a few times that weekend. I thought maybe his nicotine withdrawal was altering his personality, as things did not go well between us that weekend. The following morning I decided to head back, as I had other obligations, such as Mr. Rogers. Debbie and Tim said they did not mind heading back a little earlier than anticipated, which turned out to be a blessing. These two were the best of friends, always coming to my rescue. Chason said, he would drive me part way and then I would have to go the remainder of the way home with Debbie and Tim, which suited me fine. My intention of taking this trip was in hopes that he would cough up some of the money that he owed for his involvement in the calendar. I was waiting for him to hand me some cash or a check, but he made an excuse that his car payment and rent had cleaned him out. He said that by the end of next week he should have some money, and would send it to me.

At the halfway mark we stopped for breakfast. It was hot, and I did not want to leave Gizmo in the car. I couldn't take him in, so I ordered what I wanted and then went back to the car to tend to him. Gizmo would be fine, Chason told me, and wondered what was wrong with me checking on him every two minutes. I told him it was sizzling outside, and I was not about to put my precious boy in harm's way. If I had been stupid enough to listen to this idiot, I know Gizzie could not have survived. I truly believe, he wanted something to happen to him to get back at me; at least that's what his actions proved. If anything would have made Giz ill or worse, he knew, I could never forgive myself. I would put myself in harm's way before I would allow anything to happen to my precious pet.

Once everyone finished, Chason just jumped into his car and was gone in a flash, with barely a goodbye to us. Reaching inside my purse, I had to laugh when I found some instant coffee packets with the name of the inn imprinted on them, which I had previously stuck in his suitcase. From whom was he trying to hide his whereabouts?

After I arrived home, it was not long before I received an interesting call. Chason had bought a car from a PD captain friend of his, and had been making some payments to him. When he defaulted on the loan, the captain called me and wanted to know where he was living. I told him I did not know the address, but would look into it and see what I could find out. All Chason had given me was his phone number, nothing else. I started playing detective, calling around up North, where he said he worked and lived. As luck would have it, I found a man who said that he knew who Chason was, and did not like him. He said, Chason was full of hot air, always mouthing off about great financial adventures and how in the past he had lived the rich life. He said, he knew a phony when he saw one. This guy worked at the car dealership where Chason had been employed, and knew where he lived and where he got his morning coffee. He supplied me with Chason's address, which was a motel in a not so desirable neighborhood.

After receiving the info on Chason, I decided to put the investigative skills I had learned on the job in to action. I made a few calls and found that the phone number for Chason was disconnected. I found the number for the restaurant where he hung out, and gave them a call. I talked to a very helpful employee who said he knew who he was, and did not like him. He told me Chason was living with a woman and gave me her name. I thanked him for all his help and he wished me luck in tracking him down and nailing his you know what to the wall! I called information and was able to get a number for the woman he was living with. Calling that number, I spoke with her son, who was initially very hesitant to speak with me, which was understandable. Once I told him that I was looking for Chason in order to get some money he owed me, he seemed to open up. I explained that Chason had been part of a calendar business that fell through and he did not hold up his part of the deal financially. He was not surprised and said, he thought he was broke, and was taking financial advantage of his mother. Unfortunately his mother was crazy about him, and he did not want to be the one to jeopardize her relationship. He said, his mother went through a very acrimonious divorce and this was the first time she appeared happy in a long time, but Chason gave him the creeps. He would sit on the couch for hours and just stare at the TV and not speak to anyone while watching "his shows". He felt there was just something not quite right about him. I had never personally witnessed this silent behavior, but as the kid said, he was weird, and nothing this jerk did surprised me. He also told me that he was lazy. He thought, he was about to get fired from his car salesman job, and he happened to mention the dealership where he was working. I thanked him for his help and told him again that I was only interested in retrieving some of the money he owed me for our failed project.

As we were speaking, I heard him say something to someone who had apparently just entered the room and as it turned out, it was his mother. I could hear him briefly telling her who I was and what I wanted. She got on the phone and started shouting profanities at me. She said Chason was her man and that he was the best f____ she ever had. She said they screwed in every room and on every piece of furniture in the house. I told her, I was not at all interested in their sex life and the only reason I was calling is that I wanted the money he owed me from our business deal. She continued to yell further obscenities and I decided that it was time for me to hang up. This woman appeared to be totally out of control, and in dire need of professional help! Especially since she was exhibiting this behavior in front of her son!

After this conversation, which really had me shaken up, I phoned Chason's ex-buddy, to whom he owed money for the car. He was very grateful to learn where Chason was currently working and told me Chason was in for a big surprise, as he planned to repossess the car at his place of business. And if that didn't work out, he would look further into obtaining his recent address and go from there. He promised to keep me posted, once he accomplished his mission. I told him, it would be quite entertaining to be a fly on the wall and see the expression on Chason's face, once he discovered that his wheels were gone. He agreed, but didn't think that he would hang around once he had possession of the car; it just wasn't worth the confrontation.

A few days later I was talking to one of the detectives who knew Chason. I told him what a flake he turned out to be. That was no big surprise to him. He had heard that Chason was writing bad paper all over the county and wouldn't be surprised if he was involved in some shady deals. That gave me the idea to run him through the bad check computer index and see what I could come up with. Lo and behold, there was an outstanding warrant for him in Riverside County for writing bad checks! I pulled the working papers and saw that everything matched up. An overwhelming satisfaction of sweet revenge started pulsating through my veins. I phoned the issuing agency and learned that the warrant was still valid. I was overcome with joy, barely containing my delight. I have to say, I would never be that person today, one who took such pleasure in getting revenge, nor would I ever conduct such a down and dirty head hunt. At the time I felt justified, but today I have learned to let most things go and let them resolve themselves on a different level. I know who is in charge and that all of us will have to answer for our actions. As the saying goes, karma is a bitch. I told the officer I was speaking with, that I knew where the suspect could be located. The Riverside officer asked me to call the police department in the town he was living in, and relay the information to them. As shameful as it sounds, at the time I felt pure elation as I placed that call.

I spoke to a sergeant at the Paso Robles Police Department and advised him of an outstanding warrant being valid on an individual that was residing in their jurisdiction. I asked if they could assist me in serving the Riverside warrant, and was told their agency would take care of the matter. I did explain to the sergeant a bit of why I became involved and why I was forwarding the information to them, rather than to the Riverside PD. He understood, and assured me that they would handle the matter.

Two days later, my roommate, a young girl working her way through college, called me at work. She sounded frantic. She said, some big burly guy came knocking on the door, threatening her. He asked for me by name, and she told him I was not home. He told her in no uncertain terms to tell the "blonde bitch" to back off or there was going to be a real problem. Based on my roommate's description of this individual, it didn't sound like anyone I knew.

I thought I better inform my sergeant of this development and of my involvement in getting Chason arrested. Much to my amazement, he sided with me, stating that he never liked him when he worked here and always thought he was a flake. He also said he did not like anyone being threatened and if it happened again, the police were to be called immediately. Boy, a sigh of relief fell over me as I knew I had somewhat overstepped my boundaries, but as my sergeant pointed out, Chason had broken the law, and he should have to answer for his actions.

The warrant was served the following day. Chason had to appear in court in Riverside, in order to settle the matter. As a result, he also spent a night in jail. Oh how sweet the taste of revenge was to me at the time! It also pleased me greatly to know that it would be a major inconvenience for him to have to travel such a distance without his car to make that court appearance. Of course I am sure the woman in his life was more than happy to accommodate him. I actually felt sorry for her, for sooner or later she would learn the hard way what kind of person he was. It didn't sound like she needed more grief in her life.

Through my personal investigation I also learned that Chason was married, and had been for over a year. I actually spoke with his wife; one day they had a fight and Jason took off. She had not heard from him for months. She added that it was just as well, as she was fed up with him and his lies. She also mentioned his drinking problem. Chason could not hold his liquor and would become very belligerent. That conversation recalled to my mind a New Year's Eve party, where Chason and I joined Debbie and her husband Tim and friends for a celebration in Laguna Beach. After downing several vodka tonics and wine, which he managed to spill all over the front of me, he was ready to duke it out with some of the guys. Nobody really knew why, and we just tried to calm down the drunk. After that altercation, his tears started flowing, as did his nose. He kept repeating that he wanted me to love him, because he was so in love with me that it was driving him crazy. Because he was so drunk, I didn't tell him the truth, which was that I really couldn't stand him. Believe it or not, I never even let him kiss me during our entire relationship. The thought of it was repulsive to me. I was just very needy at the time he came along, so I closed my eyes and pretended I was somewhere else when we had sex, but I never let him kiss me. For some reason, that just seemed too intimate and I couldn't do it. Oddly enough, after the first time he never tried again, when I turned my face away, nor did he ever ask me about it, or mention that he thought it was strange. He was probably afraid that if he brought it up, he might not like the answer. Once he started dangling carrots in front of my nose by promising to buy me an expensive home and a five karat diamond, I took the bait like a starving big fish. He also promised to help with the calendar business and help me financially. As his captain friend mentioned, Chason just had a way with the ladies. He thought it was his large stature, and the way he made a woman feel protected. All of this was more than I could resist.

His wife went on to tell me that he had previously been married; she was not sure how many times, but from what she could determine, it had to be quite a few times. She told me she thought all he did for a living was try and live off women as his retirement from the police department was not much, and getting free room and board was how he supplemented his income. She finally told me to make his life as miserable as I could; she would celebrate and support it to the fullest. After hearing her story, I counted myself one of the lucky ones who never let him move in and live off me.

I received a call from a television network that was airing court cases and was asked if I would be interested in appearing and presenting my case before a judge on a nationwide program. I told them I would be more than willing, as I could possibly be rewarded by the network for my losses. They said they would have to contact the other party and would get back to me. A representative from the station called a day later and said they had reached the defendant, and they were told by him that he would not go before a judge or appear on TV. I was not surprised by his decision, but was also disappointed at the same time. It would have given me such satisfaction not only to see him squirm, but also to maybe get some of the money I felt that was owed me. Besides, I love center stage, and this would have been an exciting adventure. But he wasn't stupid, he knew he didn't have a chance in hell of winning, and would only look like the fool that he was.

I also filed a Small Claims Court suit against him, timed so that he would be served with my civil suit while he was appearing in criminal court. It worked just as I had planned. Maybe this guy learned something from this experience; that there could be a price to pay for taking financial advantage of people, but mostly for screwing with people's emotions. I bet I am the only female in his life who managed to put him through the grinder like that. While I never got any monetary compensation out of the deal, the thought of having been instrumental in having his cheating and lies catch up to him, was extremely satisfying.

18 MORE POLICE YARNS

Getting up at 6:00 AM was not a favorite routine I enjoyed, but I did like my job. Debbie, my good friend and partner at work, and I had adjoining desks at the back of the bureau, which at the time was a large open room where we could see and hear most everything. We definitely had some detectives who could only be called "characters", very fun loving and ornery, always playing practical jokes and looking for ways to shock people. One day one of the more outrageous detectives, Olis, came up to our desks, reached his hand down inside his pants, and proceeded to inform us that he had come down with a bad case of the crabs. As you can imagine, we were speechless and just stared at him with our mouths hanging open in shock. All of a sudden, he pulled his hand out of his pants and threw two big black live bugs at us! We jumped up screaming and ran into our lieutenant's office, hiding behind him as if he was going to protect us from the invasion of the big black bugs! The poor lieutenant had no idea what was going on or why the two of us were shrieking at the top of our lungs. Olis hadn't expected such an extreme reaction from us and hurriedly scooped up the defenseless bugs and headed out the door before the lieutenant could confront him. Once we calmed down and told the lieutenant what happened, he actually found it quite amusing. Olis later told us it was just two harmless June Bugs and that he disposed of them in a humane manner, setting them free. He knew we were animal activists and would never have forgiven him if he had stomped on them; truth is, they were probably too big to stomp anyway; they would've made quite a mess out of his shoes.

Once the commotion was over and we felt safe to return to our desks, we told another detective what had happened. He took pity on us and decided we needed a treat for being such good sports. He went home and returned with a mixer full of Piña Coladas. He went back in the Detective Bureau storage room, where he couldn't be spotted, and poured us each a glass garnished with some fruit. He brought them to our desks. We were laughing so hard that we attracted the Bureau Captain's attention. He was curious enough about what was so amusing, that he strolled over to our desks to find out. We told him the Olis bug story, while trying to hide our drinks under our desks. The Piña Coladas gave off a strong tropical scent of coconut. Several times he sniffed, asking what that smell was. Debbie told him, she was wearing a new exotic perfume, and he seemed to buy that story.

It was good that most people thought Debbie was sweet and innocent, for, if he had not believed her and had investigated further, discovering the drinks, we would have all been in big trouble, and most likely would have been disciplined. Although back then almost everyone in the Bureau was a big drinker, coming back from lunch with alcohol on one's breath was a common occurrence. The brass did frown on this unacceptable behavior, and were trying desperately to change this practice. As time went on, they did succeed in putting a stop to it, and certainly no one would dare do it today, but in the earlier years it was very common to have a couple of cocktails before returning to work, many times the brass even joined us. All that was required was that you maintain some semblance of composure. You could not come back in an obviously drunken state. And you had to be capable of getting your work done in a timely manner. If you could do that, no questions were asked.

Rich, one of our Check Detectives, who was a prince of a guy, used to take Debbie and me to the monthly fraud investigators' meetings. The gatherings were informative, but above all a lot of fun. The detectives from other departments and the bank investigators would treat us to a few vodka tonics with our lunch. Back in those days there weren't a lot of women investigators, and we weren't hard on the eyes, so we got our fair share of attention, and we loved it. As much as we enjoyed these meetings, it could be torture returning to the office after those drinks and sitting behind a desk for the remainder of the afternoon. The detectives were lucky, because they could head out of the office and do their investigations in the field, which kept them awake, although rumor had it that some of them were known to find a nice big tree to park under for a few winks. But as tortuous as it was to be desk bound the rest of the day, it was worth it, and we never turned down an invitation to a meeting!

I recall one birthday luncheon, when everyone just seemed to be in a very festive mood, and I went overboard with the Vodka tonics. On these special occasions I would try to refrain from taking any Valiums, or whatever the doctors had me on at the time, so I could thoroughly enjoy myself.

Because of my agoraphobia, and the fact that I couldn't drive more than two to three miles from work or home, the restaurant we went to that day was within my driving range, so I drove. This is still true to this day, although if someone is with me, and I feel comfortable with where I'm going, I can drive farther, but never on the freeway. As it happened, I chose a very bad day to be the driver. Once back at work, I had no memory of the party ending, or of driving back to work. This was the first and only time I ever drove drunk. I had driven after drinking before, but never drunk. Thank God, I safely made it back to the department, was able to park my car and get up the stairs, but I definitely did not recall doing it. I started downing the coffee, and as I started sobering up, it hit me that I should have been arrested for drunk driving. Very scary! Once I started heaving and running to the bathroom, no one said anything to me with the exception of Debbie. She was feeling no pain either, and as usual, just found me amusing. Leave it to me to always be Debbie's entertainment!

Surely, everyone knew that I was tipsy, yet no one was preaching to me. They didn't have to. In my heart I knew this would be the last time I would do anything so reckless and stupid. If I ever got caught up in the moment again, I would either call for a ride, or sit there until I sobered up. As time went on, I found that drinking was far better for me than the pills the doctor prescribed. I have a morbid fear of hospitals, and when my good friend was in one for the last few weeks of her life, I found that I could go and see her if I drank just enough to take the edge off. It started me on the path of using vodka tonic for medicinal purposes. I used alcohol to help me handle stressful situations. Not to say I didn't drink sometimes just for fun, of course I did. It wasn't always vodka; I enjoyed a scotch now and then, as I heard it was the best thing to drink to avoid hangovers. I also developed a taste for cordials, and a glass or two of wine also helped to soothe the nervous system. I figured, if it helps getting me out of the house and function, allowing me to live a somewhat normal life, then it is a good thing; much better than pills. I did have a drink on occasion when I drove, but I never let myself get out of control again. Debbie said I was a much better driver when I had a drink, and she is right. It relieves some of the tension and fear I have of being behind the wheel, so I am more relaxed. It is hard to believe that I used to love to drive, and would even take whole day trips by myself. I laugh when I recall driving to Oceanside to see a guy in the Marines, whom I was dating. I was driving a 5 gear shift sports car, would have a soda in one hand, a sandwich in the other, and manage to smoke; all at the same time!

One day I left work to go home and check on my dog Gizmo and my cat Kidders. I pulled up in front of my garage and attempted to open my car door. After several unsuccessful attempts, I started looking around, trying to figure out what was wrong. To my horror, I discovered my skirt had become stuck in the car door, and there was no budging it. I sat there pondering my options, which seemed pretty bleak. I finally decided I had no choice but to remove my skirt. My garage door opener just happened to be broken at that time, too, so all I could do was exit the passenger side door, and make a mad dash for my gate, which had to be unlocked. Scanning the neighborhood the coast was clear, with the exception of the neighbor across the street, watering his front lawn. I saw him turn to the side and thought, it is now or never, I better make my move. As soon as I exited the car, out of the corner of my eye I could see him make an abrupt turn, facing in my direction. I could see his hose go up in the air, sending water flying everywhere, as he stared dead straight at me. No doubt he was shocked to see me standing there trying to unlock my gate with nothing on but a sheer pair of panty hose! I never used to wear underwear underneath my panty hose, obviously not a good idea if you're getting your skirt stuck in the car door! Once inside the house, I quickly grabbed another outfit and went outside, attempting to pry the car door open, in order to remove my skirt which was hanging on the ground. My neighbor was still in his front yard, and once he spotted me, I got a hearty greeting from him. I decided to just let his imagination run wild; I would not try to explain to him what had happened.

Even with all my tugging and pulling, there was no way this skirt was budging from the door. I phoned work and spoke with one of my favorite detectives, explaining my dilemma to him. After an outburst of laughter, he proceeded to tease me about how these unusual things always seem to happen to me, and how much my neighbor probably enjoyed the peepshow, and then offered to meet me in the police parking lot in a few minutes. On the way to the department, I could see part of the skirt flying in the air and hear the other part flopping on the ground, I was pretty sure there would be no salvaging it. Passersby noted the article flying out of my door and some surprised me with a friendly wave. After arriving in the lot, my buddy, Tom, greeted me with a crow bar and a chuckle; within a few seconds he popped the door open and set my skirt free. This wasn't the first time he had come to my rescue. The skirt was trashed with oil all over it, and black marks from the asphalt. Oh well, I learned a couple of valuable lessons that day, always wear underwear under your panty hose, and always make sure your clothes are properly tucked in before you shut the car door.

Prior to learning this valuable lesson about panty hose, I had another embarrassing moment. One morning I was walking from my car to the police department and could hear one of the detectives chuckling behind me. I was in a hurry, since I was running late as usual, no matter that I lived only 5 minutes away, so I didn't bother to turn and ask him what was so funny. I entered the police building, made it all the way up the stairs and to my desk, before one of the nicer detectives pointed out to me that the back of my skirt was tucked up in my panty hose! Once again I was just bopping around with my bare butt hanging out for all to see! I tried to shame the detective who followed me in the building without saying a word, but no apologies were forthcoming from him; he just laughed hysterically.

On another occasion I arrived at work and was part way through my day when one of the detectives approached me and told me I had a department store security tag hanging off my skirt. Sure enough, I looked down and there was one of those big white security tags hanging securely on my skirt! The detective got some tools and tried to remove it, but it wouldn't budge. So off I went home to change clothes, knowing I would have to take the skirt back to the store, knowing that with my luck the security alarm would go off on the way back in! I wondered how many people noticed that tag hanging off my skirt during the course of my day, and never said a word!

Another time I was sitting at my desk eating a salad with blue cheese dressing. I accidentally spilled some on my skirt and immediately noticed the blue cheese dressing start eating a hole in my skirt! As I was bending down trying to stop the spread of the hole, I wheeled my chair right over my skirt, leaving black tire tracks on it. Another skirt bit the dust. Debbie of course was laughing hysterically; I never ceased to entertain her.

I had this bright blue dress that I just loved, it was very form fitting and figure flattering, and I thought I looked extremely attractive in it. One day one of the detectives told me I looked like a Q Tip with my bright blue dress, white hair and white shoes. Once he put the idea in my head, I couldn't help secretly agreeing with him. Later that day, while leaning over the same detective's desk, discussing a case, all of a sudden he looked down the front of my dress and said he could see all the way down to my toes! After that day, I never felt the same way about that dress!

I remember one outfit I had that was reminiscent of Michael Jackson, denim with all kinds of chains and metal stuff hanging off it. One day at work I walked out to the lobby and there was a citizen sitting in the lobby. She stared at me, looking me up and down from head to toe; I was just thinking: Wow, she must think I look really good, when she suddenly said "They let YOU work here?" Trust me, it was NOT a compliment. I never looked at that outfit the same way again either.

And then I had my infamous "zipper dress". It was a really cute short denim dress that had a zipper all the way down the front and it could be zipped or unzipped from top or bottom. I'll never forget at one of my parties, after downing a few too many vodka tonics, I thought I was just the cat's meow and started dancing around provocatively, trying to impress my boyfriend whose band was playing at the party. I was slithering around on the dance floor between people's legs and then decided I could really make a splash by flying down the stairs. Apparently during the course of all my shenanigans, my upper zipper had gone down and my bottom zipper had gone up so that they were almost meeting in the middle! A couple more dance moves and I would have likely had nothing securing my dress but an inch of zipper in the middle and everything would have been hanging out for all to see! But fortunately one of my friends who still had her wits about her approached Debbie and told her she better tell me in a big hurry that my zippers were about to meet in the middle. Fortunately Debbie did warn me before I gave everyone a full body peep show, but they still saw enough. I say fortunately, because Debbie didn't always warn me, sometimes she was just as ornery as the detectives!

With all the levity in the office, it was amazing how much work did get accomplished. In any workplace there should always be a little time for laughter, without the threat of getting into trouble; happy employees are better employees. My friend Tom and I would take on the characters of Morticia and Gomez from the Addams Family and tango up and down the aisles while laughing hysterically at how clumsy we were.

It only took a minute, but brought laughter to a lot of people.

One time I went to work while still suffering the remnants of a cold, something I wouldn't normally do because I didn't believe in people going to work sick and spreading germs around. I often chided co-workers for doing it. The rule was, if it was over three days, you were no longer contagious, and it was my fifth day of being sick. Even so, I still had a runny nose and it seemed like I was constantly blowing it. One of the detectives caught me honking away. As a joke, he started telling everyone, he caught me picking my nose, something I would never do! And so began a constant stream of wise cracks and jokes at my expense. I got several cards with pictures of kids digging deep, and one of those rats even put a decal on my cubicle partition, depicting a kid with his finger up his nose. The detectives really enjoyed yanking my chain, and especially enjoyed my very unladylike responses. I think one of the detectives, by the name of Dennis, came to work just so he could torment me. He would pull the rubber from the bottom of his shoes, which had all kinds of nasty looking stuff stuck to it, and put it on my desk with a note stating "pick a winner". After this had gone on for months, I decided it was time for payback; I just had to think of something really clever.

One of the girls who worked in the Narcotics Bureau solved my dilemma. She gifted me with a big rubber booger, much like the rubber dog poop that we've all been subjected to at some point in our lives. It really looked authentic, and I thanked her profusely. It was just what I needed! I placed the gnarly looking thing in one of my nostrils and let out a very loud fake sneeze. I pretended to wipe my nose and then threw the Kleenex away, being sure to leave the fake booger hanging out of my nose. The detective who first started the nose picking jokes let out a howl and screamed at everyone in the room to come and look at the boogers coming out of my nose!

One of the guys was talking to a victim on the phone and abruptly hung up just so he could see. Someone shouted to look at me now; I was the original "booger lady". One of the detectives sitting nearby, Adam, took pity upon me and quietly told me to wipe my nose because something was hanging out of it. You could really tell he felt badly for me. But he was the only one, the rest of the guys were laughing uncontrollably. Some of them couldn't even talk, they were laughing so hard. Adam repeated again that I should please listen to him and wipe my nose NOW. I put the Kleenex up to my nose and suddenly flicked the booger at the detective sitting in front of me, who had so rudely hung up on his victim just so he could laugh at me. He let out a loud squeal as it soared through the air and landed on the top of his hand. Of course believing this was a real booger, he started stuttering curse words while trying desperately to get it off him. Because it was soft rubber, it kind of stuck to him, and it took him a few seconds to realize it was only a harmless piece of rubber. I got them good, and they had no choice but to admit it. After this, the nose picking jokes came to an abrupt end, much to my relief. But heaven forbid, they just leave me alone, they immediately went back to jabbing me about my being a vegetarian, mooing and clucking and regaling me with their hunting stories.

19 JESSIE AND MR. ROGERS

It was the weekend and time to go back to Mr. Rogers. For another one of those "I wish I could forget" moments two of his nurses and I accompanied him to Bob Burns, his favorite restaurant, located at Fashion Island in Newport Beach. After ordering our lunch, we were all chatting when Mr. Rogers suddenly grew very quiet. We asked if something was wrong and he just said he wasn't feeling quite up to par. Boy was that an understatement! Once our luscious food arrived and was placed before us, Mr. Rogers proceeded to throw up all over the table, drenching everything in vomit. I started retching and it took every ounce of self-control I had not to throw up myself. The poor folks sitting in close proximity just sat in shock, not lifting a fork or saying a word. Mr. Rogers was of course extremely embarrassed, and you can imagine how the rest of us felt, we would have been eternally grateful if the floor would've opened up and swallowed us right at that moment! One of the girls ran into the kitchen and told the cooks we needed a lot of napkins, another understatement, and some help in cleaning up the mess. I thought it was a lot to ask of the poor waiters, so we did our best to clean it up, all of us gagging as we worked at mopping it up. After paying our bill and leaving a BIG tip, we made a hasty exit. Mr. Rogers kept saying we could stay as he felt better now and wanted some lunch, but we discouraged him. We told him we no longer had any appetite and if he was that sick, it was probably not a good idea to continue with lunch.

What are the odds of this happening again at this same restaurant, you might ask? Well let me tell you. Many months later we bravely gathered for another outing to Bob Burns, against our wishes. But Mr. Rogers was insistent, he really missed going to his favorite restaurant. We just hoped the restaurant personnel had forgotten the last incident. If they had forgotten, it wasn't long before they got a nasty reminder. As soon as our lunch was placed in front of us, the poor old guy started retching and threw up all over our food, again! This was a pretty upscale restaurant with an upscale clientele which made it even more humiliating. These were not people used to seeing such things, especially in a nice restaurant, where they were trying to enjoy an expensive lunch. It was just an incredible mess and once again we tried to clean it up as best we could, not leaving the worst of it for the poor restaurant staff. If I were in their place, I probably would have just rolled up the table cloth and thrown it all away! Needless to say, we never went back to this establishment. Not only did we not want to show our faces there again, but I doubt we would have been welcomed with open arms. We felt it was Mr. Rogers' Manhattans before lunch that were not agreeing with him, but there was no discouraging him. He was a man who was used to getting his own way and he wanted his Manhattans, so he would have his Manhattans, consequences be damned. And telling him no, was not an acceptable alternative, unless you wanted to see all hell break loose.

Not long after this second incident, Nurse Ratchet as we often referred to Nurse Jessie, came under scrutiny. One of Mr. Rogers's attorneys became suspicious of some of the transactions that were taking place with Mr. Rogers's bank accounts, and she caught wind of it. How she became aware of this, I never did find out. She barred his nursing staff from his home and took over. It was learned from one of his nurses shortly thereafter that Jessie was drilling him and influencing him by giving him cigarettes and alcohol which he had been weaned off of due to his poor health. The nurse became aware of this when she stopped by unannounced at his home and insisted that she be let in, but was denied entry into his home by Jessie. She said she could smell the smoke and could hear Mr. Rogers asking for one of his favorite Manhattans. She became very alarmed and phoned one of his attorneys telling him that she thought Jessie was trying to brain wash Mr. Rogers and maybe trying to kill him, in order to cover up her theft from his bank accounts and misuse of his credit cards. She told the attorney that this had been going on for almost a week, and that she apparently had held Mr. Rogers a captive in his own home. This nurse called me and apprised me of the situation. I told her she definitely did the right thing contacting the attorneys, although she should have called them earlier, once she suspected what was transpiring.

During this time, for several months I had not been working for Mr. Rogers, as Jessie and I had a falling out, and she told me I was no longer employed. This occurred when she attempted to give me a thousand dollars, saying it was from Mr. Rogers. The only way we were given bonuses were through the attorney's office, not by her handing monies to any of us. I had asked Mr. Rogers if he was aware of this; he said he had not given her permission to give me this money. I was not sure of her motives as to why she wanted me to have this cash. She found out that I had approached him and questioned him on this, and then went ballistic, telling me to leave.

The same day his out of state attorneys learned what Jessie was up to, a Private Investigator was assigned to protect Mr. Rogers. Jessie had called one of the nurses and asked her to stay with Mr. Rogers as she needed to leave. All this went down on the same day the nurse had made the call. This was perfect timing, as the investigator and his assistant contacted the nurse, spoke with Mr. Rogers and told them both that an investigation would be taking place. The investigator proceeded to lock down the premises, changing the locks on the doors and code on the garage opener. They also placed a large locking device on the entry gate.

I would have loved to have seen Jessie's reaction the next morning, when she returned to Mr. Rogers's residence and found she was locked out. She phoned Mr. Rogers's residence and was told by the investigator that she no longer was to have any contact with Mr. Rogers or she could be taken into custody. He told her an investigation of her activities in the employ of Mr. Rogers has been initiated, and that a restraining order would be in effect immediately. She started crying hysterically, claiming that she did nothing wrong, and did not understand the accusations made against her.

I thought it wise to turn on my phone recorder and get whatever information I could from Jessie, should she decide to call me, as I expected she would be thinking that I was the culprit who burned her, due to our falling out. As expected, Jessie phoned me, yelling obscenities and insinuating that I had been the one who had contacted the attorneys and got her locked out of Mr. Rogers's home. I told her I had not done any of it. (Had I known what she had been up to, I would have placed that call.) When I could get a word in edgewise, I told her that if she had done nothing wrong then she had nothing to worry about. I told her "you know that the nurses and I had done nothing wrong during our employment with Mr. Rogers" and she replied "oh I know that". I told her at the time she was acting irrationally and should consider contacting a shrink; that she definitely needed help. I still have the tape of that conversation in my possession.

This was a very stressful time for everyone, as all the past and present employees were put under the microscope and drilled by the P.I. Jessie had created a situation where charges could be brought against her. She put everyone in a precarious position because of her actions. The investigation went on for several weeks and it was the final determination of the P.I. that Jessie was the perpetrator and the only one that was responsible for wrong doing and could be prosecuted for her involvement with Mr. Rogers and his financial affairs. The problem was Mr. Rogers refused to have any charges brought against "his Jessie" and would not testify against her.

Because of her greed and her psychopathic state, (later it was learned she was bi-polar along with other mental problems) she went over the top, convincing Mr. Rogers to help her purchase new clothes for her two adult children and on a bigger scale, new cars and two condos in the South County area of Orange County. She managed to convince him to do this by plying him with the cigarettes and alcohol and having him sign contracts and deeds, while he wasn't totally aware of what he was signing and agreeing to, after a few martinis or Manhattans. This was her strategy when she shut the nurses out for those few days. Again, Jessie was his "darling girl", as he called her, and she could do no wrong. Mr. Rogers had most of his faculties and nothing ever escaped him. So in his heart of hearts he had to know, at least to some degree, what she was doing, but he did not want to acknowledge it, or see her behind bars.

A few weeks later, she really went over the top, and started writing checks on her joint account with her husband, which she had removed from the trunk of his car without his knowledge. He had placed them there in order to conceal them from her, but you couldn't keep anything from her. When it came to her wanting something, she was relentless. She could sniff things out like a rat. She cashed a number of these checks and went on a buying binge. She proceeded to have a tummy tuck as well as purchasing expensive items for herself and for one of her lovers. She moved out of their home, taking all the credit cards she could find. Jessie then moved into a very exclusive condo on the Bayfront, where she was later asked to leave, as she was harassing other tenants, one of whom she flashed by knocking on his door and pulling her long coat open for him to view her naked body. There was one incident in the bar at the condo's club, when with a fork she stabbed a man whom she had been hustling. The police had been called, but the patron did not want to press charges. Jessie had used the credit card funds to re-do the interior of the condo, which totaled about $15,000.00 dollars. With all the money that she spent, her husband had to put their home up for sale to pay off all her debts that she had incurred.

Not long after being banned from the club's facilities and the condo she had leased, she hopped on a plane bound for Israel. She told people that she wanted to see Jesus. Officials were apprised of her actions and were able to contact family members regarding her irrational behavior and requested that they immediately come and get her. Shortly after arriving back on U.S. soil, she started experiencing pains in her abdomen. She was admitted to a local hospital where she was diagnosed with a very serious infection, most likely caused by her liposuction procedure; it had spread through most of her abdomen. During the exploratory surgery she went into shock and never recovered. She died that same day.

One has to have empathy and some forgiveness toward one who was so mentally ill, even though she created a lot of havoc for most everyone she came in contact with. Jessie was a complete control freak and was always stirring the pot and setting one against another. It is hard for me to fathom that I was in high school with this girl, and was one of her bridesmaids in her wedding. She changed so much over the years, becoming more demanding and controlling; after she got married and had her children, her personality and actions

278

had turned around a 180 degrees. Her illness had taken over and she lost it mentally. No matter what she did, one has to feel some sorrow for someone so sick.

After Jessie was banned from Mr. Rogers, he and the family called me and asked if I could come back to work on the weekends. I accepted the offer, as I missed Mr. Rogers and his staff, and the job I had. Once Jessie was no longer in charge, it was a totally relaxed environment. His beautiful home on the bluffs overlooking the ocean was a paradise. Sitting on the hillside, enjoying the most astounding panorama, it made me wonder how a person like me deserved to be there.

The nurses and I were always treated with respect and spoiled on top of it all. For lunch, always at the best of restaurants in town, he insisted that we all accompany him, urging us to order whatever we wanted. Ever since that time, my taste buds no longer tolerate the offerings of fast food chains, which I never really cared for.

About six months after returning to work for Mr. Rogers, he became quite ill with a kidney infection and was admitted to the hospital. Within two weeks of his stay, he passed away. It was heartbreaking to lose him. All of us girls loved him a lot, as he treated us like his own family. Mr. Rogers had a way about him that commanded attention and respect. You couldn't help but feel that you were protected by his very presence. His grandsons arranged for a beautiful burial ceremony for him. Several of his attorneys from the east coast were also attending to honor him. It was a very sad time and I was sorry to have to close this chapter of my life.

20 More Police Shenanigans

Several of my co-workers from the PD and I would head to the PD gym after work. After sitting at a desk for ten hours a day, a walk on the treadmill and lifting a few weights helped to relieve the stress. There was a new cop who was always there at approximately the same time we were. He was a strange looking dude with extremely large ears, so large as to be distracting. One would have thought he would've sought help from a plastic surgeon. I don't intend to be mean spirited, I actually felt very sorry for him, because surely he was the butt of jokes his whole life. Seriously, Dumbo would have been envious if he ever laid eyes on these flaps. He did some strange stuff, which made me wonder if being teased as a child caused his weird behavior. When he rode the exercise bike, he would always polish his shoes; not something you see very often in a gym. He would never acknowledge you at any time. A friendly hello was completely ignored. He didn't seem to fit in, or be "one of the boys", and his coworkers often commented on some of the unusual stuff he did in the field.

I guess he felt he didn't fit in either, because he ended up leaving our Department, going to work at another local Department. We later heard that he was arrested for being a peeping tom, and was fired from his job. Apparently there had been reports of a peeping tom in one particular neighbor-hood and it turned out to be him. He would wear a dark sweatshirt with the hood pulled over his head, pretending to be jogging while peeping in women's windows. No wonder he wore the hood, he would have been too easily identifiable by his ears. It was obvious that the guy had some real problems, and you had to wonder how he ever passed a psychology test. Maybe the shrinks just felt sorry for him, too.

It seemed like there was always one detective in the group who suffered the brutal ribbing and pranks of friends, and was picked on relentlessly by the rest. He had a grating personality at times, but was blessed with a generous heart. His warm and fuzzy side appealed to the women, but didn't go far to ingratiate him with most of the men. He always treated the ladies well, and would even go out to our favorite diner, bringing us breakfast or lunch.

One day Carl had enough of the heckling from the guys, and came up with a brilliant idea. He headed to the pet food store and returned with cat and dog cheese treats. Debbie and I knew they were pet food, but he swore us to secrecy. We had no problem obliging. He filled the candy dishes on our desks to the brim with the goodies. The guys were notorious for not being able to pass up free food and they dove into the cheese puffs and pretzel bites, at least that's what they thought they were. The first batch disappeared in a few of minutes, so we filled the dishes again. As the guys scarfed the stuff down and even commented on how good the cheese puffs were, Debbie and I remained completely straight faced, no easy task under the circumstances; we should've won an Oscar for that! Once quite a few of them had gobbled up the treats, Carl started going around the bureau scratching himself like a dog, lifting his leg as though he was going to pee on the desks and asking if anyone was itching since eating the cheese puffs. The guys were used to Carl's weird antics, so they pretty much just ignored him thinking he'd really gone over the edge this time.

It was not until the next day that the truth came out. While some of the guys were asking if we had any more of the cheese puffs and pretzels, Carl stepped in and announced that anyone who wished to have some more could purchase them at PetSmart. He pulled out the empty boxes to show them what they really had eaten. Some of the guys had to give him credit for pulling off such a prank and started playing along, running around the room barking and meowing. But several of them became incensed. Of course, these were some of the biggest pranksters around; they could dish it out but couldn't take it! One even wanted to file a police report against him and several were concerned that they could get sick after eating food meant for animals. In reading the labels for ingredients, it appeared that they were probably healthier than the human variety. No one had gotten sick after eating them.

After this stunt, Carl really had to look over his shoulder, because the guys who had always taunted him were really out to get him now. But they didn't intimidate him. He would even bark and scratch and meow occasionally just to taunt them. His hecklers never forgave Carl for pulling off the ultimate payback.

One night after work, a group of us decided to get together at the local pizza place for some beer, bonding and food. Most everyone from the Bureau showed up, even Carl. Though he was not well accepted by some of the detectives, they normally tolerated him, and we ladies were glad that he joined in. One of the sergeants we'll call Larry, had a tough time controlling his drinking and got quite blitzed. He was one of those loud obnoxious drunks, but because we liked him, we just laughed it off and tried to ignore him. This night he apparently didn't feel like being ignored, so he proceeded to open the zipper to his pants and let little Pedro peek out. He started swinging his hips in front of Debbie and me, so we would be sure to see what was swinging to and fro. Needless to say, we were shocked and judged it to be a good time to make a swift departure. Before we could get away, Carl started making some strong accusations against the sergeant, understandable under the circumstances. We didn't want to get involved, because we were friends with both of them, and it was known that these two had butted heads many times in the past. This was the window of opportunity for a payback, and Carl took full advantage of it by berating the drunken sergeant.

An internal affairs report was filed by the sergeant against Carl for insubordination and for breaking a napkin holder at the restaurant, which was supposedly an unintentional accident. We were all shocked that Larry would file a report against Carl after he had pretty much wagged his weenie at us in a public place! But the sergeant was so drunk that he completely forgot, or maybe purposely left out that detail, expecting that no one would dare bring up his part of instigating the confrontation with his lewd behavior. Once the investigation started, and it came out what he had done, he became so stressed out that he started contacting all the girls who were present that night, in an attempt to convince us that we hadn't seen what we thought we saw. He said there was no way he had exposed himself to us, all he had done was put a pencil through his zipper as a joke. Of course we knew better, we knew what we had witnessed; we weren't the drunk ones in the bunch! He even contacted several of us at home, pleading with us to go along with the story he had concocted. He said it would be the end of his career and he had a family to take care of. As it turned out, he needn't have worried. The captain in charge of Internal Affairs was his good friend and he basically dismissed what we had to say, even though it was the truth. And he knew very well that the sergeant had been in hot water before, with his uncontrollable drinking and lewd behavior.

At a football game not only full of HBPD employees but also full of officers from other departments and their wives and girlfriends, he had pulled his pants down and mooned everyone. There was no formal action taken against him for that incident. Another time a group of us were partying at our favorite watering hole. The sergeant proceeded to get fall-down drunk; no one wanted anything to do with him and no one wanted to take him home. He lived in South County which was about a thirty minute drive or more from the club. There was no way he could have driven himself home. Somehow they conned me into letting them load him in my car, so I could take him home and let him sleep it off on my couch. Debbie helped me drag him, the dead weight of his drunken body scraping over the sidewalk and stairs, dumping him on my couch. I thought, what if his wife is frantic, not knowing where her husband is, so I decided to call her. I somehow read the wrong number on our personnel roster and ended up calling another police officer who was a real enemy of his. I didn't know they were enemies at the time, so I told him what had happened. You could hear the delight in his voice, as he told me he was going to enjoy having some fun with this, which he did, by harassing the sergeant at every turn, and adding the latest incident to the complaint that was already being investigated.

Another time we were all at a City Employee Night at Old World in Huntington Beach and again this very sergeant got rip roaring drunk and dropped his drawers for all to see. No one reported this incident. What can I say, he was a very likable guy when he wasn't dropping his drawers and wagging his weenie.

Larry ended up escaping the chopping block, thanks to his Captain buddy. The only formal reprimand was that he be required to attend alcohol rehab. Apparently, his close call really scared him, because he agreed, and up until his retirement, he was known not to have a drink. And believe it or not, once the investigation was completed and he quit drinking, he was promoted to Lieutenant. It does pay to have friends in high places, especially back in those days.

As for Carl, who really hadn't done anything but yell at the sergeant about his bad behavior, he became a target of constant harassment by his co-workers and superiors because they liked Larry and felt Carl shouldn't have ratted him out for his actions at the pizza place, even though Larry was the one who initiated the complaint. There was no logic or fairness to this thought process, but when you're popular, you can do no wrong. It's always the unpopular guy's fault. They started making all kinds of allegations against him, such as that he was going home several times a day when he should have been out in the field investigating his cases. He denied this, stating he only went home for his lunch break, but still an investigation was launched. He was also accused of using profanity at another sergeant and another investigation ensued. While all of these investigations were going on, he foolishly created a flyer poking fun at the captain who had protected Larry and who was known to have it in for Carl. He didn't name him by name but everyone knew what captain he was referring to. Back in those days flyers came out almost on a weekly basis, poking fun at someone, and everyone took it all in fun. Carl figured, since he didn't name anyone by name, he was safe. But this captain was not laughing, and another investigation was initiated. In defense of all of these accusations, he filed a formal complaint claiming harassment and proclaiming his innocence. Those of us who knew him, found some of the allegations against him unbelievable, but we weren't privy to all of the information contained in the investigations. After several years of dragging through the courts, his case ended up being dismissed. However, he was awarded an honorable medical retirement. As for Larry, he enjoyed his position as Lieutenant for several more years before retiring.

I had been working a complex forgery case that had occurred at one of our local Ralph's Grocery stores. The suspect had used a counterfeit driver's license in order to cash a check and purchase a few items. He had hit this store on several occasions, and Ralph's was out several hundred dollars. Debbie and I had been promoted to Civilian Check Investigators in the Fraud Division. Later this position was upgraded to Civilian Investigator, but of course, no pay raise accompanied the title change, as was customary when it came to civilian personnel. When a civilian position was restructured, about the only means of securing a pay raise was by filing a grievance with the City, which required a lot of research and documentation, and sometimes could take years to process, and no guarantee of success at the end. Of course, if you had friends in high places, who would go to bat for you, then your odds increased dramatically. Basically if PD management wanted you to be reclassified and get a pay increase, they could make it happen, otherwise you were on your own to "fight City Hall".

But let's continue with the forgery caper. I had previously gone to Ralph's to show a photo line-up consisting of six photos of different individuals, one of them being a possible suspect in my case. The victims had not been able to identify him. I earned my new title of "Investigator" when, after a lot of digging, I was successful in obtaining a photo of another possible suspect who resided in Anaheim. Unfortunately, the acceptors of the checks were again unable to positively identify the suspect in the photo as the person who had passed the checks in their store. Too much time had passed, and with the high number of customers passing through, it was difficult for any of them to recall the suspect's appearance. However, there was one employee who was somewhat sure the suspect in the photo was the guy he had accepted the check from. Of course since the checks were forgeries, the name on the checks did not match my suspect, and our forensic handwriting expert was unable to positively ID my suspect's signature as it appeared on his driver's license, as the same signature that was used to cash the checks. All forgers use aliases, and this guy was no exception.

But I wasn't ready to give up yet. I had an address in Anaheim, CA for this possible suspect and the only way to ID or eliminate him was to pay a visit to his residence. As civilians who don't carry guns, we never went to a suspect's residence without being accompanied by a police officer. I convinced two of our detectives to accompany me and Debbie to Anaheim, in order to check out the address. We stopped for a Code 7, (lunch time) the most important code to a police officer, prior to going to the residence. While we were eating lunch, a call came over the radio from Fountain Valley PD requesting assistance from our department in serving a warrant in Anaheim, as they knew that officers from our department were in the vicinity. One of our more gung ho detectives jumped right on it, and said we were available. Debbie and I looked at each other and asked what we would be doing. Steve, our overzealous leader, said we would have to see how it played out, whatever that meant.

While finishing up our Code 7, detectives from Anaheim PD rolled up, accompanied by Investigators from the D.A.'s office. It so happened that they were about to serve a warrant at the same apartment complex where my possible bad guy lived. I showed one of Fountain Valley's detectives a photocopy of my suspect and right away she said she knew of him and his true name. She said he was a druggie, very active in passing fraudulent checks, and had been arrested quite a few times in the past. She said they would assist us in our attempt to contact him after we assisted them in serving their warrant.

While our detectives assisted FVPD in serving their search warrant, FVPD requested that Debbie and I, along with one of the investigators from the D.A.'s office, search a storage unit at a nearby location. I was told I would drive one of our detective units to the storage unit. We had to back track several miles to the storage area and my stress level was escalating by the minute. Because of my agoraphobia, I wasn't comfortable driving, or sometimes even being outside my comfort zone, and Anaheim was way outside my comfort zone. I was starting to have a very bad feeling about this whole caper. As always, whenever I had to travel outside my comfort zone, I carried a flask with me with a strong mixture of Vodka Tonic. I started slugging back a few to calm my frazzled nerves as we travelled to the storage unit.

The storage facility was located in the City of Stanton. The Investigator from the D.A.'s office said we would have to rummage through the unit where Anaheim PD's suspect had property stored. Debbie immediately said she would be responsible for writing the inventory list, leaving me with the task of digging through the items in the unit, which turned out to be some of the worst crap I have ever encountered. Fortunately the guy from the D.A.'s office furnished me with a pair of gloves before he was picked up and taken to help with the search warrant. So Debbie and I were stuck with the dirty job, or I should say I was, since Debbie managed to not even get her hands dirty.

I began sifting through pieces of soiled shredded papers in an attempt to piece together some sort of evidence. There was a discarded Kotex Pad that had a growth on it that I'm not sure even a scientist would have been able to identify. Several rotting pieces of fruit, which could have been bananas at one time, were stuck to some of the papers. I tried my best to match up some of the pieces of paper and to find evidence, but this task was not made easy with all the gross disgusting things growing on and stuck to the papers. Debbie just laughed hysterically each time I came across one of these nasty things, the look of horror on my face probably was pretty funny, but at the time I wasn't laughing with her. I was just frantically trying to get done before I caught something or some creepy crawly landed on me. I figured I would have to go home and burn the clothes I was wearing.

I hadn't heard the word "cooties" in years, but I couldn't get it out of my head that day! Debbie continued to encourage me to dig on, telling me what a great job I was doing —yeah, right! She was so delighted that her penmanship was far superior to mine so she could write the inventory list and only had to observe the mostly unidentifiable disgusting objects from afar.

After two hours of this torture, I had emptied out the bin. It was so hot that day, that my clothes were sticking to me and my hair was damp with perspiration. This did not make for a happy Norma; I've never liked the heat, and have a propensity for losing my cool when I am hot and sticky. So through no fault of my own, the only recourse I had was to take a few more shots from my flask in order to maintain my sanity. About the time we were wrapping up, the D.A. returned in his own car and said he would put the evidence in his car and Debbie and I would have to drive the Huntington Beach unit and the Fountain Valley unit to the residence in Anaheim. I tried my best to convince him that it would be okay to leave one of the cars there and pick it up later on our way back from Anaheim. When logic didn't work, I even tried whining a bit, but he totally ignored the sound of desperation in my voice. So I found myself behind the wheel of the FVPD detective unit. Because of my agoraphobia, I hadn't driven a car by myself outside my three mile comfort zone in years, so my already fragile nerves were on the verge of sending me spiraling into a full blow panic attack. Thank goodness, I had filled my flask to the top with mostly Vodka and I proceeded to chug it down.

The D.A. had us follow him, and I could see Debbie ahead of me with a huge smile on her face. She was cracking up because she knew I was on my way to getting plastered. She always thought I was a better driver when I had some drinks, so she wasn't worried about that. But boy, if the PD knew what I did, I would have been behind bars! But a girl has to do what a girl has to do, and I did it! It wasn't as if any of this was my idea!

Once we caught up with our detectives and the cops from Anaheim at the location where they were serving the warrant, they had us stand back over by the apartment where my suspect might be living. FV officers knocked on the door of their bad guy and once the suspect became aware of what was going on, a scuffle ensued. The cops were jumping on the guy and finally wrestled him to the ground. As all this commotion was going on, the door to my possible suspect's apartment flew open and then almost slammed shut when they saw the police, but not before one of our detectives managed to get his foot in the door, preventing it from being closed. They called Debbie and me over and we entered what had to be the most filthy, foul smelling room anyone could ever imagine. It was a one bedroom apartment and it appeared that two females, one small child, and my suspect all resided in this tiny space. The young boy was the son of one of the women who was later determined to be a hooker and a druggie. It was obvious the kid had problems; we were told he was autistic. He was only eight years old. It saddened us all to see him being subjected to this hell.

Before any of us could move around inside, we had to kick layers of discarded newspapers, clothing, and unidentifiable objects out of the way. I saw a couple of cockroaches scurry through the garbage on the floor, which freaked me out and almost made me head for the hills. On the kitchen counter were open cans of tuna and spam with a couple of bottles of mayonnaise that were no longer the color of mayonnaise. You couldn't even see the sink and counters through the dirty dishes and spoiled food. None of us had ever seen anything quite like this, not even the seasoned cops. The thought of "cooties" started running through my head again. Now I knew for sure, I will have to burn my clothes as soon as I got home!

The suspect I was looking for was sitting on the couch and could hardly move; he was completely stoned out of his mind. One of our detectives called Debbie and me into the bedroom where a porn movie was playing on the TV. We were told by one of the females that this was the little boy's room. In one corner of the room were stacks of crusts from what was once white bread, now green with mold. On the dresser were old syringes with dried blood, lying right out in the open, where the child could reach them. Stacks of filthy clothes were piled in heaps on the floor and on the bed, which was soiled with blood and one could only guess what else.

I had to get out of there and get some air, the stench had me gagging! I ran outside and lit up a cigarette and, when no one was looking, took a few more swigs from my flask. I felt like I was having a nightmare, and was hoping someone was going to wake me up any minute! As I stood there puffing away and gulping my Vodka, trying to calm my nerves, I wondered what could drive people to such extreme lows, to live in such filth, and especially to subject a child to it.

FV detectives joined us at the apartment, and one of them escorted my suspect to a bench, out in front, where he was cuffed and ordered to sit down. She told me to interrogate him to see if he would admit passing the checks. Then she just walked away, leaving me all alone with this stoned felon. By this time I was visibly shaking, in spite of the Vodka, but the fear of making a fool of myself won out over the urge to get the heck out of there. So I showed him the checks in question and asked him if he had passed them. Believe it or not, without any hesitation, he admitted he had. My first thought was whew; maybe I'm done now and can go home!

But the compassionate part of me kept me glued to the spot as I tried to get through to the suspect about the error of his ways, although he was so stoned, I'm sure he didn't hear a word I said, or even if he heard it, I'm sure he wasn't comprehending it. I told him, he was still a young man and could turn his life around and that if he didn't, he would end up in the morgue very soon. He just sat there and stared blankly at me with a bit of saliva running out of the corner of his mouth, never responding. I was so nervous, it was just he and I out there, for what seemed like an eternity, but I couldn't leave him alone since he was cuffed and basically in our custody. I kept thinking he could just leap up and take off and what could I do to stop him? I certainly wasn't going to tackle him, they didn't pay me enough for that kind of shit. Hell, they didn't pay me enough for anything I'd been through that day! Finally one of our detectives came to the rescue and took over the interview. I'm sure he was relieved to have me out of his hair, but as a final parting word, I reminded him that he would have to answer to the Lord someday and I hoped by then he had turned himself around.

I was ready for another few shots from my flask, and another few puffs; my nerves were shot and I felt like I was ready to explode. I was so relieved when I saw the detectives escorting my suspect and the two females to the police vehicles for transportation to HBPD Jail. I thought, now I could just relax and take it easy on the way back to the station, and finally get my nerves under control. Unfortunately, that was not to be, my rather sadistic supervisor Steve told me I would have to drive one of the units back to the station while my friend Debbie got the cushy assignment of being the passenger in the car with the male suspect, while another detective transported the two female arrestees. Before I even got a chance to protest, and trust me, protest I would have, Steve threw the keys at me, ordered Debbie in to the other car, and off everyone went! There was nothing I could do, if I didn't jump in the car right then, they would leave without me, and I had no idea where I was or how to get back. So, once again, I found myself alone behind the wheel of a strange car, in a strange place, way beyond my comfort zone. I think I was kind of in shock that this could happen to me twice in one day!

Steve told me to get on the radio if I needed anything, except he forgot to tell me, or possibly my Vodka soaked brain didn't comprehend, which channel to use, and there were quite a few to choose from. Not being familiar with the police radio, I started hitting buttons and learned later that I was on orange channel which goes out to all the police agencies in Orange County. I was still taking swigs from my flask until I finally emptied it; now my security blanket was gone, too. Even though I was a little buzzed, it wasn't enough to stop panic from setting in. At least, I had the presence of mind to know, I probably reeked of Vodka. I gobbled down some mints I had in my purse, and prayed that once back at the station, no one would notice the smell of alcohol emanating from my pores. Maybe the stench from rummaging through garbage all day would disguise it; I didn't know which was worse.

The detective in the lead unit, James, promised me he would stay in the slow lane, so I could follow him. But soon he started moving over and speeding up. I immediately reached for the radio, turned on the button that I thought was the correct one, and in my quivering voice said "Jimbe, you are making me nervous, get back in the slow lane." I also told him I would never forgive him if he tried any fancy driving with me behind him trying to keep up. Unbeknownst to me at the time, I was being transmitted to all Orange County police agencies, not just HB. Debbie told me, even the male prisoner was incredulous to hear me talking like that on a police radio and asked "She doesn't really work with you guys, does she?" Debbie told me he just sat in the back seat howling as he listened to my radio calls. He thought it was so hilarious that even the seriousness of being arrested didn't keep him from laughing hysterically. Before I knew it, we were approaching the freeway, and I do not do freeways; no way, no how. You couldn't give me enough alcohol to make me do it! I literally screamed out over the radio "You better not be going on that onramp Jimbe, cause if you do I will kick your butt from here to eternity!", again broadcasting to all of Orange County. I also found out I failed to turn off the radio when I wasn't talking to the detectives, so all my muttering and cursing to myself was also broadcast and heard all over Orange County. No doubt there were cops all over the County who were laughing their head off, but also dumbfounded, wondering who this crazy woman was on their police radio.

We finally made it back safe and sound to the department, hours after our day had begun. I was shaking uncontrollably by this time, and the only thing keeping me from a total melt down, was knowing that I was done and I was going home. I figured I would be able to make it that far, since it was less than five minutes away. But once again, it was not to be, I was told I had to respond to the jail to book Cummings, something I had never done before, and now I had to do it in a booze addled state. I thought God had to be playing a very cruel joke on me, for I just didn't know how much more I could take in one day.

I know it's probably hard for most people to understand how traumatized I was, because for a normal person it probably wouldn't have been a big deal. But for someone with agoraphobia, who rarely ventured out of Huntington Beach, never drove alone, except in a three mile radius from home, and had spent the day being subjected to all kinds of depravity, not to mention guzzling Vodka all day long, it was extremely traumatizing. I'm not exaggerating when I say it was nothing short of a miracle that I was still standing up.

Steve came up to me and said "You reek of booze". He was aware I had been drinking during the day but he had not said a word until then. I asked him what he expected after all the crap he had put me through. He knew I had problems, but almost seemed to delight in my horror and anxiety, because he just kept putting me in one predicament after another, like I said, he is a bit sadistic.

One might have thought that seeing me shaking uncontrollably and reeking of booze, Steve might have taken pity on me and sent me home, but no. Instead, he handed me some gum and told me to chew it before I went to the jail to book Cummings. What a guy! I chewed all the gum at once, hoping to camouflage the overpowering odor of Vodka. I proceeded with the booking process and somehow made it through, I'm not sure how, sheer willpower and fear of making a bigger fool of myself, I suppose. It was almost 7 PM by that time, way past the end of my normal work day, and I was feeling like I had been hit by a Mack truck. The alcohol was wearing off, and all I wanted to do was to beam myself home. I had visions dancing in my head of being in my jammies warm and cozy and safe in my clean bed, after burning my clothes, of course. In spite of everything, I was feeling blessed to only live 7/10's of a mile from the station, so within five minutes I would be pulling into my driveway, entering my house where it was quiet, and attempting to regain my sanity and sober up.

Once I recuperated, and it took a few days before I really felt normal again, I had to admit it was quite an adventure. I never really liked boring office work and it did make for a great story, I know. Debbie certainly enjoyed telling it to anyone who would listen! We did, of course, leave out the part about the Vodka; this would not have been acceptable to the higher ups. I just thank the Good Lord above that he took good care of me that day. It was truly a blessing that I didn't have an accident between the Vodka and the anxiety and the panic. I let Steve know what a liability I was and how it wasn't very smart on his part to place me in jeopardy and the Department at risk, had something bad happened. I reminded him that forcing me to drive when he knew I was drinking was totally irresponsible, not to mention dangerous. He promised he would never do anything like this again, but I knew him well, and didn't believe it for a minute; Steve was ornery and could never let an opportunity for a laugh pass by.

22 LADIES OF THE HBPD

Dahlia

Some of the girls in the bureau had a dress code all of their own. One of them by the name of Dahlia, aka: "DD", commonly showed up wearing a body leotard scooped down to her navel. Obviously there were no complaints from the detectives, but the brass thought it far too distracting and even though they tactfully approached her on the subject, she would just shrug her shoulders, say O.K., and show up the next day wearing something even more provocative. In reality, there wasn't anything they could do to her. She seemed to enjoy rubbing their noses in that fact. She would occasionally mention the big "harassment" word, which had the intended effect of sending them scurrying back to their offices in a big hurry. She definitely had a will of her own, and put herself high on a pedestal. She truly believed she was a hot number, but in reality, she was pretty plain looking. I did applaud her for her self-confidence though, the way she acted, you would have thought she was the next Marilyn Monroe.

Maggie

Then there was Maggie, a very attractive girl, blessed with model looks. For a while she took the pains to dress attractively and presentably, which landed her a detective who was an up and coming expert in the computer field. But after she had foot surgery, and had to wear a cast on her foot, she started showing up to work in baggy sweats. This did not go over well with the brass, but again they were most tactful in dealing with her, always fearful of a harassment suit being filed. If her sweats had looked like she had not slept in them, they might have cut her a little more slack. She still managed to lasso the nice good looking detective who eventually left the

Department for a very lucrative career in the computer industry. The two of them did marry, but ended up in divorce a couple of years later. Her husband had always made it clear, he wasn't ready for children, but Maggie got pregnant anyway, which likely led to the demise of their relationship.

There were times when I got annoyed with Maggie because she always wanted to be the center of attention. One night I was meeting an English pro golfer friend, whom I had met on one of my nights out, for a happy hour get together. I invited Maggie to join us. Tony and I were more than just friends and he was only in town for a couple of days. I had asked Maggie to come along only because I was feeling badly for her. She and her detective boyfriend were having a spat, and I thought it would help her to get away from her problems and have a few drinks, and I also wanted her to meet my current love interest. After a couple of margaritas, she decided to put the hit on him right in front of me. He was somewhat taken aback, but obviously flattered by the attention of this attractive woman. This did not sit well with me, as I have a strict friend rule; we keep our mitts off each other's guys, no matter what. Just because she was having a few problems with her soon to be spouse was no excuse for infringing on my territory. Although I had the urge to reach over and grab her by the neck and shake the crap out of her, lucky for her, I hadn't imbibed excessively, so I behaved like a lady. Neither of them had a clue that I was simmering inside and just wanted to throw them both into the bay! But I simply grabbed Tony by the arm and told him it was time for him and me to have some alone time together. That was the last time I ever invited her as a single woman to meet one of my boyfriends.

Gloria

Then there was Gloria, who was the head secretary and the matriarch of the bureau. She knew how to keep the men in line and when she spoke, they listened. You couldn't ignore her; she demanded attention. Gloria had the potty mouth of a drunken sailor; one of her favorite words was the "F" word. She was the only person in the entire Department who could get away with letting the "F" bomb fly whenever she felt like it. To this day, no one would dare to confront her about it. This language was natural to her, and everyone expected her to use it and if you didn't like it, it was tough s___, as Gloria would say. Gloria's heart is and has always been in the right place. She's a very kind, caring person, and a huge animal lover, the type who would use her last penny to take care of them, something I have great respect for. No one else has ever came close to having the devotion and loyalty to HBPD as Gloria did for over forty years. She finally retired after forty years, but not because she wanted to. The City offered what they call a "golden handshake", giving a retiree an extra 7% in retirement for the rest of their life. Since she was already maxed out on her retirement, it didn't make sense for her to pass up this "free money". After she retired, she was allowed to stay, on a part-time basis, but once the part-time program came to an end, she got a kick in the butt out the door! While this was no surprise to me, Gloria was extremely hurt. The current climate in the PD is one of indifference, once you are through; it's kind of like "don't let the door hit you on the way out!" It's very sad; it hasn't always been like this. In the old days you would see retirees wandering the halls on a regular basis, now it is rare for any of them to return to visit.

Sheila

One gal who I would like to forget entirely, Sheila, had a penchant for dried skin. After a day basking in too much sun she would end up burning and then peeling. She would rip the skin off the exposed parts of her body and then proceed to pop the dried stuff in her mouth. Not only was this a common practice, as she was a beach bunny, constantly ending up with a bad burn, but would chew the dried cuticle from her nails and ingest it. At times she would be digging at her scalp, and then placing what we thought was dandruff, in her chops. We would sit there and attempt to ignore her to the best of our ability or run to the nearest bathroom and dry heave. She did not last long at the PD, as she had put in for a position for the City of Orange where she landed a job in the morgue. This was the perfect position for this woman. I often wondered if she was also attracted to other people's dry skin, dead or alive.

Loren

Loren is another interesting lady who also does not want to say goodbye to the boys in blue. She has also worked there for over forty years, and would not have retired if not for the "golden handshake". She is now volunteering part-time at the PD, just so she can remain part of the group. It is difficult to understand why she would do the thankless job of handling bicycle thefts for free, because this is a woman who definitely likes the green stuff! When I first came to work at the PD, she and I worked the swing shift together in the Records Bureau. We became good friends and would spend holidays together with our respective beaus. She married one of the cadets, but their relationship soon failed as he liked to spend money and Loren liked to hoard it. They just couldn't come to a compromise. They say money issues are one of the biggest reasons for divorce and that was what caused the demise of their marriage. Her second husband was one of our officers, and she was totally crazy about him. She somehow managed to talk him into joining her Dempsey dumpster diving, looking for coupons or labels she could use with her coupons to save a few pennies. Everyone thought it must be true love because this was a macho type dude and the vision of him digging through all that trash behind grocery stores at night, was difficult to comprehend. But so much for true love, he soon tired of getting his hands dirty and found himself another lady who not only didn't clip coupons but who also wanted a family; something Loren had no desire for.

It isn't that this girl needed the money, her house was paid for and she made a decent salary. Her folks had also left her quite a bit of cash, along with all of their very expensive antiques. She simply did not like to spend money, she was beyond frugal. I've always been a firm believer in smelling the roses along the way, because one day it might be too late, but apparently not everyone feels the same way.

Kerri

Loren is not the only frugal lady to grace the PD. Kerri is an older gal who was married for a short time, and came from the city of New York. Her parents were well to do, they owned gas stations and bars, and once her parents passed away, she came into a great deal of cash. She has a beach house worth well over three million and an up-scale house in the desert that is paid for. All of us wondered why she was toiling as a secretary in the PD when apparently she was well heeled. We came to learn that she liked the social aspect of the job; it was convenient, as she lived only five minutes away, and the extra cash did help to pay for property taxes, which are huge. Still, she does not appear to enjoy what she has. Her beach house would be a perfect party house for most of us, but she lives in only one part of the three story six bedroom home. She used to have a roll away bed in her dining room area where she would sleep along-side her dogs. Today I do not know what her accommodations are, but it sure looked uncomfortable before. What a waste not to enjoy your entire castle! The old saying is very true about the different strokes for different folks. Don't get me wrong, she is a very nice person who loves her four legged friends and takes the very best care of them. She and I would go out to breakfast once in a while, and then that came to a halt, once I retired. I got my nose out of joint a bit, but understand that for some people it's kind of out of sight out of mind. We still exchange birthday and Christmas gifts but it's very rare that we ever get together, and we only live 5 minutes apart. She just doesn't seem to be interested. Fortunately that is not true for everyone.

Debbie

My dearest friend Debbie remains close; she is like the sister I never had, and the world's best friend, more like family than friends, and I know it will always remain that way. Cheryl, whom I met at the PD and have known for over thirty-five years, is still one of my most valuable friends whom I also consider family. Unfortunately she lives in Colorado and I can't travel, so I only get to see her once or twice a year when she visits California. But I am blessed to have two long term wonderful friends.

When Debbie came to work, she was just pushing twenty-one. I was so lucky to have her as my partner in crime, as I am sure I have mentioned before. She was married to Tim shortly after she started her job and Tim later became our photographer in the calendar business I had tried my hand at. They did part after several years. To this day, Tim would give anything if he could reverse their relationship and connect once again. This would never work, as Debbie remarried and has been Mrs. Dove for over nineteen years. But they still remain friends to this day.

Several years after her divorce from Tim, I encouraged her to date one of the detectives who was absolutely crazy about her and made it known to anyone who would listen. She was not the type that liked to mix her business life with her personal life, but after much pressure and persuasion, she decided it would do no harm to have one date with the highly infatuated detective. This was the best move of her life as she has a man who absolutely treasures her beyond anything in life, and that includes golf! He also got himself one of the best wives he could ever hope for! More on the story of The Love Doves later.

Jade

One of the most unusual women in the bureau was Jade. This gal had attitude and was always right, and no matter how much evidence was laid before her, she would never alter her opinion. She latched onto Debbie and it concerned me that she may not be the best influence on Debbie, but they became good friends and it all worked out in the end. There was one occasion when she announced very loudly for all to hear in the detective bureau, that I had a mental illness. Debbie was standing nearby, and I could tell it took her by surprise to hear Jade make such a statement. I tried to defend my agoraphobia and panic attack problems, explaining it was not an illness like being a manic depressive, or any other serious illness that would land someone in a straight- jacket, but she kept on and on and would not relent. She had to see the effect of her harsh words on me, the hurt and embarrassment, but it did not seem to matter to her.

I kept trying to explain that it was brought on by my anorexia, which had brought me to the brink of dying several years ago, and how it affected my nervous system. I told her, never before had I heard the term mental illness connected to my problem, not even by my doctors. But this lady was the authority. At length, I even started thinking that maybe she was right. I just never looked at my problem in that light. I always felt it was like someone who had a morbid fear of spiders, or some other object, that could cause them to panic. My remaining major concern was that she should not have been so outspoken in front of all my co-workers. I had worked so hard to keep my problem under wraps for so long.

As I've mentioned before, cops had a difficult time truly understanding an illness such as mine. Living in this state most of my life already made me feel inferior and incompetent, to say the least. I always tried to remember my gentle and kind mother telling me that I was OK; that living in a comfort zone and staying within my three mile driving range from home was just fine, and that no one had the right to challenge it. She reminded me that if they did, this would be the kind of person to avoid; that I didn't need their approval, nor did I need to seek their friendship; who needed friends like that? Her words of wisdom always helped to take the sting out of other people's meanness. There is nothing like the love of a parent who loves you no matter how weird you might be! Over the years, I have learned to accept myself and my limitations, and I no longer think that I am so bad, after all I've experienced.

I did forgive Jade, and as time went by, I really enjoyed spending time with her and her family. She would invite Debbie and her husband, and me and my guy Joe to their home for holiday dinners, which were always wonderful. She and her family went out of their way to make us feel welcome, and the spread was always delicious. Occasionally we would all get together and go for dinner and entertainment. We were crazy for one of the lead singers in a group who did a lot of Tom Jones and Sinatra songs, and found ourselves showing up almost every week to his gig. There were some really memorable times, and it did make up for the way she could get under your skin at work. For some reason, away from the job she was a lot more fun and pleasant.

Jade was also addicted to gambling, specifically Keno. Every chance she got, it was off to Laughlin, or the local bar or donut shop where you could play Keno. She was fairly lucky at picking out those bouncing balls on the Keno board. The more she won, the more she played, until her luck started running thin. Some of us worried that she might go too far and mortgage her home, just so she could continue to play the games; that's how addicted she was. Once her husband discovered how much money she was losing, her gambling time was definitely curtailed. He was livid, to say the least. But she was addicted, and she still managed to fit in some gambling when he was traveling for his job, which was often.

Her marriage consisted of years of ups and downs, some her fault, some his, but they somehow managed to stay together until she passed away. But the gambling always remained a very touchy subject between them. Jade and Debbie used to take trips to Laughlin all the time, but those trips definitely came to an end, once Jade's husband discovered her losses. It made Debbie sad to lose her gambling partner, but it was probably the best thing for her, too, at least financially. Jade still sneaked off to the local donut shop to play Keno every chance she got, clear up until she became too ill to leave the house.

Over a year ago, she developed a constant cough, which at first was misdiagnosed. Eventually they discovered that she had a rare form of lung disease. She was a smoker, but according to the medical books, this disease was not brought on by smoking, and usually only affected Asian women. After enduring lung surgery, and then surgery to her brain also, as the cancer had spread throughout her body, she passed away.

It was difficult to watch her decline, to see her with the side of her head shaved, and staples running up the entire surface of her skull, especially because she was always a very physically and emotionally strong woman. For a while, after her surgeries, she could still sit and visit, talking as if nothing had happened to her, although she would tire fairly quickly. She was a tough old gal, and if anyone could beat the odds, she would be the one, but it wasn't to be.

During one of Debbie's visits, Jade made her sneak out and buy her some lottery tickets, right under her husband's nose. Debbie was nervous about getting caught, knowing how Sean felt about her gambling, but since Jade was so sick, she made some lame excuse about having to go interview a suspect who lived nearby, and then she would come back and pick up her husband, who would stay and visit with Jade. Sean seemed to buy the lie, at least he never said anything. Jade had sent Debbie to her local watering hole, the donut shop, and when Debbie told them that she was there to buy Jade's tickets, all the patrons inside started asking about her. It was clear, that she had spent a lot of time at that donut shop, and made lots of new gambling pals. She was pretty much out of it the last time Debbie was able to visit with her. Her kids had her sitting in her beloved garden, picking weeds, but mentally she was barely lucid. She hardly acknowledged Debbie's presence until she got ready to leave and then she looked up at her and said "win the lottery". Jade and Debbie always had a deal that if one of them won, the winner would pay off the other one's debt. So even though Jade's gambling days were over, she still held out hope that Debbie would win for them.

Aggie

Lastly, one of our most memorable characters at the PD was little Aggie. She was a feisty, four foot little lady in her late eighties when Debbie and I befriended her. It was actually Debbie who took her under her wing at first, as they worked for the same supervisor, and had related job interests. She had a sharp memory and great wit, and she could tell jokes that would make a sailor blush.

This woman was like the Eveready Bunny, who seemed to go, and go, and go. We would take her on our shopping sprees, and then to lunch, where she would count her pennies before ordering. Now this woman did not have to work, but like some others, it was her social time. She had plenty of money in the bank, and also stashed throughout her house, according to her. She always carried a fistful of cash in her wallet, usually a thousand at a time, in case she found something she wanted to buy.

When it came to ordering something a little pricier on the menu, she would check her wallet and then ponder her decision, whether she really wanted to spend the extra two dollars to get what she wanted. And if she got something she wasn't happy with, everyone knew it! She would throw a histrionic fit and get this really nasty look on her face, and just pout through the whole lunch. One time she ordered spaghetti and they garnished the outer edge of the plate with parsley flakes, not even on the spaghetti, and you would have thought they served her a skunk. She put on her pouty face and complained loudly, the whole time trying to brush the flakes off the plate like they were poison.

But the worst part of all of our lunches was at the end, when it came to leaving the tip. Every single time she would quite loudly say something like "why are we paying for her college?" causing Debbie and me to cringe. Now we're talking two or three dollars as her portion of the tip, from someone who easily carried around a thousand bucks at all times. Her little hand would start to quiver and then she would make a fist, clutching the two bucks tightly until she reluctantly put it in the tip tray. We always told her, she only needed to throw in two or three dollars and then Debbie and I would leave extra, so we didn't short change the waiter or waitress, whom Aggie tended to run ragged with her special requests. I have to admit, I'm guilty of keeping them running, too; they never served enough butter to make me happy.

There was one waitress in particular at one of our favorite spots, who really catered to, and fawned over Aggie, treating her like her own mother. After several years of knowing this lady, she decided to leave the state to marry her true love. Since we found that she was more like a friend than just our waitress, we decided to give her a going away gift. Debbie and I both brought her a gift and also left her a nice tip. Aggie didn't bring a gift, but asked us what she should leave for a tip. We told her we had each left her $20. You would've thought, she was going to fall out of her chair! She took her well stuffed wallet and started shuffling through the bills with a look of great concentration, as though she was looking for something specific, or pondering a huge decision. She finally pulled out a five dollar bill, and didn't look any too happy about even doing that. She was absolutely sure that five dollars was so generous that she clutched that bill in her little hand until the waitress came by and then she grabbed her hand and put the bill in it with a flourish, as though she was giving her a hundred dollars, not five.

Debbie and I always thought it was sad that at her age she lived so frugally, even though she had plenty of money, and could have used it to enjoy the final years of her life. She lived in a mobile home that was really uninhabitable, at least I would never have lived there, or even stayed there for any period of time. She had lived there for 50 years, and had done nothing to it in all those years, not even cleaning the carpet! And I'm sure the walls were full of mold. We tried to talk her into having someone come in and clean, but she was too embarrassed to have anyone see her mess.

Before Aggie admitted to us that she had a lot of money, we assumed that she was near penniless, since she lived so frugally and was still working in her 80's. So we got volunteers, young kids from the Search and Rescue program at work, along with Debbie's husband and a Lieutenant from HBPD, to go over and clean up her yard, after she got a warning from the mobile home park. It was an all-day undertaking and those kids worked their butts off. Aggie never offered them a penny for their efforts, and actually complained for days afterwards about one of her favorite plants being damaged. Debbie and I were shocked that she would complain about anything; out of the kindness of their hearts, all those people had devoted their own time to help her, because they thought she was poor, when in fact, unbeknownst to us at the time, she could have easily hired someone to do it.

My partner, Joe, also volunteered twice to trim her trees, which was a pretty big job, and while she did break down and buy him a bottle of wine, it was the cheapest bottle she could find, and he never drank it. She had a daughter, with whom she had a love/hate relationship, mostly hate, and she was always telling us how this daughter was trying to take her money. Whenever the daughter did come to town, which was very infrequent, she would stay at her mother's dirty place and attempt to clean it up somewhat. Her husband would tag along and do some work around the place also, and it was always understood that they expected to be paid for their services. Aggie always gave them anywhere from a few hundred to a couple thousand for their efforts, but they were greedy and it was never enough to satisfy them. When they stayed with her, they constantly wanted to go out to eat, and Aggie always paid, they never even offered. She paid for all their groceries and gas and whatever other expenses there were while they were there. Even though I didn't envy them having to clean that house, this was still their elderly mother and I found it appalling that they only helped her if they were paid. It never failed, that Aggie would complain long and loud after they left, about having to give them money, and about her daughter cleaning and moving things around. Knowing the condition her house was in, no matter how little respect I had for her daughter, I thought she did deserve kudos for tackling that mess and I was always surprised to hear Aggie complain about it.

Aggie could be very demanding at times. She got nervous when her gas tank got below ¾ of a tank, and she would have one of the guys from the police shop, where she worked part-time, top off her gas tank and then pick up lunch for her afterwards. They took care of all the mechanical work on her car for free, they even took her car to the carwash, basically ran most of her errands for her. She never even offered to buy them lunch to repay their kindness. One of the mechanics, Frank, who worked with Aggie for many years, took her under his wing and treated her like his own mother.

When she had an accident one night coming home from work, it was the end of her driving days, which was really a Godsend for others on the road, but the beginning of the end for Aggie. Once she lost her independence and her ability to get to work, she seemed to deteriorate rapidly. It was left to Debbie, Frank, and me to help her get to the grocery store, doctor appointments, etc., since, as usual, her family was nowhere to be found.

Once she became housebound, she decided that she wanted a cat to keep her company, because they were easy to care for. Debbie and I tried to discourage her, because she had never liked cats before, complaining about them pooping in her yard. We didn't think her house was a good or safe environment for a pet, nor did we think she was physically capable of taking care of it. She kept asking us to take her to shelters to look for one, and we just kept making excuses, hoping that she would forget about it.

One day her daughter showed up at Aggie's with a cat that one of her friends needed a home for. It figured! Her daughter never gave her a darn thing, and then she would show up with a cat... the last thing that Aggie needed! All I can say is: that poor pathetic cat! Aggie wanted the cat to be a lap cat and keep her company, although we had explained over and over to her that cats weren't like that, they aren't like dogs; they go where they want when they want. The cat wouldn't come out from underneath the bed, which was now in her living room, so Aggie and her daughter bought a leash, dragged the poor cat from underneath the bed, and leashed it, foolishly thinking she could make it stay with her on the bed if it was on a leash.

Well, dear reader, if you've ever owned a cat, I don't have to tell you how that worked out. The cat disappeared, together with the leash. We would ask Aggie every day about the poor cat, and she would just say, she didn't know where it was, but she could see that it was eating and pooping. Now mind you, this was just a very small mobile home, so that cat must have had to search long and hard for someplace to go where she couldn't find her! Aggie became antagonistic towards the cat, because it obviously didn't like her, so I finally persuaded her neighbor, who was a big cat lover, to take the poor thing. Aggie was none too sad to see it go.

As Aggie's physical condition worsened, causing her to basically be housebound, Frank went way beyond being a friend to more like being her devoted son, pretty much on call twenty-four hours a day. He wasn't married, so he was in a better position to be accessible to her than Debbie or I. But sometimes she did take advantage of his kindness. If she wanted a ham sandwich late at night, she would call him and ask him to get her one, even though she knew he had to work the next day. He lived at least fifteen miles or more from her, so it was not an easy, five minute task for him, but he never refused her. I think all of us were afraid to deny her anything, because we didn't know how much time she had left. He would stop by and see her almost every day, making sure she had plenty to eat and was taking her medicine. He would go over on the weekend and organize her medications for the week, and do her grocery shopping when she no longer was able to. It was difficult for all of us to watch her sudden downward spiral. Up until her accident, she had been such an active person for a woman in her 90's. In spite of her faults, we still loved her, and on her good days, she was a joy to be around.

In the end, she did take care of Frank financially, which the poor guy truly deserved, after almost a year of being on constant call for her. Not to mention the many years before that, running her errands and being her good friend and confidant. When her condition worsened, and she knew, she was at the end of her life, we did our best to comfort her. Just when she started feeling better in the hospital, and we all hoped, she might actually be on the road to recovery, she suddenly passed away. On our last visit with her, she was sitting up laughing and talking, acting perfectly normal; then, just a couple of days later, she was gone. Her daughter and her husband immediately tore a path to her mobile home and ransacked the place, grabbing all her jewelry, which was high end stuff, and sifting through the whole place, looking for her hidden money stashes. It turned out, she had several hundred thousand dollars, making it even sadder that she had chosen to live her final years in a pig sty.

When Debbie and I visited her, we were never able to stay long, we just couldn't handle the smell of mildew and filth and stale food, it would literally turn our stomachs. One time Debbie had to run over to the front door for fresh air as she actually started to gag; she didn't want Aggie to see that and hurt her feelings. She made up some story about looking at one of Aggie's outdoor plants. Aggie would call Debbie at all times of the day and night, keeping her on the phone for hours, lamenting over her daughter's lack of attention and poor treatment of her. She even complained that she was afraid of her daughter at times. Debbie never cut her short or complained, even though it could be stressful having to console her all the time. We still find it so sad that she denied herself so much pleasure, just to ultimately leave her hard-earned money to a grandson she barely knew and who never had time for her until he thought she was dying. Even then, he only paid her a couple of visits. It's just really hard to fathom the mentality of someone who has the means for a better life but chooses to live in squalor and filth, just to leave their money to virtual strangers.

Heaven forbid her daughter would spend any of Aggie's money on a service for her! After her passing, Frank and a neighbor decided to have a small memorial at the mobile home park, where she lived. Many folks from her mobile home park came, bringing refreshments. One of the ladies handed each of us a candle, and we all said a prayer for her. It was an uplifting gathering. We all had our stories to share about Aggie and her antics, which were many.

One month after Aggie's passing, Frank was found dead, slumped over in his patio chair. This poor man, who had just retired, and could finally enjoy his life with no pressing obligations, was gone. He had become such a good friend to so many, and would be missed so much. Frank was very spiritual, and we all knew that he was with the good Lord above. We often thought about what would have happened to Aggie, if he had passed away before her, he was such a good friend to her, and took such good care of her. I believe she would have been shattered. But she was a tough little old lady, and would have survived. And surely, Debbie and I would have stepped in and would have made sure that she was OK.

Frank was only in his middle sixties, not old by today's standards; he should have had many more years to enjoy his life. There was a very nice memorial service for him, and many people from the PD attended, even a lot of old timers, who had been retired for a while, reinforcing what a good man he was.

23 COPS AND ROBBERS

At work several days later, I received a call from the front desk. The receptionist told me there was a guy on the phone trying to locate me. I told her, it was OK to put him through, never thinking it could be the guy from The Hop, since I never gave him my phone number or any encouragement at all. But I was wrong, he had tracked me down! I politely told him I was not interested, and would appreciate him not calling me again. Most men do not like rejection, and he was no exception, he did not take it well. His little flare of temper just proved to me once more, that my instincts were right; he was bad news.

That particular day, Debbie and I had a photo lineup we had to show to one of Debbie's case victims. We borrowed one of the Detective units and off we went. We passed by one of the local banks, where we noticed a couple of guys sitting in an old beat up Cadillac convertible right in front of the bank. One of them appeared to have a handful of what appeared to be credit cards and was shuffling them back and forth. It looked very suspicious, so I decided to get on the radio and call in that incident. I asked the dispatcher to run the license plate, in order to see to whom the car was registered. I just had a feeling that these were bad guys. The dispatchers did not like civilians to play cops and robbers. You could almost hear them moaning and groaning before they responded to our request. In a few minutes, a black and white pulled up and asked what we were up to. We pointed out the individuals in the car and told the officer what we had observed. He looked at us like we were a couple of idiots, but went ahead and checked the guys out. He asked us to leave, seeing as he had the situation under control.

As it turned out, they were not doing any illegal activity inside the bank, like passing forged checks. The officer got on the radio, saying that our intuition was way off. Shortly after this, we found out that the officer did in fact impound the car, as the driver was wanted for questioning in a molestation case, on which one of our vice detectives was working. This detective quietly commended us for locating a suspect he had been looking for. It was nice knowing our female radar was still working after all.

Although the street cops probably preferred that we stay safely out of sight at our desks in the Detective Bureau, our detective supervisors encouraged us to go out in the field. They didn't want to have to send a cop along with us when we did a photo lineup, or interviewed victims. It was fun to get out of the office sometimes, and certainly far more stimulating than sitting at a desk listening to disgruntled victims accuse us of doing nothing on their cases.

Sometimes the victims were worse to deal with than the suspects. All of us gave 110% to our jobs and assisting citizens, but some of them just didn't understand our procedures, and were difficult, at best, to reason with. They wanted their cases solved, the suspect arrested, and restitution right now. They didn't care about evidence, and procedures, and all those silly things required to make a case, before you can arrest someone.

For obvious reasons, we weren't allowed to go looking for suspects on our own, or interviewing them, since we were not trained to protect ourselves and did not carry a weapon. We did, however, get involved in some situations that made us nervous, because we weren't really prepared to handle unforeseeable dangerous events that might occur, but most of the time we found it very exciting, and it made for good stories! I could totally understand the adrenaline rush cops got when they got the bad guy! There were many occasions, though, when we interviewed suspects alone in a closed interview room. This practice later came to a halt, as it was putting us in a precarious position, since you never knew how a suspect might react to questioning. If something had happened to one of us, it would have been a huge liability for the City. All in all, we had a good and solid job, which was fun at times. Most of the time, supervisors and co-workers were great. But there was always one or two, whom you might fantasize throwing off the balcony. One, in particular, was a sergeant in the Economic Crimes Unit, who ended up being my sergeant three times. This supervisor had a sadistic side, and for some reason he set his sights on me. Once he discovered that I had nervous problems, he took full advantage of this knowledge, and, on several occasions, created such a hostile atmosphere for me that I thought I was going to have a breakdown.

I only called in sick when I was in bed with the flu, or too ill to move. This supervisor did not believe in calling in sick, and would phone you at home, usually when you were sleeping, letting you know that after three days out, you would have to get a doctor's release before returning to work. And then he would try the guilt trip; he would mention how your work was piling up while you were gone. I used to be so fearful that he would kick me out of detectives and put me back on a graveyard shift, that it made me even sicker. One time he even stood in our cubicle and quite loudly demonstrated a person having a panic attack, laughing all the while. It was obvious that he did it to humiliate me, since everyone in detectives knew that he was referring to me. For all these years I have tried to keep this problem under wraps, and when he learns about it, he makes it his mission to broadcast it to everyone, and to embarrass me as much as possible.

Although I suffered the brunt of his nastiness, I certainly wasn't the only one. He oftentimes made unprofessional comments about employees who called in sick. Debbie suffered from debilitating menstrual cramps and would occasionally call in sick. He loved to lecture her about how he didn't believe menstrual cramps really existed, and when his wife complained of them, he would tell her that she just needed to exercise. But Debbie was one of his favorites, so she didn't suffer his wrath at anywhere near the level that I did. Several times he attempted to pit us against each other, but his attempts failed, because we had become such good friends.

Something that will always bother me, is that when I was hard up for cash, I had sold him two of my best ship paintings for a pittance. The only consolation is that he really did take pride of ownership in my paintings and displayed them prominently in his home. I actually won second prize in a local competition for one of my paintings and was able to sell almost everything I painted.

I have seen this sergeant a couple of times since he was my supervisor, and always got a kick out of his reaction when I would approach him and give him a sincere hug. I've grown up a lot since those rough times, and like my grandma always said, "You catch a lot more flies with honey than with vinegar". How true this is!

A popular place, at the time, to have a few drinks while listening to live music, was The Hop. Going to The Hop was always exciting, you never knew whom you would meet, or what would happen. This particular evening turned out to be more annoying than exciting, a fitting end to a miserable weekend. There was one guy who would just not leave me alone. He kept asking me to dance, and I repeatedly declined. Once I realized, he wasn't going to give up, I relented and got up for a dance. As it turned out, my first instinct about him was right. He kept telling me over and over again that I was a woman in flux, and he knew what to do to fix that. I told him, he must be clairvoyant, because he knew nothing about me, and he wasn't a very good one, because he was way off base. Nothing I said would shut him up; he just followed me off the dance floor and kept up his annoying and misguided advice on how to fix the problems he presumed I had. I finally had enough and told Debbie, we had to get out of there as soon as possible. But she was having a good time, and I didn't want to be a party pooper, so I hung in there and just tried to look as bored as I could, hoping that this idiot would get the message and take a hike.

I made the mistake of telling him, I worked for the police department, hoping this might scare him away, but it didn't deter him one bit from his endless prattle. I wished he was someone I could be interested in, although odds are, I would have been turned off by anyone who tried to analyze me and my life without even knowing me. After what seemed an eternity, we finally left, and I hoped I had seen the last of him.

24 RANDY

Debbie and I couldn't kick our addiction to The Hop. Every couple of weeks, we looked forward to a night of fun, dancing, and if we were lucky, meeting someone interesting. This particular night I met an interesting character who appeared to be a free spirit with a great sense of humor. I love a good sense of humor, and I found his very appealing. His type always fascinated me, regardless of appearance. He had some physical attributes that might not have appealed to everyone, but I found him attractive in a weird sort of way. He was on the short side, and almost looked somewhat out of proportion, as his head seemed to belong to a larger frame. Despite this distraction, his eyes were the Paul Newman blue, and he sported a headful of dark, thick hair, which aided in cutting down the size of his noggin. His Italian personality was extremely charming, and he knew how to use the attributes that he possessed.

After an hour of conversation, he said, there was something I should know about him as he started to lift up his shirt, and proudly displayed his upper torso, which had a defibrillator implanted in his chest cavity. He proceeded to tell me the whole story behind this contraption: His heart periodically would stop beating, and when this occurs, electric pads are used to shock his heart back into action. I felt a strong sense of empathy towards him, admiring his pluck that no matter how serious his condition appeared to be, he was not allowing it to slow him down. He believed in living life to the fullest; he was not afraid of anything. The manner in which he was shooting down jiggers of Tequila made me a believer. Even with his physical disabilities, he was able to get out on the dance floor and shake it up. At the end of the evening it was the same approach: "I'd like to see you again; may I have your phone number?" I decided, why not? And gave it to him. I was always interested to see if a guy would follow through with a call.

The next day, the phone rang early, and sure enough, Randy was true to his promise of phoning, and asked if I would be interested in going out for dinner that evening. I declined, as I was exhausted from the night before, and needed to pull in my horns the following day. I was never a two-night partier. I'm sure my drugs, keeping me calm, had a lot to do with it, and probably mixing a couple of drinks with them was not the smartest move on my part. I told him, perhaps another time, and thanked him for thinking of me.

I did not hear from him again, but did bump into him a few weeks later at The Hop. He told me, he did not call back, as he thought, his physical problems were a turn-off. I assured him, it had nothing to do with it, that I was just not up for another night on the town. This evening he proceeded to tell me about his mom and grandmother, and that he was very close to them. He was currently living in their apartment house in Huntington Beach. Randy also said his uniquely different sister, who sounded like a gangster when she spoke, also lived there, along with her current husband and two kids. Randy said it was your typical Italian family, joined at the hip. He asked me if we could really get together, and I responded by accepting an invitation for a dinner at one of his favorite spots, planning to get together the following weekend.

I had mixed emotions about getting involved with this character, as I really could not read him too well, but I had nothing else happening on my social calendar. He became quite evasive when I asked him the normal getting-to-know-you questions, and I was just not sure where he was coming from or where he intended on going.

He did tell me that he had been married and had a daughter, to whom he was not close. Randy said his ex-wife did not have favorable things to say about him, and was sure that she managed to poison her mind against him. Once he got sick, his wife hit the high road, and didn't want anything further to do with him. Then he turned around and said that she was a "Twiggy" when they first got married, and after the birth of their daughter she put on an immense amount of weight, and he said he could not deal with it, as she refused to do anything about it. Randy said it was actually he who decided to end their relationship.

I asked him about his illness and what had occurred to create his problem. He replied that it was just one of those things that happen to people; another vague reply. I kept prodding and asking him questions, and was finally successful in getting some information on this guy. He told me, he had been on disability for the past year. Formerly, he worked as an assistant to a psychologist, administering tests to patients. His college education helped him in the past at landing good positions. I did note that he had an above average command of the English language, until he had one too many shooters. He appeared to have something between his two ears, which impressed me, although I thought it not too wise to be boozing it up when one has such serious health problems.

The following week he phoned me just about every night, wanting to get together. I explained to him that I worked a long day, ten hours plus, and was always too tired to go out during the week. We agreed on a dinner date on the upcoming weekend. When he picked me up, he said he wanted me to meet his mom and grandmother first, to which I agreed.

322

Entering the home of his parents, I was greeted with open arms by the two sweet ladies in his life, along with his stepfather, who appeared to be a warm and friendly sort. They immediately insisted that we have dinner with them, and wouldn't have it any other way. I was impressed with his folks and felt completely at ease with them, not to mention what fabulous cooks they were. Looking back, it was his family, the mom, grannie and stepdad that I was really seeking to have in my life. For several years it had always been just me and my mom, which was wonderful, but I really wanted to feel like I belonged in a real family setting. My younger brother, who lived in Mission Viejo was always working, and I was lucky to see him once a year. My older brother lived with his wife and kids in Louisiana, and I was able to visit with him at least once a year, when he came out to see Mom and me. I still felt the need to have more in my life.

After a most enjoyable evening with his parents, when he dropped me off at my home, he insisted on coming in. I was not too thrilled with the idea, but thought an after dinner drink or coffee would be O.K. Once inside the door, he made himself completely at home, which should have sent up a red flag. How could I gracefully ask him to leave without hurting his feelings? Before I knew what had hit me, he had fallen asleep on the couch. I felt like a louse at the thought of trying to wake him up and throw him out the door. So I threw a blanket over him, and proceeded to my bedroom and shut the door.

At the time, I had a roommate, Katy who had a boyfriend, Sergio who also spent many a night at the townhouse, and appeared not to know his way home. Before I knew it officially, he had moved in. I wasn't happy about the arrangement, but thought, I could certainly use the extra income for rent. The townhouse was spacious, with three bedrooms upstairs and two and a half baths, so there was ample room for three people to live comfortably, but I would have been happier to have fewer folks underfoot. Before long, Randy was showing up almost every evening at my doorstep, bringing homemade treats from his mom, and I could not resist them. We started seeing each other exclusively, as I never had an opportunity to get out and make my escape from him; he was always there. At times I did enjoy the idea, but I truly treasured my private time alone, particularly during the week; however, as I did not like being a single person on the weekends, I went along with it.

Ryan was still the number one man for me; he was always in my thoughts. Once he saw that I was getting involved with Randy, he became extremely concerned that I was hooking up with a looser. Time would prove his intuition to be right on the money!

As fate would have it, the townhouse I had been leasing was put up for sale. Moving was always, and shall ever be one of the most stressful experiences in my life; it never goes smoothly. I was never able to save enough money to put a down payment on a place. City workers were not compensated nearly to the extent that the public thinks. Private industry was far more lucrative, but I sacrificed money for job security. What we didn't get in pay, we made up for in benefits, especially the promise of a decent retirement. At my age, my focus wasn't on retirement, but I knew it was something I had to take into consideration. I had pretty much planned to work until I dropped, because spending a lot of time at home alone was not for me. Plus I really enjoyed my job, and looked forward to seeing the gang every day. It was exciting during the seventies and eighties; you never knew what would happen from day to day.

The townhouse, that I had currently lived in for almost three years, was sold. I went into panic mode. I was very fortunate to locate a smaller place just a few blocks away, which I was not crazy about, but there were no other choices in the neighborhood that I had grown accustomed to, and didn't want to leave. Being only five to seven minutes away from work was a luxury in itself. Katy had decided to get a place of her own, and asked if Sergio could move in with me, as he had no other place to go. Katy had dumped him when he refused to marry her. Randy decided if Sergio could move in, he should be able to move in, too. I wasn't ready to take this big step, so I told him he could visit, not live there.

Randy might as well have moved in; I could have charged him rent, as every time the door-bell rang, there stood Randy. My roomie, Sergio, had his eccentric ways, but was harmless. He was forever flossing his teeth as he had a horrid fear of the dentist's drill. The only problem with this was that I would find his used floss all over the floors and counter tops. If you wanted to know where Sergio had been and where he was, one just had to follow the trail of used dental floss. He would also spend countless hours in the bathroom; I could only imagine what he was up to in there, which drove my imagination wild. Some of our neighbors also thought he was a boyfriend of mine, even though he was twenty years my junior. I passed him off as my nephew, who was working his way through college and needed a place to reside. I could tell, no one was buying my explanation, which made me most uncomfortable. I felt, some of these people who appeared not to have much of a life, were viewing me under a microscope, as some of their comments were not too flattering, and there was not too much I could do about it, as I needed the extra cash to pay the rent. I would run into a lot of the neighbors at the community pool, where I would be confronted and put on the spot about Sergio.

It made me wonder what Sergio was doing when I wasn't around, that created so much interest in him and our living arrangements. I did my best to find out, but never did. There is more on the saga of Randy later.

Debbie and I enjoyed going to our local swap meet, which was one of the largest in Southern California. One day, as we were walking along, we had a brainstorm. We decided that we could make some extra money if we started selling exercise apparel at the swap meet. Being fit and staying in shape was a high priority with people in Orange County, and at that time there were no vendors selling exercise apparel. We thought we couldn't go wrong. We contacted a seller at the swap meet who was liquidating their equipment at what we thought was a fairly reasonable price. We later learned it wasn't so reasonable. They were very shrewd wheelers and dealers, and were in the process of opening up one of the first "99" cent stores in the county. They told us, sales at the swap meet were down, and they had tired of getting up every weekend morning before 4:00AM to set up their booth. We should have taken note when they mentioned that sales were down.

Debbie's husband at the time, Tim, said he would help us out and escorted us to their home where they laid out all the equipment that was necessary for us to get started. Now all we needed was a product. We scanned the papers and found a business in our area which sold bicycle clothing and workout clothes. We hurriedly made a phone call, and set up an appointment to meet at their warehouse.

We were greeted by a representative of the company who was more than eager to show us their merchandise. It was exactly what we were looking for, and our excitement mounted, thinking we were going to get a great deal on their products, since they seemed anxious to liquidate their inventory. Most bicycle tops were priced between four and five dollars and the riding shorts and pants about five dollars. Again, we thought we were getting a big bargain, but not having done our homework, and being overly enthusiastic to get started on our way to making our fortune, blinded us. We ended up shelling out $5,000.00, which was way more than what we should have paid. We no sooner shook hands and made out the check, than this guy showed up at our credit union to cash it. I guess he knew, he had two patsies, and didn't want to allow any time for us to come to our senses. We both woke up the next day with the sinking feeling that we had made a huge mistake. But now we were stuck, so all we could do was set up shop at the swap meet and hope to recoup our investment.

We had the inventory and equipment but nothing to transport it in. We could use Tim's truck, but then we had to load and unload everything every day, because it wasn't covered and it was his only vehicle. There was a lot of stuff to load at 3 AM in the morning when we were barely awake! We did luck out when a friend of Tim's decided to get a new car and trade in his old VW bus. He told us we could have it for what the dealership was going to give him, $600.00, so we bought it. He did warn us, the clutch would stick and it was a bear to drive. When Tim was not available to help us out, I attempted to drive it, which was a disaster at times, particularly when I would shift it into the wrong gear. The worst was when I thought I was throwing it in fifth as we were driving down a crowded street and ended up hitting reverse. There would be a terrible noise and we almost went sailing through the windshield. But the bright side was that we could leave everything in it, so we didn't have to unload at the end of a long day, or load at 3 in the morning.

We discovered, it was not an easy task to get a spot at the Orange County swap meet. The people who sold us the equipment furnished us with a number to call, and if we got through, we would be guaranteed a spot, which would cost around $100.00 for the day. Of course they failed to mention that it was virtually impossible to get through on their phone lines! If we could not get through on the phone lines, we had to line up in the parking lot around 4:30 AM, where lottery numbers were passed out. If you were not one of the lucky ones to draw one of the random numbers that were called, you just didn't get in, unless someone with a prior phone reservation failed to show up. We would have to remain in our van until all the numbers had been called, and then wait to see if there was a spot that we might be lucky enough to get. And you were strictly forbidden from exiting your vehicle during the entire time you were sitting in the parking lot, waiting. I found this out the hard way. After sitting for a couple of hours, I was feeling stiff and thought I would just get out and stretch my legs. The swap meet people came literally running over to me, screaming at me to get back in my vehicle, as though I had committed a cardinal sin! At first I thought they were joking and laughed, but as they got closer and I saw their faces, I realized this was no joke, they meant business! I don't think I ever moved so fast in my life, jumping back in that bus, as if wolves were chasing me! Of course, Debbie was sitting in the bus, watching this drama unfold, laughing hysterically. We later learned the reason for this rule was that they didn't want any cheating going on, no buying or selling spots among the vendors, something that would have been nice to know before they scared me half to death!

One day I stayed home from my police job and spent the entire day attempting to get through on the swap meet's lines, continuously hitting redial, and I still never succeeded at getting through. I think the whole thing was rigged for preferred vendors; we most definitely did not fall into that category. If we got lucky and got in, it was a mad rush to set up our tarp, get all of our clothes hung up, and get our display up before the patrons started showing up. Most days we didn't even make enough money to pay for our spot. Toward the end of the day, Debbie and I would get discouraged and leave Tim in charge while we went shopping. He was an asset, so charming with the ladies, and usually sold more than we did. We would go shopping, usually ending up spending more than we ever earned.

It was exhausting breaking down the tarp and packing up all of our merchandise, especially since it seemed, we usually took back almost as much as we brought. It helped when I could lie down in the van, or when we had Tim's truck to take a short snooze. My body was accustomed to siestas ever since I had been sick, and when I didn't get the time to unwind, I was worthless. Soon we got desperate to make some money. So Tim started going to the Garment District in L.A., buying merchandise that we thought would sell. We actually made more money on that, than our exercise apparel, but still not nearly enough to cover expenses.

There were occasions when we didn't get into the Orange County swap meet, and would rush off to a smaller one at a local college. After getting up early and preparing for a day of sales, it was discouraging not to be able to try and sell something. The other swap meets did not have the foot traffic like the O.C. had, so we really did not do well at all. But we were determined not to become discouraged and give up the sinking ship.

This was one of the most enervating of all of my wild ideas. It was hard enough to work a ten hour day at the police department, then fit in Mr. Rogers, and then be faced with this every weekend. Most nights I never got home, except to sleep.

After a grueling day at the swap meet I would head out for Mr. Rogers on weekend nights, to handle the night shift. My nervous system was going haywire, and if it weren't for a few medications and a couple of drinks now and then, I don't think I could have hung in there.

We did the swap meet venture for approximately a year. The only thing we made money on is when we would go to Los Angeles to the clothes mart and purchase jackets and leggings which were the in thing at the time. It was not much, but at least it helped to offset the cost of our space at the market place. Several times we got lost in the big city and ended up in some undesirable neighborhoods.

There was an incident where a big burly guy came up to the car and pressed his face against the window, demanding something. We were so shaken, we just stepped on the accelerator and got away from him and from that area we were lost in. There were not too many trips to the clothes mart without Debbie's Tim escorting us. He was a tall and handsome fellow, who looked like he could take care of himself and of us, too, so we were most grateful when he could pull himself away from his job and help us out.

When we finally had enough, and conceded that we were not going to make our big bucks at the meet, we sold our equipment at a loss, donating most of the left over clothing to charity. We did make about a $1,000.00 on the sale of the van, even after it was vandalized, which cost us $350.00 in repairs. This was our only positive purchase through this whole experience. I truly do not know how we survived the grueling hours and exhausting long days at the swap meet. It was an experience neither of us would ever consider doing again, even if we could have made a fortune.

Randy and I were in an on-again-off-again relationship. His folks were wonderful to me, which made it hard for me to call it quits. Jane, his mother, and I had become such good friends and enjoyed shopping and having lunch together. And, in typical Italian family fashion, I was often invited to their home for the most sumptuous dinners. Jane loved the police department, and wanted to work there in the worst of way. There was an opening for a part-time secretary. She put in her application and was fortunate to get hired. She was in her mid-sixties and it was quite an accomplishment for her, or anyone in that age bracket, to beat out the younger applicants. This position did not pay very much, but that didn't matter to her, she wasn't doing it for the money, she was just so thrilled to be a member of the department. She was old school, and believed you earned every penny and she definitely did.

Jane was also a very warm and caring person; her co-workers thought very highly of her. She was a tiny little thing, maybe 4' 7", but big in character and energy, she could run circles around people half her age. Jane was so thrilled that Randy and I were dating, and dearly wanted me as her daughter-in-law. I didn't want to get her hopes up, so I simply responded by telling her only God knew for sure what the future held.

Because of my traveling issues and Randy's health issues, most of our dates were pretty mundane. So one day we decided we needed to spice things up, and do something different and exciting. We decided on a three day cruise to Mexico, thinking it would be relaxing, and something we could both handle, he physically, and I mentally. We booked our passage and off we went. I had always wanted to try another cruise ever since the disastrous World's Fair cruise. One of the things I was most excited about, was playing the slot machines, even though everyone warned me that they rarely paid off.

We checked into our cabin and it wasn't too cramped, better than I expected. We had a port hole, and if you stretched far enough, you could see the roaring ocean below. At least we had fresh air; I think I would have been claustrophobic otherwise. It was dinner time, so with much enthusiasm we ventured into the main dining room, where we encountered the biggest buffet either of us had ever seen. There was so much to choose from, I spent a long time wandering the room eyeing all the delectable goodies before I was finally able to make a decision and fill my plate to overflowing.

Randy heaped his plate with crab legs and lobster, something I was deathly allergic to. We struck up an enjoyable conversation with some other passengers, seated at our table. In the middle of our conversation, I suddenly noticed that Randy appeared to be turning a strange shade of gray. I asked him if something was wrong. He chose that moment to inform me, that after experiencing heart problems that morning, he had gone to the emergency room. His heart was skipping beats and then stopping, only to kick in again with severe palpitations. He said, his doctors had given him some medicine and told him to go home and rest. I was stunned to the point of speechlessness that he would allow us to come on this cruise, not bothering to inform me of something as important as a trip to the emergency room that very morning! We could've easily re-booked for another time, but Randy, being the stubborn man that he was, insisted that he was not going to miss this trip, and that he would be fine.

After dinner we returned to the cabin, where he stretched out to rest, telling me that he would join me in the casino later. Believing that all he needed was a little rest, like his doctors prescribed, off I went to win my fortune. There were quite a few slot machines to choose from, and I had a great time hopping from one to another, although I wasn't winning anything to speak of. After about an hour and no sign of Randy, I thought I better check on him.

Upon arriving back at the cabin, I found him having problems breathing. He told me, he was going into V-tack, and would require pads to shock his heart. I frantically called for the ship's doctor. Unfortunately I learned the hard way that cruise ships are woefully unprepared for any major medical emergency.

The doctor showed up, gave Randy a cursory check, and promptly informed us that they did not have the equipment on board to help him, and the coast guard would have to be called. The captain made the arrangements, and fired up the engines, heading to Catalina, where the Coast Guard medics could take over. I'm sure, everyone on board was wondering what was going on when the ship suddenly started going full steam ahead.

When we landed in the harbor, there was a team of coast guard personnel and medics, who had the life-saving pads to jolt Randy's heart into a steady beat. From the cruise ship they evacuated him on a stretcher, and placed him on the Coast Guard vessel, where the medics immediately started to apply the electric pads to his chest. By now there was quite a crowd gathering on the cruise ship, hanging over the rail, cheering Randy on. It seemed an eternity, as the medics hovered over Randy, attempting to stabilize him. I heard one of the coast guard members ask if he was with someone, and the ship's doctor pointed to me. One of the medics approached me and said Randy would have to be "Medevacked" to Centinela Hospital in Inglewood, as they did not have the resources to help him any further.

By now the sun was rising, and I had been up for nearly 24 hours; not good for someone with my fragile psyche. I was already beginning to feel panic setting in. I'm ashamed to say, at that moment it wasn't Randy I was thinking about; my main concern was how we were getting to the hospital, not knowing what "Medevacked" meant, and trying to maintain my composure, and not panic. It was clear that I wasn't in my right mind, when instead of asking about Randy's condition, I inquired about what would happen to our luggage. I was told it would be returned to Long Beach Harbor where we could pick it up the following day. I was then helped on board the Coast Guard vessel. Randy was holding his own, but according to the medics, they could not get a blood pressure reading, and his pulse was dangerously low.

I finally got up the nerve to ask what type of transportation we would be taking to the hospital, and when I was told it would be by helicopter, my heart started racing faster than a horse at the Kentucky Derby. A helicopter! Were they kidding? I did not fly, and getting on a helicopter was out of the question. Before I even had a chance to respond, we were landing on shore, where the chopper was already circling overhead.

Once the chopper landed, the medics hurriedly loaded Randy in the back, where they started to hook him up to a bunch of machines with wires protruding in all directions. I was not asked, I was told to ride up front, with the pilot. I responded that I did not do flying of any sort. I don't know what I was expecting, I guess maybe a little sympathy for my situation, but that's definitely not what I got. One of the medics in the back yelled that if I didn't like it, I could stay on the island and take a boat back to Long Beach Harbor. He had enough problems at the moment, and didn't want to hear another word from me!

I guess I was more scared of the mean Medic than I was of the helicopter, because I found myself hurriedly climbing in next to the pilot. Thank God the pilot seemed sympathetic to my fears, and he wasn't bad on the eyes either. Hard to believe that in my heightened state of panic and fear, I still managed to take note of a good looking man! I was petrified, but the thought crossed my mind that if we crashed and burned, I would at least have a dramatic ending. Staying alone on the island was never an option; I knew I would go into severe panic attack mode, and most likely would have to be taken off the island in a damn chopper anyway, probably ending up in the hospital next to Randy. The only option was to board the helicopter and pray like I had never prayed before!

Up we went, and, just as I knew I would, I immediately started hyperventilating. The unfriendly medic yelled at me to knock it off! He had his hands full, and was not going to tolerate any nonsense from me. He threatened that if I didn't stop, they would turn the chopper around and drop me off back on the island. The pilot squeezed my hand and said, he would not let anything happen to me. I made the grave mistake of looking down, and upon seeing the ocean far, far below, my insecurities reached new levels. I loved the water, but not from this height. It seemed forever, that we were up in the sky. All kinds of morbid thoughts swirled through my mind, like: Would we ever set foot on land again? Or, would we plunge to a horrible death in the cold dark ocean?

As embarrassing as it is to admit, Randy hadn't even crossed my mind, I was too busy trying not to hyperventilate so I could avoid the wrath of the medic, saying prayers, and imagining all kinds of horrible outcomes that could befall us. But just so you know I'm not completely cold-hearted, I did hope and believe that Randy would be stabilized as soon as he was admitted to the emergency room; never for a moment did I think that he wouldn't make it.

Finally, we were approaching the hospital, and the pilot started maneuvering to land in the parking lot of the facility. This required turning in tight circles, almost like doing donuts in the sky. It made me dizzy, and I was deathly afraid that I was going to puke. I had been clutching the poor pilot's hand so hard that by now my nails had left an indentation. It had to be painful for him, but he never said a word. The pilot landed smoothly and I could feel the relief flowing through my body, I felt blessed to be alive. I had my camera with me and asked the pilot if he would mind if one of the crew members took a picture of him and me. I told him no one would ever believe this happened to me without some kind of proof. By this time Randy was being wheeled into the emergency room, so I felt sure that he would be O.K. He was far too ornery to kick the bucket.

After the harrowing experience of Randy's seizure and airlifting, he recuperated rather rapidly. Randy had decided that he deserved a new leather jacket for his birthday. We checked out the Orange County Swap Meet one Saturday morning. As a result of some new medication, Randy had a permanent erection. Don't ask me how I missed it, but I did. By the time I did notice it, it was too late, and we were already walking around the swap-meet. Leave it to Randy not to say anything! It was very embarrassing, and I asked him to carry something in front of him. He halfheartedly attempted to carry a package to camouflage the protrusion, but he was far too interested in his search for the perfect jacket to try very hard. Plus, I think, in a weird way, he might have been proud of showing off his manliness!

Once we found what he was looking for, the oriental gentleman who was assisting him, began grinning from ear to ear, barely containing his laughter. I almost died of embarrassment when I realized that he could barely keep his eyes from moving down to Randy's groin. He kept looking down and then back up at me, almost as if he couldn't believe what he was seeing, in shock and immense amusement. All I wanted to do, was for Randy to select a jacket and get out of there as quickly as possible! I could tell the poor man was trying to control his mirth with a light chuckle, but not very successfully. He just kept glancing back and forth between me and Randy's erection, with that ridiculous smirk on his face. Randy was either oblivious or just didn't care, because he didn't seem to notice the man's response. Once we got out of there, I told Randy, I would never go anywhere with him again, unless he had his privates under control. The look of disbelief and glee on that man's face is forever ingrained in my memory!

I asked Randy what kind of medicine he was taking to produce such dramatic results. He proceeded to tell me that he gave himself a shot in the penis in order to maintain an erection, and sometimes it took a while to deflate. He also told me it could be dangerous for him, if it remained erect for over four hours. I asked him why in the world he would give himself a shot before heading out for the swap meet, and he said that he was experimenting. To say he could be exasperating at times, is a great understatement!

Later that night, Randy decided that it was time for another shot, and out came the needle. Unfortunately the erection had lasted for over five hours, and started to become quite painful. He phoned his doctor, whose office was in Los Angeles, and explained his tale of woe. His doctor told him to come into the office right away, where another shot would have to be administered in order for the erection to deflate, otherwise he could be in for some serious complications. This episode occurred well before the discovery of Viagra.

It happened to be 2:30 AM when we left for his doctor's office. I was amazed that any doctor would get up in the middle of the night to assist with this type of dysfunction, but I learned later that this procedure was still in the trial stage, so it was being closely monitored. This particular doctor was one of the innovators of the procedure, and had invested his own time and money, so he felt responsible for any mishap that might occur along the way. At least, this is what he told Randy.

I waited outside in the office area, listening to Randy squeal like a stuck pig inside the examination area. I'm sure having shots administered in such a sensitive area had to be excruciating. I heard some choice swear words, along with, "you've got to be kidding" a few times. The process took over an hour, and I could hardly keep my eyes open. I had to show up for work no matter what, as I had the supervisor from hell, who would've liked nothing better than for me to give him an excuse for disciplinary procedures against me. I had just missed three days of work with the flu, so I knew, he would not be appreciative of me missing any more time from work.

The doctor finally succeeded to get Randy's erection under control. As we headed home, he whimpered a lot, telling me, he never wanted me to go through something like that; which, of course, was not at all likely, since my plumbing was significantly different from his. This experience cured him of the desire to continue using those shots; nothing was worth enduring what he had been through.

I managed to drag myself into the office, where I sat in my chair with my eyes half closed, feeling as though I had been hit by a Mack Truck. Not getting my nightly zzzz's was one of the worst physical abuses for me. I was totally worthless, but I did not let my sadistic boss know that. I had ways of camouflaging my weaknesses, and always put on a big happy face for the boss.

Randy was on many medications, and when he drank, he became a demon. It got to the point where I could not handle his mood swings and foul mouth. But before I wised up and threw in the towel, I made a very bad financial mistake and unknowingly became a co-signer for Randy on a brand new Toyota Camry. For a long time, Randy had been talking about purchasing a new Toyota. He was always paying a visit to the local dealer in town, checking out the cars. On this fateful day, he convinced me to go with him, just to look. Once there, he introduced me to this salesman he had talked to on several occasions, telling me that he was a good guy, very up front and honest. They both sat me down, and started telling me about the wonderful deal he could give us. I totally did not understand the salesman when he was explaining all the details to me. Between this jerk and Randy, I was led to believe that if I signed on the dotted line, I would not be financially responsible should anything happen – w r o n g!

When we left the car agency, I had a sinking feeling in the pit of my stomach. What stupid thing had I just done? Randy tried to convince me that I had nothing to worry about; that he was always on time with his payments, and should something happen, his mom would cover for him. He said, his mother told him on several occasions that I was always the daughter she wished she had, and he knew she would do anything for me. But I was still upset, mostly with myself, because I had let them play me, and I felt like a fool. I still don't know what I was thinking at the time, because I really did know better.

After this fiasco, my feelings of dislike toward Randy started growing. I felt used, and now with this financial thing hanging over my head, a little trapped. As promised, he was punctual with his payments, but the thought of something going awry was always in the back of my mind. I told him that I did not appreciate what he did to me, and that I should have turned in a complaint against the salesman who played along with it. After all, I didn't even like the stupid car, and $22,000.00 off the lot was a lot of money, which I could in no way afford to pay if something happened. As time went on, I realized, I couldn't get past the deep feelings of betrayal I felt towards Randy, so eventually I asked him to move out, and that it was best that we call this relationship off. But I tried to keep things as cordial and friendly as possible; I didn't want him to be so upset with me that he wouldn't continue to honor his financial obligations.

It wasn't long after Randy and I parted ways, that he went on the prowl anew and met a new victim. After knowing each other for only a month, Randy talked the poor woman into marrying him. I had no doubt that he had ulterior motives, maybe moving in with her was the only way he could move out of his parents' small apartment, as he had done with me. I was still worried about the car being in my name, so I asked his mother to have him contact me, hoping that maybe his new spouse would put it in her name. Randy did call me, but it was with disturbing news. He said the car was parked out on the street, and was the victim of a hit and run. I told him in no uncertain terms that he needed to get the car repaired, and registered in his or his new wife's name. He assured me, he would take care of it, as he knew his mother would come down hard on him if he didn't. He never wanted his mom mad at him, because it seemed, he always needed something from her, plus I'm sure he did not want to be removed from her will. She and her husband owned an apartment building in Huntington Beach that held four units, one of which was occupied by his sister with her husband and two kids, and he knew, someday he would inherit part of that property.

Several weeks later I got a call from Randy. He told me, he had the car repaired, and I shouldn't worry about anything. Again, I stressed the importance of his transferring the title out of my name. Once again, he said, he was in the process of taking care of it, and I should basically cool my jets.

Not long after this conversation, I learned that Randy and his new wife had purchased a condo in the San Diego area. I was also told that he had been arrested, after threatening his wife. He had been drinking and acting crazy, and knowing that he owned a handgun, she ended up calling the cops on him.

He served several weeks in the county jail, and before his release date, I went to my sergeant to inform him of what had happened. I told him of my concerns regarding the car. I told him that Randy's wife had called me and said that they had not made the transfer, and thought I should know where the car was. She said she didn't want to have anything to do with the car, or with Randy; she was through with the relationship. I asked my boss if I had the right to pick up the car, since my name was on the title, and he actually stressed to me the importance of doing just that.

The car was in the San Diego area, and I needed two people to help me out, because I didn't do freeway driving, and San Diego was way outside my comfort zone. My good friend Cheryl offered to drive me, and I asked my neighbor, Joe, to go with us and drive the car back to Huntington Beach.

Cheryl, Joe, and I headed to the area where I was told the Toyota was sitting abandoned. We finally found it, parked under a tree, filthy and covered bumper to bumper in bird droppings. We cleaned the windshield as best we could, and

Joe drove the car back to my house, where I locked it up in the garage. I didn't trust Randy, so I knew that I would have to find another location to store the car, once Randy was released from jail. Luckily, I had a neighbor friend who had a vacant spot in her garage, and she kindly offered it to me for as long as I needed it.

Once Randy was released from custody, he phoned me, demanding to know where his car was. He said he went looking for it, and was told by his estranged soon-to-be ex-wife, that I had picked it up. I told him I was liable for the car, and since he had failed to transfer it out of my name, I had no choice but to recover it, and try to sell it. I knew that I was going to lose money, but it was worth it to get out from under the responsibility of having it in my name. He didn't take the news as badly as I had expected, he just said he would buy something else. He could be very volatile and verbally abusive when he didn't get his way, so his calm reaction was an unexpected blessing. Now all I had to do was to find a buyer. It took a lot of research and advertising, but I got lucky and found an interested party, who was willing to pay almost what I was asking for. It was just a blessing to get out from under the debt and responsibility, even though I took somewhat of a loss. Another hard lesson learned in life.

One particular night, Randy stopped by and wanted to talk with me. He was in one of his rare, serious moods, and talked about how he had made so many mistakes in our relationship. He said, he knew, he was out of line a good deal of the time, and wondered if I had it in my heart to put it all behind us, and try to work out our differences. He was choking on his words. I knew how difficult it was for him to express these emotions and apologize for his contribution to the demise of our relationship. His false pride had always been an albatross around his neck, and I let him know it. When all was said and done, I was not convinced that I should give him another chance, so I told him that while I still wanted to be his friend, I was no longer interested in a romantic relationship. I told him I was dating someone rather seriously, and I was happy with the new man in my life. I explained to him that my fragile nervous system simply couldn't handle all the peaks and valleys that a relationship with him entailed. My drinking had increased and I was a nervous wreck most of the time. I couldn't live like that any longer. And in spite of his promise to change, he was who he was, and while he might have been able to be "good" for a while, ultimately, things would return to the way they had been.

At one point he had pushed me too far; it hit me all at once while I was at work, and the flood gates opened up. I started crying uncontrollably, and began hyperventilating and choking, having a terrible time catching my breath. I ran into the little room inside the bathroom, where there was a cot and where I spent many a lunch hour napping. I figured, at least my co-workers wouldn't see me losing control. But I was sobbing so loudly, that everyone who came in to use the restroom, could hear me. Before I knew it, my friend Debbie and another co-worker, Joanie, came in, and said they were taking me home at the request of my boss. I was in no shape to go home and be alone, so we ended up driving around until my friends decided to take me to see my doctor, who was only a couple of miles away. I was in such bad shape that I didn't even want to get out of the car, so Debbie went in and talked to the nurse, who told her to take me to the nearest emergency room. Once there, the E.R. doctor appeared to be having a bad day, and was very abrupt with me. He ordered a breathing treatment, and yelled at me to lie down and be quiet. I told him, the only way I could breathe, was to sit up. He became very irritated with me, showing no sympathy for my plight at all. All I wanted was just to calm down and be able to catch my breath. His rude behavior actually added to my stress and caused me to start hyperventilating again. This man was in dire need of some bedside manner classes!

I had an inhaler for my asthma, and earlier I had used it at least thirty times. When they first put me on the breathing machine, I thought, I was going to pass out from so much inhaled steroids. But after about thirty minutes, I started settling down, and my breathing began to normalize. I was so surprised and touched by my personal doctor's receptionist who had come to the E.R. with a bagful of cookies to cheer me up. Acts of kindness, such as this, always remain in your memory. I don't know if it was the cookies, the breathing machine, or the caring treatment my friends showed me that finally put an end to my misery. After many hours, I finally snapped out of it. I'm sure it was a combination of all those things, and in spite of the E.R. doctor. After a few hours of shaking, crying, and hyperventilating, I probably lost close to five pounds. However, I do not advise this as a weight loss measure for those who want to shed a few extra pounds.

Regardless of the negativity associated with my relationship with Randy, I still cared very much about his family, and was very close to his grandma, whom I enjoyed visiting on occasion. Ever since his mother died, I felt it was important for me to spend time with his grandma. She missed her daughter so much, as most parents would, but even more so, because they lived together most of their lives, and were very close. She had a really rough time adjusting to the loss, but being a very strong soul, she handled it as well as anyone could. She was approaching her nineties, and it was amazing to me, how she held it together as well as she did. At any age it takes a huge chunk out of one's heart when a loss of a child occurs, it just goes against nature.

She and her family came to the states from Sicily when she was in her teens. She was from an old school of thought, and relied on her faith to pull her through tough times. She also loved her vino and pasta. I think keeping busy preparing meals for the family, helped her keep her sanity. Having family and friends over to share a good meal was a driving force for her; company was a necessity to help keep her sadness at bay.

25 RANDY'S DEMISE

One fateful night I was home after having visited with the grandma for approximately two hours, when an unthinkable tragedy occurred. I received a phone call from one of the captains at work, who was aware that I knew Randy and the family. He also knew that Jean had worked for the PD, and that Randy was one of Jean's children. He told me, Randy had been murdered by his brother-in-law and he wanted me to know before I heard it from anyone else. He asked me to come in to the PD for an interview, thinking maybe there was something I could add, assisting in their investigation. It took me a while to grasp what he was saying. Murdered? Randy had been killed? Once it sunk in, the flood gates opened up. I just couldn't conceive that something so terrible had happened to someone I had once cared about and lived with, it just seemed like a bad dream, and I kept hoping that I would wake up.

I went to the police department that night, as soon as I was able to calm down and get my bearings. The whole family was there, including Randy's sister and grandma. I spoke with his sister, Anna, who told me it was her husband, Donny, who had stabbed Randy numerous times, and then shot him with Randy's own gun. After the murder her husband had taken off, and the authorities immediately issued an all-points bulletin for his arrest. I asked how the grandma was, and she said grandma was in the kitchen fixing dinner, and had witnessed the whole incident, but was holding up pretty well considering the circumstances. Apparently, Donny forced the front door open and immediately lunged for Randy with a knife in his hand. The grandma ran into the room and witnessed him stabbing Randy repeatedly with this knife. She then saw him grab the gun Randy had placed under the pillow on the couch, where he had been resting, and started firing several shots at close range at Randy. Donny then took off running, jumped into his car, and left the scene.

Randy did not die immediately. Anna heard the gunshots, came running downstairs from their second story apartment, and saw Randy covered in blood. She phoned 911. The police responded in minutes, along with the paramedics.

When the paramedics arrived, Randy was still alive, gasping for air. He told them he could barely breathe and was begging for them to help him. They did all they could to save him, but ultimately he succumbed in the emergency room.

Knowing that the family would not want to spend the night at their residence, I suggested that they should come to my home and try to rest for the evening. After I arrived home and prepared some sleeping space for them, I called Joe and told him what had happened. I asked him if I could spend the night at his apartment, so the family could have enough space to sleep comfortably. He knew how upset I was, and said yes, without hesitation.

Once Randy's family arrived, so did a really pesky fly. It came buzzing around my face numerous times, landing on my hand several times. I was so shell shocked, I started thinking maybe this was Randy's spirit flitting about. It just would not go away, but I put up with it, because in the state I was in, I thought: you just never know. The hour was late, after midnight, and it was unusual for a fly to be so active and to pay so much attention to me. After about an hour, I was running out of patience and did come close to swatting the little bugger, but I refrained. It was just a very strange occurrence, and I have never forgotten about it. It is strange, the games your mind can play on you under such duress. At any rate, I was able to help everyone get settled and told them, I would be at Joe's, which happened to be just two houses away from mine.

I tried to sleep, but was just too stressed out, unable to clear my mind, tossing and turning all night long. I could visualize Donny with the knife in his hand plunging away at Randy, and then picking up the gun and shooting him at close range. I could picture the blood running from Randy's body, and the look of horror on his face. I thanked God that I left the residence two hours before this happened. If I had witnessed such a horror, I probably would have had a stroke. I know it would have been something I would have had a terrible time coming to grips with, and I probably would have had nightmares for years to come had I witnessed what happened.

I was grateful for one thing though, I was off work the following day and didn't have to try and explain to my co-workers, what happened. In some respects, (I know it's a terrible thing to say), I was also somewhat embarrassed by the whole tragedy. I felt as if a very private part of my life was now an open book. People would know, I had been in a relationship with him, and cops can be very judgmental, particularly the homicide detectives. Randy was not your ordinary type of guy, he was someone they would likely have looked down on. With so much personal information accumulating in the hands of the investigators, I believed, they would be judging me in an uncomplimentary manner, which I found later on to be the case. There was one detective in particular who was very condescending in his remarks towards me. This was very hurtful to me. Most of us do not want our personal lives to be scrutinized and discussed, particularly when we have to work with the same individuals who are criticizing and judging us.

On the evening news the following day, the story was one of the top features. Donny had not yet been apprehended. I had supplied a photo of Randy holding my beloved Gizmo in his arms, which appeared on TV, as well as in the local papers. I still hadn't really grasped the reality of this gruesome murder in my mind. It was just too horrible for me to get a grip on it, until a few days later at work when it hit me full force.

I was taking a break outside to try and relax for a few minutes when one of the girls in the training division, Susie, came out and joined me. It had been stressful, to put it mildly, to return to work and face everyone. Most of the detectives were sympathetic when approaching me, but there were a couple who were obviously keeping their distance. I could see in their eyes the look of what appeared to me to be disgust. Maybe I was wrong and misread their glances, but I didn't think so at the time.

While I was on that break, I started talking to Susie, and once she said how sorry she was for what had happened to Randy, I burst out in tears and started shaking uncontrollably. I couldn't believe how the dam had so unexpectedly opened up and for approximately thirty minutes, I could not stop sobbing. I wished I had a Valium at this point, as I was in the throes of hyperventilating. Later, when I gained control, I felt badly that I had unloaded on Susie. The poor girl was just trying to be nice, and once I started freaking out, she didn't know what to do. I felt like a fool, but there was no controlling my emotions at the time. I so wanted a Valium or at least a very strong vodka tonic! Back in those days when I could still drink, I could usually count on alcohol to help calm my nerves. But I would have to wait until I was off duty.

When I got home that night, I heard on the news that Donny had been arrested and was taken to Orange County Jail.

Randy's sister also called me, and told me the news with a sigh of relief. She said she knew her husband had a criminal background for minor offenses when she married him, but never thought he could commit such a violent act. Anna said, he had come a long way since they had married, and that he was a good stepfather to her two boys, but what he had done, was still inconceivable to her. She went on to say, she and the family were making funeral arrangements for Randy, and would let me know once everything had been settled.

Anna contacted me several days later, and gave me information regarding Randy's memorial service and funeral arrangements. In the interim, Donny had been apprehended and had been placed in Orange County Jail, pending his arraignment. He had not fled far from his former home, located in the Lake Elsinore area, where he was taken into custody without incident. I was surprised that he had not attempted to flee to Mexico, or at least somewhere remote from his last stomping grounds.

Randy's funeral service was held at a local cemetery, not long after his violent death. It cannot be said that his demise was unprovoked, as Randy was a constant instigator of turmoil with his sister and Donny. I was told, he even resorted to calling her employer, to make disparaging remarks about his sister. It was one thing to be bickering with her, but threatening her livelihood was really crossing the line. But still, no one deserves to have their life end in such a cruel and violent manner. When he mixed alcohol with his medications, Randy often became irrational, out for the blood of anyone who made him angry. He was known for calling people and going into a drunken rant. He was a man of many moods and temperaments, to put it nicely; you never really knew which Randy you were going to get. I have to be cautious about disparaging the departed; I don't want his spirit coming back and haunt me in something more sinister than a fly!

Prior to the graveside service, while at the funeral parlor, my body was overcome with cold chills. Because of my relationship with Randy's grandmother and the other relatives I had grown so close to, I felt obligated to attend the open casket service, but if I could have avoided it, I certainly would have. The room was filled with family and friends as well as past girlfriends. One lady in particular was extremely emotional. I later learned, she was a second cousin, with whom he had a fling shortly before his death. She went up to the casket and bent down and kissed him on the mouth. I was impressed that she loved him enough to do that, but there was no way I would place my mouth on a corpse, I don't care who it is. Maybe that sounds heartless, but I always heard that the chemicals the embalmers use on the deceased are very toxic. Plus, it's just something I simply find to be morbid.

The ceremony was short and interjected with a bit of humor by the priest. I know Randy would have enjoyed the quips he came up with. One remark stood out in my mind: "Not everyone appreciated who Randy was, because he definitely did march to a different drummer." The pastor got that one right! He went on to say, his rough exterior could be unappealing to some, but he did possess some redeeming qualities. The pastor talked about how charming he could be, and about his sense of humor. He mentioned his great love of animals and family, the two character traits that I admired most in him. He went on to make some other favorable comments, which helped to balance the not so positive opening of the eulogy.

I did force myself to go up to the casket to pay my final respects to Randy. I could see where the knife marks had been sliced onto his arms and hands. I did not know exactly where the bullets had hit him, nor did I actually want to know. The whole thing was so gruesome and mind blowing to me, to think that I was once close to this person, and now here he was, laid out in a casket, his life taken from him in such a violent act. It was very hard for me to grasp the whole concept of me having been involved with a murder victim.

Randy's estranged daughter, with whom he had little contact in the past few years, was present. She was a single mom with a young daughter. When she was first born, Randy wanted to adopt the baby girl. He felt his daughter was not capable of raising a child on her own. He had asked me at the time if I would take on the responsibility of aiding him in caring for the girl. This was his idea, not his daughter's. I toyed with the idea, but ultimately declined to take on this huge lifetime responsibility. Randy continued to try convincing me to do it, saying that he was fearful that his daughter's drug use would put the child in harm's way. But I stuck to my guns, reminding him that I had a full time job that would make raising someone else's child extremely difficult. Plus his daughter was not particularly agreeable to his proposal, so there probably would have been a long drawn out custody battle. She told him repeatedly that she was not about to give up her daughter to him or to anyone else.

I felt a huge relief after hearing this, because who knows if I would have eventually buckled under his pressure. My only hope was that she would do right by her baby daughter, give up drugs and raise her in a loving environment.

At the funeral home, his daughter spoke to Randy's second cousin (the one he had his final fling with) and to me, stating that her dad regretted two decisions in his life: the mistakes he made with her mother, who was his first wife, and with me.

He said, we were the only two women who were decent and caring, and that he should have tried harder to work out the problems in these relationships. She said we were the ones he had loved and respected the most. Hearing this was comforting to me. There was satisfaction in knowing, he wasn't totally blind to a good thing when he had it. I took one more glance at Randy, and said a prayer for him.

The next day was his graveside service. When I pulled up and saw the crowd gathered around his burial plot, I was amazed. I did not realize how many friends Randy had in his life. I knew his family accounted for many of them, but there were people I never met or knew about. I found a spot standing by one of his relatives as the priest gave another eulogy, and it, too, was filled with humor that had the whole crowd chuckling. It was an uplifting ceremony; one I'm sure he would have enjoyed, and maybe he did. I'm just glad there were no flies bugging me at either of the services. That would have been unsettling!

After the service, we were all invited to his grandma's house for a luncheon in his honor. Many showed up and shared stories about their experiences with Randy. There was no doubt, he had a wild and humorous side to him. You could tell that he was truly liked, by some of the tales people came up with. His ex-wife was also present. This was the first time I had met her. She was a quiet woman, and rather large. I had seen photos of her when she and Randy were together, and she was a skinny thing at that time, but those days were obviously long gone. I knew one of the reasons Randy had left her was due to her weight gain after she had given birth to their daughter. From what I understood, she gained an enormous amount of weight with her pregnancy, and was unable to lose it. It seemed very shallow to me that he would have divorced her based solely on this. I'm sure there were other issues involved in their relationship that led to divorce court; there always are.

His cousin, with whom he had been fooling around, made a very loud and obnoxious statement to the crowd, "Look around, here is all of Randy's harem. Boy, he was a busy little man". She followed with a hysterical laugh, punctuated by stony silence from the crowd. This unfavorable outburst obviously did not set well with the family, and she was cold shouldered for the remainder of the day. Not a classy lady!

I had a brief conversation with his ex-wife, and found, she was not much of a conversationalist. I think she uttered maybe three or four words, and that was it. She most likely felt very uncomfortable, as it had been several years since she had seen the family, or had contact with them. Also, not knowing most of the people present, had to be awkward for her. I didn't stay too long, as I also did not feel like joining in with the small talk. I made an appearance just to show support for his grandma, more than anything else.

It was not long after Randy's passing, that his grandma passed away also. I was glad that I had been able to spend time with her the few months before her death. She was so appreciative of having the company, and always wanted to feed me every time I walked in the door. I don't know how the family managed to stay trim and slim, the way they downed their pasta! And grandma made the best, ever. "Mangia, mangia" was their slogan. They always had open arms for everyone who entered their home, and there was usually a pot of pasta to go with the open arms!

Her memorial service was a touching one. The room was filled with many relatives and friends. Her one son came up to me and said this family was very fortunate to have such a good friend as I was. This was a wonderful compliment for me.

I'm glad I could help the family through some very trying times. I was always treated as one of their own, and that meant a lot to me.

As it turned out, I had attended three funerals for this family; Jane, Randy, and then grandma. This caused a lot of sadness in my life, for quite some time. After the grandma was gone, I never went back to the house. His sister and I were never close, so there was no point in me returning. This was another chapter in my life that was closed.

26 JOE

An opportunity arose for a short get away to the mountains. I loved Big Bear, so I gathered my courage and asked Joe if he would like to join me and some friends for the weekend. I held my breath while I waited for his answer, and when he said yes, I'm sure he could hear my huge sigh of relief. If he hadn't been interested, I could have been jeopardizing a great friendship by scaring him off. When my friends and I rented cabins, we never knew what we were getting until we got there. On this particular trip, there were not enough bedrooms for everyone so I asked Joe if he would mind if we slept on the couch in the living-room. Debbie and her boyfriend at the time offered us their room, but I insisted that Joe and I would stay on the couch. I wasn't ready to take the sexual plunge with Joe; I was more interested in getting to know him better.

It worked out great and Joe and I slept together with our heads meeting in the center of the sofa. I felt very secure with him and knew in my heart that this might just be the guy I had been praying for. We had a great weekend sliding down the mountains in our saucers and sipping toddies by the fireplace. I was really sad when the weekend came to an end, but I still have special memories of our first weekend together.

It was time to get back to work. I was always attempting to put some type of order back in my life. Getting involved in cases and doing my investigations was fuel for my brain, and helped take my mind off the past horrific events. Joe turned out to be such a great support system, and so was my terrific pal, Debbie.

My nerves were not in the best of shape, though, and I realized that it was going to take a while to totally settle back into a somewhat normal routine. Making matters a bit more stressful, my roommate decided to move out and take up residence with his girlfriend. This put me in a financial pickle, as on my own I could not afford the townhouse I was leasing. They say, everything is in the timing; it just so happened that Joe was in a similar situation, and was looking for a place to call home. It appeared, my luck was about to change for the better. We talked, and decided that his moving into the townhouse I was leasing, would benefit both of us.

I had been enamored with Joe for quite a while. He was a tall handsome man, very soft spoken, and I felt that he had a kindly spirit. I had a crush on him the moment I laid eyes on him. When I would go to the local pool, he would come out and keep me company. We had many great conversations and he was a very decent, normal man, completely different from Randy. He had been dating someone, and when I asked him about her, he told me, they had parted ways, because she wanted him to leave the state and move to the Oregon area. This was not something he was willing to do, because he had a teenage daughter whom he took care of most weekends, and he would never leave her. This news was music to my ears.

With our romance heating up, I was ecstatic! One evening he professed his love for me, and I returned the sentiment.

Debbie and Tim's marriage had been on shaky grounds for some time. Before long, they separated, and then shortly thereafter it was divorce court. Tim was totally destroyed by the separation and would come to my house with a bottle of champagne and get completely hammered. With many tears he would tell me how sorry he was about screwing up by indulging in a one night fling. Debbie could not come to terms with what he had done, and could not forgive him for his indiscretion. She started dating a guy who was crazy about her. Like most of the guys who knew her, he wanted to get to know this lady better.

We all needed a fun-filled getaway, so with her date, Mark, we four decided that a trip to Las Vegas was just the ticket. This would be a monumental test for me, agoraphobic as I am. I had not been anywhere too far from my home grounds, so this was going to be a milestone in my life; that is, if I survived it.

Since I had stopped the medications, vodka was now my sole tranquilizer, as I have mentioned before. On this occasion, before taking to the road, I made sure to have a fifth stashed in my overnight bag, and for the car ride, I took along a 7-Up bottle filled with this liquid relaxant, mixed with a splash of soda. For me, going through a desolate area, such as the open desert, is the very worst scenario and a true test of the nerves. I would have never made it, had it not been for my liquid refreshment. There remained one problem: that of sobering up, and then realizing that you are not close to your safe haven, which is home sweet home.

Las Vegas is not the place for persons with severe nervous disorders. There is so much commotion, lights flashing at every turn, and noise! I enjoyed my few trips back in the sixties and seventies, when the town was not yet so spread out, and the casinos were less flashy and more comfortable in my way of thinking. Each time I visited this town, I felt a sense of doom and gloom. One could possibly term my experiences as being in the presence of evil. I hyperventilated in those days also, but not to the extent that I did on this particular trip. Back then, I was on Valium and other assorted doctor-prescribed drugs.

Had we rested sufficiently before hitting the night life, my full blown, out of control, panic attack may not have occurred. Debbie's friend had family at the Hard Rock Café that night, and invited us to join in with them. Since this fellow had driven us through that God-forsaken desert, I felt an obligation to at least show up and give it my best effort. I was pushing my luck at the time, and I just couldn't swallow any more vodka at that point, to carry me through this ordeal. When we arrived, the volume of the music in that club, along with all the loud chatter from his family and friends, was more than I could handle. After an hour of this nerve shattering cacophony, I looked at Joe, and told him, we had to go, as I was feeling ill.

We took a cab back to the hotel, where I started hyperventilating, choking and gasping for air. When we arrived back in our room, I was in a full blown panic attack, with no stopping in sight. The whole night long I shook, sobbed, attempted Yoga to calm down, breathed into a paper bag and felt that horrible cloak of doom hovering over me. Nothing worked. I could not get a grip on my condition, and it would worsen each time I attempted to calm down. Shaking and crying seemed to be the only thing that helped, if that's what one would call it. I felt so badly for Joe, and didn't want to ruin his stay, but I had no control whatsoever over my condition. He tried to comfort me throughout the night, while I in turn encouraged him to rest. I had thrown a blanket on the carpeted floor to lie on, in order not to keep him up the entire night, as all I did was thrash about on the bed, disturbing him. At length, sunlight came shining through the window; this is when I caught a few winks, only to wake up and start shaking violently again. With all the shaking I took off five pounds on this trip; not intentionally, of course. It's a hell of a way to lose weight; not one that I would recommend, by any means.

Joe convinced me that a hearty breakfast might be just the ticket. I cleaned myself up and managed to restrain my body to a slight quiver, enabling us to go downstairs for something to eat. I felt as though I was on a planet that I did not wish to visit, and getting through breakfast was a challenge, as I tried to hold together my shattered nervous system. Earlier in the night, Joe had suggested that I should visit the emergency room, but that was the last thing I cared to do. It was probably stupid on my part to fight going there, as a shot to calm me down might have helped. At the time it just sounded too overwhelming, and I'm sure, my alcohol content would have registered off the charts, where taking a tranquilizer of any kind might have only added to my misery.

After breakfast I thought, I would attempt to get some more rest, but it never happened. The shakes and gloom hung over me, and there was no letup in sight. Debbie wanted to help out, but I discouraged her from coming up to the room. I thought it bad enough that I had ruined Joe's trip, I didn't have to put a damper on hers also. I insisted that Joe visit the casino and try to enjoy himself.

Once he walked out the door, I let loose again, and started in with another major round of hyperventilating. I phoned a friend and started unloading on her, explaining my doomed trip, and the inability of getting a grip on my nerves. She suggested that we head home as soon as possible.

When Joe returned and witnessed the state of my condition, he said that he was going to rent a car and that we should head out. He was fearful for me, if I went through another night like the previous one. I was so disappointed not to have overcome my out-of-control condition and to have ruined his trip. I so much wanted to play the machines, but couldn't keep myself from shaking. I was fearful that seeing me, people would freak out, and the added stress of trying to concentrate on poker would not have been an intelligent choice.

We packed our bags and headed out in a cab to a car rental agency. Before doing so, I gagged down a couple of vodkas in preparation for hitting the open road. An hour or so outside Vegas, we stopped at the "Last Stop" and it was there that I felt like hitting a couple of one armed bandits, along with gulping down a few more drinks. I have never been lucky with gambling, but I was determined to give it a try, regardless. After all, we had travelled a long distance in order to enjoy a few pulls of the one arm bandits. There was a band in the lounge that sounded pretty good, so we had another drink and listened to a couple of songs, and then we hit the road.

I did pretty well until we hit Buellton. I had totally sobered up, and really did not feel up to any more booze, but started worrying about the rest of the trip home. It would be several more hours before we pulled up into our driveway, and I wasn't going to make it, as I started freaking out again. One more stiff shot, I told myself, and that's what I did. I thought I was going to surely die from alcohol poisoning at this point, but I didn't feel there was any other alternative. Down the hatch she went and with many prayers, we made it home. Those last few miles, I kept thinking of my favorite movie character, E.T.: Home! That's where he wanted to be. And me, too. I thought for sure, that this would be the final chapter of our relationship, as my performance should have been enough to scare away any guy, no matter how patient and kind. But I lucked out!

Whoever coined the phrase "There is no place like home" said it all. I was never so grateful to be inside the door of my townhouse. After all the hours of hyperventilating, shaking, and drinking, it was miraculous that I did not experience a heart attack, or worse. Poor Joe, he really was such a great sport during my traumatic experience. It takes a special individual to hang in there, particularly when they don't really understand the problem. Debbie's boyfriend tagged him right, when he called him Saint Joseph!

Joe had seen all my flaws by now, and still claimed to love me. What a blessed girl I was! To have, at last, such a man of character and values in my life; a man with a gentle, kind heart! God had answered my prayers! From that time on, I no longer had Ryan in my thoughts. Joe was the man I had been waiting for. Ryan had retired from the force and moved out of state. Eventually his wife did divorce him and left him a broken man. This was the story that spread among his friends at work. I felt a great deal of sadness for the both of them.

After Joe moved in with me and settled in, I put the pressure on and spoke to him of marriage. He immediately froze, and said this was not the time to jump into such a commitment. My feeling was, if he truly loved me, he would want to sanction our relationship with wedding bells in the near future. My feelings were hurt, without a doubt. Joe is the type of fellow who has to think long and hard before making any move whatsoever. I knew this about him, and resolved to learn some patience, and give it time. Joe was the kind and thoughtful man that I had been seeking, it did not hurt, either, that he was very handsome. It was worth sitting back and letting our relationship play out.

I remember our first encounter when we spoke, my lip broke out in beads of perspiration, and I was hoping that he had not noticed. This sort of thing just didn't happen to me. He was so soft spoken and sexy with his thick dark hair framing his handsome, rugged face. He was a carpenter and years of working out in the sun not only tanned his chiseled face, it also added lines of distinction that were movie star attractive. His 6'0" frame was imposing with strong, muscular arms and shoulders, which I loved having wrapped around me. I felt protected and adored.

In the beginning, when all romantic encounters are at their peak, we were joined at the hip. Inseparable. This lasted for quite some time, and I was beaming with such elation and exuberance that everyone who knew me, noticed that I was a changed lady. After a couple of years passed, our relationship changed into a more relaxed comfort zone. There was always one problem on the horizon: Other women.

When you have a handsome fellow in your life, ladies on the hunt take notice, and think he is fair game. After all, he was not married to me. You have to have your radar on high alert, and be most vigilant watching the hungry crows out there, lest they snatch up your man. It is a malicious game that females play, and it drains the trust and confidence you once had in your relationship. It puts you on edge, to put the term most mildly.

With a comely fellow in one's life, there are pitfalls. Men are much to blame, as most of them like their egos continually stroked, and one can do just so much to fulfill their unrealistic needs. I can somewhat understand this stance, as I, too, required much attention, and the more they paid attention to me, the better I felt about myself. What a misconception this is! You learn this as you age. It really means nothing, except that you are insecure, and really could use some counseling, which I did seek. It is a tremendous letdown, though, as you age and your looks are behind you. I used to think, "What will I do with my life if I can't attract the opposite sex?" It left me with a very hollow feeling. I was accustomed to that ego feed. How shallow a person I was! This was the reason I started my starvation quest, and almost died for wanting men to pursue me, because I looked good. Thin had to be the key, or so I thought! The usual therapy consensus was that I was in search of a father figure. This most likely was one of the many hang-ups that burdened me.

Regardless of the pitfalls, I was, and am very blessed, as this was, and is a man who puts up with many of my downfalls. He understands and endures my panic attacks, and above all, my agoraphobia. My solo driving range being only two miles or so, requires that someone else who knows how to drive be in the car with me, so I can head out to my favorite Fashion Island Mall in Newport Beach, which is approximately six to seven miles from my home. Shopping is one of my delights and a ruination, or it used to be. High fashion and dressing tastefully and with class is a must in Orange County, if you want to stay in the game. I thanked God on a daily basis for my dear friend Debbie, who made sure that I could go shopping and to lunch a few times a month. On occasions, Joe would drop me off if Debbie couldn't make it to the mall, and then come pick me up. It was not as enjoyable without Debbie, but if there was a super sale, I sure didn't want to miss it. Of course, if the nerves set in, and I started feeling vulnerable being on my own, I carried a flask with my favorite vodka for such emergencies.

I now had a chance to introduce Joe to a few of my co-workers at a special anniversary party we were invited to. Everyone was impressed with Joe, and really impressed that I had finally chosen wisely. Rob and his wife were without a doubt the most in-love couple I have ever known. Rob worked in the same unit Debbie and I did. There wasn't a day he didn't rave about his "bride", even though they had been married for years. He could barely wait until 5:30 rolled around, so he could get home to her. They had been married for many years, and they had become like one person, if that's possible. They did everything together. Whenever you spoke with Rob, he would always use "we" and never "I", and she was the same way. Janie had dropped in at the department on a couple of occasions, and I had the pleasure of meeting this very sweet and humble gal. Many of the cop's wives were bitchy, as I am sure they were always worried about their husbands being tempted by one of the female coworkers. In a way, I didn't blame them. Women tend to love men in uniform, so they had many temptations. And back in those days, it wasn't unusual for them to succumb to those temptations. The divorce rate in our department was equal to most other police agencies, which is much higher than the norm.

Rob had been in police work for over thirty years, and was on the verge of retiring. He and Janie were so excited about his retirement and being able to spend 24/7 together. They had planned a long overdue month of travel abroad. They had saved and planned for this for quite a few years, and Rob would come into work every day, grinning and doing the daily countdown to his retirement. They had also planned to move to a lake home, which they had purchased for their retirement. Both of them were such thoughtful and kind people, of whom everyone thought very highly. Their marriage was one to be admired and envied.

We all hear true stories of tragic love affairs, but not often do we personally know people involved in those tragedies. Two weeks after Rob retired, and shortly before starting out on their trip, they were sitting on the couch together enjoying an afternoon cocktail and discussing their travel plans, when Janie fell over and collapsed onto Rob's lap. She died instantly. Later it was learned that she had experienced a heart attack. Janie was in her mid-fifties and had no prior health problems. Their lifestyle was a sedentary one, according to their cousin who happened to be a sergeant on our police force. They were not into the California fitness fad and just enjoyed a laid back style of living.

Rob could not accept and adjust to his loss. His drinking became a morning through night routine, taking the place of eating. So many people offered to help him, and the members from his church stepped in to console and encourage him, along with the priest, but he could not, and would not do anything to save himself. Rob was on a self-destructive path of no return, and nothing that anyone said or did could change that path. He ended up drinking himself to death, dying of a broken heart.

I had called him several times, telling him, this is not what God wanted him to do. He would tell me, he was trying to get control of his life; that he was not trying to commit suicide, as it was against his religion. He said, he just couldn't eat, but refused to go to the doctor to get some help. Family members and friends would bring him food, but it would just rot in the refrigerator. I wanted to go by and visit with him, and try to inspire him to rise above his sorrow, but I fell short of the courage to do it. People said he was beyond recognition; a skeleton of himself and I just didn't want to see him in that condition. He and Janie had no children, but they had a nephew, to whom they were very close. They also had a dog that they loved so much; she was their child. I thought for sure that Rob would want to hang in there for the dog they both treasured, but even his love for her just wasn't enough. After Rob passed away, their nephew adopted the dog, so she ended up in another loving home, fortunately.

I so often think of the two of them and hope that they were re-united in heaven. I prayed for Rob too, hoping God forgave him for his self-destruction. It was heartbreaking to know how much these two people meant to one another, and the joy and anticipation they had of a whole new life before them once he retired, and then see it end so tragically. Theirs was the truest love I have ever witnessed.

There was a certain attractive detective, who just could not take his eyes off Debbie, and he didn't mind if everyone knew it. He was so enamored of her that he took me aside and asked if I thought she would be interested in going out with him. Guy knew that we were good friends, and hoped that I might put in a good word for him. I liked him, so I told him that I would do my best to convince her to go out with him. Debbie had a lot of male pursuers, but was not in a relationship at the time.

I had a long talk with Debbie, and after many "I don't date co-workers", I told her, she had to throw her rule book aside and give Guy a shot. I told her it wasn't as if she had to marry the man! I later had to eat those words; but I was happy to do it.

Unfortunately he was going through a very nasty divorce. His soon-to-be ex, Lee, was determined to make his life as miserable as possible, for no apparent reason other than greed. She acted like a woman scorned, but actually it had been she who had been having an affair with a married co-worker and ended her marriage to Guy when Guy discovered the affair.

After the pain of the affair and the divorce lessened, Guy did have a funny story to tell about it. Prior to the end of the marriage, Lee threw Guy a 40th birthday party at their home. Dick, one of the guests, was the co-worker with whom she was having the affair. Dick had also been a co-worker of Guy's at one time. During a conversation at the party, Dick told Guy that one day he was "going to have a house just like yours", little did Guy know that he actually meant it literally, and would eventually end up marrying Lee and moving into Guy's house.

One of Lee's missions in life was to drain Guy of every penny; she even told him, all he needed was enough money to rent a small room somewhere. Guy had two children with Lee, and she never missed an opportunity to demean him to his kids, or to drag them into the middle of their disputes. Guy, on the other hand, took the high road and never badmouthed their mother, hoping that one day they would be smart enough to figure out on their own, exactly who did what to whom. When he married Lee, she already had a daughter, Laura, whose real father had committed suicide. He grew to love Laura, and she was the main reason he ended up marrying Lee. But during the divorce, Lee managed to poison Laura against Guy, which hurt him terribly, because he had always loved her like his own. Lee's harassment and ugliness didn't end until both kids turned 18 and there was nothing more she could do, although it didn't stop her from trying to cause problems. In the end, Guy is a better person for the way he handled the situation, and tried his best to protect his kids from the ugliness. It paid off for his kids, too, thanks to their father's positive influence; they are both good, hardworking adults. The years of dealing with Lee's shenanigans and lies, and being dragged into court, did take a toll on both Debbie and Guy. It is somewhat of a miracle that their relationship survived.

Guy was a super sport, and didn't mind me tagging along sometimes on their dates, particularly when we headed out to our favorite local nightclub, The Hop. He would dance with both of us. One night he sweated through his shirt so badly that Debbie had to buy him one from the club. It was lucky that they had his size, because he was a weight lifter, and not easy to fit. The downside was the shirt was white, with a high collar, which made him resemble the Pillsbury Dough Boy, but he took the ribbing good naturedly.

There was a special occasion, when Debbie and Guy invited Joe and me to go along for a professional glamour shot at a local photography studio. They put so much makeup on all of us, you needed a knife to cut through it. Although Debbie and I indeed thought we looked glamorous, poor Guy and Joe were less than excited about being "made up". But they were good sports and suffered through the make-up and sexy posing, without so much as an eye roll. Afterwards, we girls decided that we couldn't waste all this glamorous makeup, so we persuaded Guy and Joe to take us to The Hop to celebrate. I think I pushed my luck with Joe a little bit that night, but fortunately he went along with it and ended up seeming to enjoy being in the company of such good looking women!

Guy and Debbie started dating on an almost daily basis, and before long they were sharing a home together. They lived together for quite a few years before taking the plunge and eloping to Las Vegas. I was so disappointed that I was not there to witness their ceremony, but due to my own fear of traveling, I couldn't make it. Debbie was just as happy to have no witnesses. She always had a hard time expressing what she calls "mushy" sentiments, especially in front of people. She always said, if she'd had her way, they would've just done a drive-through wedding.

Guy always said, one day he would buy a beautiful house with a swimming pool for his gorgeous wife, because she had always dreamed of having a pool. They moved several times, and did finally settle down in a new community backed up against the mountains in South County, where Debbie got her dream saltwater pool. She is a sun bunny, and relaxation for her is lounging by the pool, with a good book, so she was in heaven.

27 THE TRIAL

During the many years I worked as a civilian investigator, I received numerous subpoenas to appear in court to testify. Usually the suspects would end up pleading out before it ever got to the point of a trial. Several times I did have to show up at court, but at the last minute the defendant would plead out. Having to testify was one of my worst nightmares. If the climate in the courtroom was light and I could joke around a little, I thought I would be all right. In high school, I loved vying with my classmates to be the center of attention. Getting up in front of my peers and showing off was euphoric to me. To my horror, I discovered, that the atmosphere in a courtroom is not like it is portrayed on the TV sitcoms. A little levity now and then would be a welcome relief for the tension that hangs over a room full of hostile and uninviting attorneys, judges, and suspects. The serious and tense situation made me more up-tight than I could handle. When I thought of being in that witness chair and facing all those people in the courtroom, I would talk myself into a near state of panic. Every time I managed to escape the hot seat, I thanked God for taking pity on me. I avoided the hot seat for so long, I convinced myself it would never happen.

I had been investigating a forgery, and the defendant had an Italian name. For some strange reason I thought, with a last name like that, wouldn't it be something, if he was a relative of a well-known mafia family; as if every Italian was somehow related to the mafia! I didn't dwell on it too long, because the case was solid, and the bad guy would surely plead out. But boy was I ever wrong, and my streak of good luck came to an abrupt end.

The district attorney handling the case called me into his office and told me, this case was most likely going to trial, and coincidentally, the suspect was a relative of a known gangster of years past. Just thinking about testifying against the relative of an infamous gangster nearly put me in a state of collapse! I explained to the D.A. that I had a foolproof case, and a trial just couldn't happen. I went over the facts in my case and pointed out that there was little question as to who was responsible.

The DA explained to me that the defendant had procured one of the most renowned defense attorneys in Beverly Hills, and he was going to fight the charges. I never could figure out why a guy like this would be involved in a case that resulted in such a small pay-off. I pretty much assumed he had made a mistake and was just not about to cop out to it. I had talked to the suspect on several occasions, telling him to clear it up with the bank, and the problem could easily be settled out of court. He assured me repeatedly that he would contact the bank manager and attempt to clear up the matter. But for some reason he never followed through. I received my subpoena, and learned that this was going to be a trial by jury, and I would be called on the case. It really did not sink in, even after I received the summons. I was so terrified of testifying, that I convinced myself that he was just screwing with the system, but would ultimately clear it up before it got to court. Much to my chagrin, I found myself summoned to court. And without a single drop of vodka to get me through!

Greeting me at the door was the defendant's attorney. My partner at the time immediately told the attorney that this was my first case in court. A big mistake! He responded by stating he would take good care of me. The tone and manner in which he phrased this comment alerted me to the fact that he planned on dissecting me the minute I stepped up on that stand. And I was oh so right!

Outside the courtroom, there was a group of well-dressed people huddled together, speaking in whispers so no one would eavesdrop. They were there with the suspect, even before his slick up-town attorney gestured towards them, pointing his finger in my direction. I could feel all eyes fix on me, and I could tell exactly how they felt about me by their cold piercing expressions. Right then and there I resigned myself that I would most likely pass out on the stand.

We no sooner entered the room and sat down when they called the case. I walked up to the witness chair and collapsed into it, dumping all my paper work on the floor beneath my feet. I never had the opportunity to organize them after that, so my case notes were totally screwed up. The judge immediately told me to step down out of the chair, and very sternly said "Ms. Johnson, you have to be sworn in" and then shook his head, totally disgusted with me. As if I wasn't already panicky enough, now I had ticked off the Judge! In my state of complete fear and anxiety, I had simply forgotten all courtroom protocol. When I lifted my hand, I was visibly shaking, and I could hear chuckles throughout the courtroom. I looked at the DA and he was glaring at me.

During our earlier conversations, he had told me in no uncertain terms that he did not want to lose this case. I was afraid I was not going to be able to comply with his wish. Right at that moment I really didn't give a rat's ass if I did screw up, I just wanted this nightmare to be over. Most people might not have had a problem with all of this, but this was definitely not for me. If I had looked out into that courtroom and seen at least one friendly face, or one smile, it might have helped to ease the tension, but all I saw around me was hostility, even from those who were supposedly on the same side as me!

I did a quick sweep of the jurors, trying to find what I hoped to be a friendly smile. The judge was an older man, extremely salty and demanding, and I could tell immediately that I wouldn't be winning him over to my corner. I glanced at the defendant, who happened to be a drop dead gorgeous hunk, who should have been up on the silver screen, not sitting in a courtroom, accused of committing forgery. He might have been gorgeous, but his eyes belied a cold and soulless man, a man whose sole intent at that moment was revenge against me! I didn't know if it was real, or if my mind was playing tricks on me, but I could have sworn that I saw something under the coat of one of his family members that looked like grey steel. My mind was going in so many directions that I just couldn't focus. My response to the first question thrown at me was that I had to refer to my notes. This was acceptable procedure, and this was my response to all questioning thereafter. With his angry eyes, the DA just threw daggers at me; I knew that if I messed this up, I was in deep you-know-what!

It didn't help much to look at my notes, because they were all a big blur. I didn't know what I was saying most of the time, I just prayed that I didn't sound like a total imbecile, and was getting at least some of the facts right. Half the time I was incoherent, and the judge kept badgering me, telling me to speak up. I actually wished I would just pass out and be put out of my misery. My nervous system did not handle this type of tension well, and I could feel myself on the verge of hyperventilating. Fortunately, the judge ordered a break, just in the nick of time.

I thought I was through testifying; wrong again. On the break I must have lit up three cigarettes. All I could think about was what I wouldn't give for a nice cold vodka tonic. Why didn't I take a slug or two before stepping into Dante's Inferno? What was I thinking? I was shaking so badly, that my partner was getting worried, and suggested that maybe she should ask the judge to take pity on me and postpone this for another day. Chances were slim to none that he would show an ounce of empathy towards me, so I told her not to bother. I half-jokingly told her, I was never going to return, because I would be on the first plane out of the country!

When I was called back, it was the Beverly Hills lawyer's turn to drill me. And drill me he did! It was brutal. I never pick at my nails, but I found myself digging at them, messing up my nice silk manicure. Had I been hooked up to an electroencephalograph, my brain waves would have been a straight line. I felt, I just couldn't take any more, when the questioning finally ended. There were several times during my testimony, when I knew, I answered incorrectly. The defense attorney kept badgering me, and all I could say, was "let me refer to my notes".

When I was finally allowed to step out of the chair, one of my big feet caught on the leg of the chair, almost landing me face first into the wooden box surrounding the witness chair. Again there were notable chuckles. I fully expected that I would get a lot of flak after my unprofessional attempt at testifying for the first time, but surprisingly, it was only one co-worker who gave me a bad time, and that was our court liaison officer. She point blank told me, if I could not handle myself in the courtroom, I had no business being in the position I had been assigned to for the past twenty-five years. This lady always carried herself in high regard, and thought she could run the whole show, even telling officers how to handle themselves in the courtroom. I was in no mood to be harassed anymore, so, very undiplomatically I set her straight. I told her I managed to get through it, and if she did not approve of my performance, she could get stuffed!

Once my partner and I were on the road, I convinced her that I had earned a shooter or two. We stopped at a great bar on the way back to the department, and I downed a double shot of vodka, which I felt I fully deserved. Although it took some of the sting out of the past few hours, the shakes were still hanging on.

Back in the office, no one said anything to me, which was a welcome relief. The next day I received a call from the district attorney, who informed me that the jury had voted in my favor, and the defendant would have to make restitution as well as probation. I told him, that was nice, but I guess I didn't sound convincing enough for him. He lit into me, saying what's the matter with you? Don't you care about the verdict? This case had been a feather in his cap, because he had won against a big-time Beverly Hills lawyer. He was excited and expected me to share in the excitement. I explained to him that I was just worn out, and couldn't get excited about anything, except the fact that I survived the ordeal. Thankfully, I never had to deal with this guy again, as he went on to private practice, and bigger and better things.

The weekend came and I knew I must be suffering the after effects of the physical and psychological trauma I had experienced. Post-traumatic stress syndrome is what I figured it was when I just could not stop shaking. I realized I should have been on tranquilizers during my ordeal in the courtroom. I shook so hard that I shed almost five pounds during those couple of hours. I know it must be difficult for most people to imagine how this experience affected me; if your nervous system is out of sync, it is something you have little control over. Considering the grueling circumstances, I thought I really did quite well. I won the case, and I didn't lose control of my bowels in the process. I think the jury felt sorry for me after the drilling I went through, and that might have weighed on their minds when they voted in my favor. Although I have to add that I did have a solid case against this guy, and more likely, this is what the jurors based their findings on.

It was about three years later when I received another subpoena and was called back into that infamous court. I was going to testify once again. Only this time there was no jury or hot shot Gucci shoed defense attorney to tear me down. Debbie's husband, who was the burglary supervisor, offered to drive me to court, as it was far out of my driving range, and I would never go without someone there for moral support anyway. This is the sign of a true friend. Not even my own supervisor offered to take me. This time it was not nearly the drama or trauma of my first round. It was cut and dried stuff, and my case was solid. All I had to do was answer yes, and that's why I was mad having to go through this. The jerk should have pled guilty, and it would have been the end of it; no courtroom appearance for either of us, a waste of taxpayer's dollars. I was so relieved when it was over. Immediately I had a craving for a vodka tonic. Deb's hubby said I looked mad the whole time I was sitting in the hot seat; I told him, I was. This case should never have gotten this far, and testifying would never put a smile on this lady's face; not ever!

I'm on duty: Taken shortly before retirement

Debbie decided to transfer to a new position in the Department. After having her as my partner in crime for 20 years, adjusting to a new one was a challenge. She put in for a position where she was the only one in her office, and the only individual responsible for her job. She had finally been called to testify in her first case, and while she did okay, it wasn't something she cared to do again. Plus she could see the changes occurring in the bureau, so she decided it was time for a change. She said she really didn't enjoy investigating cases, even though she always did an outstanding job.

More and more responsibility was being placed on us, and of course there was not enough financial compensation to make it more appealing to someone whose heart maybe wasn't totally in it. I, on the other hand, had nowhere to transfer to, unless it was the graveyard shift in Records, and that was not an option. Working days and having weekends off were well worth my hanging in there, despite the dreaded court appearances and some other disdainful duties that went with the position. I actually enjoyed the investigative complexities of my job, and getting the bad guy was rewarding. Plus I enjoyed the detectives we worked with; they were always entertaining us with their dark humor and practical jokes. I was truly blessed to have such a good position in the department. And when I was left on my own until I did get a new partner, I felt an overwhelming obligation of duty and think I did an above average job of running the show. Not too bad for a gal who only managed to achieve a few credits in junior college.

During this period of transition, my mom was doing poorly. After all, she was pushing ninety-four. She could no longer care of herself, so, with the financial assistance of my two brothers, we placed her in a semi-private residential home, where there were only three to four other ladies sharing the living quarters. She got along very well at first, but it didn't last long. She wanted me to care for her, but there was no way I could do it while working a ten plus hour day. It bothered me terribly, when she would get upset with me for not allowing her to live with me. The guilt just consumed me, but I couldn't have done it while working full time.

There were so many problems that accompanied her dementia. She would get up at night and wander around. On one occasion she fell and broke her arm. Even at the residential home, with people there to watch over her, she still managed to hurt herself. She would doze most of the day, and at nighttime she was wide awake and would not quiet down. Joe and I were living in a small two bedroom townhouse; there was not enough room to have a caretaker with her, one of whom she would have needed at all times. On top of that, the cost was prohibitive to hire someone to stay with her twenty-four seven. I couldn't stay up all night and keep a vigil over her so she didn't hurt herself. It was heartbreaking to have her so unhappy with me. All I could do, was to try my best to ensure her safety and comfort, and attempt to make her understand the circumstances. She suffered another fall, injuring her shoulder and ending up in a hospital.

I remember taking care of her in my apartment the first time she hurt herself. She stayed with me for approximately seven months. I did everything possible at that time to care for her. I gave her my bedroom. In the morning I prepared a lunch, which I packed in a cooler for her, and made sure that she had breakfast before I left for work at 7:00 AM. My bedroom was upstairs, and I did not want her attempting the stairs while I was not there. It was a draining experience, but one I never regretted. I loved my mom and under these circumstances, wanted her smiling and as happy as possible. I sure did not want her in pain, and did all I could to help her.

After the seven months, as I recall, I had a meltdown. I just couldn't keep up the pace of taking care of her; at times she could be very demanding. My younger brother was working on her apartment in Balboa. He did not want her coming home until he completed the painting and cleaning. Being the perfectionist that he was, it took him a very long time to finish the projects that he had started at her place. This went on the entire time she had been staying with me. My brother had his job to go to and allotted as much time as he could to fixing up her place. I recall threatening him, in a sisterly loving manner, to cut off his hair if he took too long to complete what he was doing! His hair is long and he likes it that way, even though it hides his handsome face. He took me seriously, and a couple of weeks thereafter, mom was back in her cute Balboa apartment that she loved.

I wondered why I hadn't threatened him sooner. I had roommates while all of this was going on, and they were none too happy that once she was able to manage the stairs, she was on the couch in the living-room, watching her TV shows most of the day and night. My Mom's long stay at my place was infringing on their privacy. I understood where they were coming from. They did not want to disturb her, but at the same time they wanted some space and time to enjoy the living room and watch their own choice of TV programs.

Returning to her last accident, it really took the wind out of her sails, and I could see, it would be down-hill for her thereafter. She quietly died on Labor Day, and I missed being with her for her last moments. I had just left the hospice where she had been confined, and went home to take a brief rest before I would return. When I woke that day, I had the most peaceful feeling come over me. I sensed then that she had gone home to the Lord, and that she was in the best of hands. It was a true blessing when she passed away, and at the same time very difficult for me, as I sure was missing her, even in her confused state. It is never easy to lose a parent at any age or stage of life, but we have to understand and accept that God is the one in charge, and it is His will. My mom did so much for me all my life, and there is no one on earth that will ever love me as much as she did. She always told me, I was the sunshine in her life, and I knew it to be true.

We had a touching graveside ceremony for her, where the pastor from my church gave a short but beautiful eulogy. My brother and his wife, a handful of relatives (we do not have many in this area or for that matter anywhere else) and good friends attended. We were so surprised, when about a dozen of the detectives from my unit joined us in the short celebration of my mom's life. This meant so much to us. The guys I worked with at that time were very special people, and with all my heart I appreciated what they did, not to mention how great my friends were to us during this very sad time.

A few months after her passing, right before Thanksgiving of that year, my precious cat Tinkers and I were cuddled in bed catching a few extra winks. Joe had left for work and all was still. Suddenly, the light on my dresser came on, startling my cat, and her fur was standing on end. I called out, thinking Joe must have walked in, and turned the light on; but there was no answer. I was sure that before retiring, I had shut the lamp off; there was no explanation as to why it would just turn on. Looking around, I saw nothing unusual until I heard the dresser drawers rattling. Boy, this got my attention, and there was no rest after that! The cat started hissing, and my heart took off, racing faster than I could keep up with it. Once the dresser drawers were no longer banging, the cupboards in the hallway off my bedroom started opening and closing. I shot out of that bed and grabbed the phone, trying to reach Joe, even though I knew he was nowhere close by. I thought, maybe he had staged this whole bizarre episode to get me up and moving. When I got him on the phone, I was breathless, and he had a hard time understanding me. He told me, we would talk about it when he got home. Finally, things quieted down, and there were no more incidents that morning. I checked the light on the dresser, and found that when it came on so unexpectedly, it was on the middle setting, when it should have been on the first, after being turned off completely the night before. I turned the switch once, and it came on the brightest setting and then I turned it off. I checked the three way bulb and all was in working order. How could the light have turned on in the middle and not on the first setting? I would have thought I was hallucinating, if not for my cat's reaction. She sensed that something unusual was going on; otherwise her fur would not have blossomed out like a threatened porcupine; and never before had I heard her hiss so loudly! I also have to add, there was a chill that filled my room, running shivers all up and down my spine.

Could it have been just my nerves? Who wouldn't have been on edge after such an experience?

I was not a believer in spirits wanting to hang around and spook people. No way did I buy into this idea until that experience. I came to realize that there are just some things that can't be rationally explained. This experience definitely made a believer out of me!

When I finally was able to talk with Joe and tell him the whole saga of my morning events, he just chuckled, saying. I probably was having a bad dream. I told him, if it were just me involved, I might believe that, but the way my cat reacted, convinced me that it was no dream, but a real event!

I spoke with an elderly lady friend afterwards, and explained to her what had happened. She always boasted of having special gifts and of being clairvoyant. Her theory was that my mom, who apparently did not wish to leave this earth just yet, paid me a visit to let me know she was still with me in spirit. I really did not go along with her beliefs of such an afterlife, where spirits were left to haunt the living, even though they might be friendly ones. Being of Christian faith, when one dies, the soul either ascends to heaven or goes down to hell. I just could not rationalize in my mind that spirits were prowling among us.

But I experienced another unusual event that I could not explain. I felt a presence lurking around me when I was in my bedroom. Once again, several of the cupboards in the hallway next to my room were rattling. I recall running into the living room and pulling Joe off the couch, so he could witness what I was witnessing. Once he entered the room, everything became still. Obviously he thought my imagination was running wild once again. I know what I have heard and seen to be legitimately out of the ordinary, and no one will convince me otherwise. Cupboards just don't rattle randomly, and light-bulbs don't pop on of their own accord.

When I spoke to my good friend Cheryl, who now resides in Colorado, and is of strong Christian faith, I explained to her what had occurred. She firmly believes, there are spirits that do exist among us. Her suggestion to me was to stand in the doorway to my room and say a prayer aloud, telling the spirit to pass on, and go where it will have some peace, where it belongs. I took her suggestion and stood beneath the door jamb and loudly told whoever was there that it was time for them to move on. As soon as I finished my prayer, the lights in the adjoining bathroom came on. They came on twice and shut off twice. It was eerie, but my prayer worked. The light fixture in the bathroom had never done this before, you turn the switch on or off, it never flashes on and off on its own. I felt a weight being lifted from my shoulders, after this had happened. I never again experienced something so unexplainable.

At a luncheon with my co-workers, I told them all about my twilight zone experience. One of the girls decided that I was probably a witch in a previous life and I had subconsciously called upon another witch from my past; I probably rode a broom alongside of her. I didn't care for her analogy. I wasn't sure if she was trying to make fun of me, or if she was trying to send me a message of some kind.

I had several good bosses, but one in particular was outstanding, whom I count as a friend. To this day Debbie and I get together for his birthday, accompanied by Gloria, the former chief's secretary. We enjoy gabbing about grandkids, politics, and of course, reminiscing about the really good old days; they sure were not like what they are today. Rich was always so helpful to all of the civilian employees, and did not look down on us with disdain, as some of the detectives were inclined to do. Some cops did not like us playing the role of Police Officers, when our bosses assigned us to perform some police duties. Going out in the field, interviewing victims, accompanying the guys on search warrants and various other activities made the job far more challenging and interesting. It was better than sitting in front of a computer all day, breathing recycled air. Some men thought it was not appropriate, but Rich was one of the few who encouraged it. There were several incidents when I needed to take my dog, Kookie, to the vet, which was beyond my driving range. Rich often volunteered to help us out, picking up Kookie and me, placing her next to him in the front seat of the detective unit, and off we'd go to the vet's. Wish I had taken a picture! It was great to know that if we had a problem, we could approach him with our latest dilemma and he would step in and lend a helping hand; this was offered to all the civilian workers in the bureau.

It must be (and I'm sure, it is) a drain on Joe to cart me off to the dentist and doctor appointments if they are beyond my secure driving range. Joe also accommodates me by dropping me off at the mall and picking me up later. I'm so fortunate that Debbie often joins us so we can share the high of bargain hunting and then relax in an upscale restaurant to unwind. Not too many guys would put up with this. He would also like to travel, but that is not on my to-do list. It took years for me to get my head straight enough to be able to travel to Big Bear for a weekend, without the use of medication. Of course I had Vodka to rely on if an attack was imminent. Recently I am able to travel two hours in the car to hit one of the Indian Casinos for gambling. What a feat this was! Double-Double poker is one of my passions, as it is for my friend Debbie. With Joe behind the wheel, we both (Debbie and I) await with bated breath to hit the casino grounds. Joe does not enjoy gambling that much, as funds are tight and he has to watch his budget. We commend him though for taking us, as we spend the whole day there, barely moving from our chairs hoping to hit that royal flush! When football season is in full swing, Debbie's husband Guy chauffeurs us ladies to our favorite Indian casinos! There he can kick back and enjoy a cigar and a game in the lounge. Wish football was a year round event.

My friend Debbie and her husband Guy are such a blessing to me. With their tight schedules they always find the time to take me out shopping and dining. They are the very best of what friends are all about and I treasure them both. At holiday times, Joe and I are always included in their family gatherings. They have a home which should be featured in American Dream Home magazine. Everything is state of the art, and immaculately organized. I do not know how they manage this and work a ten to twelve hour day each week. I always say, God knows when to put the right people in your life.

28 RETIREMENT

The time rolled around for me to think of retirement. I felt the boot on my butt as the young attractive girls (one in particular, who was eyeballing my position) were getting all the attention and kudos from the boss, and also from the detectives in my unit. It seemed as though once I hit sixty, I was older than dirt in the eyes of these guys, and no longer significant. They were interested in the young, cute and hard bodied girls in the mini-skirts and tight spandex skirts. In all honesty, the one I am specifically referring to, was not only attractive, but also smart, and fast as a road runner on the computer. It was intimidating and disheartening to realize that I was no longer the fair haired child, as I had been for many years past. When you stay with an organization for that long, as you age, you become less appreciated and less important as the younger people come in and take over. All of your knowledge and experience doesn't seem to count for much. It's the same old song and dance everywhere, as you age, you are treated very differently, and usually not for the better.

The medicine for my heart problem made me so tired that I would sometimes doze off right at my desk. One time I toppled over and hit my head on the partition alongside my cubicle. Thankfully no one noticed, or if they did, they were silent about it. My mouth was hanging open and drooling, I'm sure. Not what anyone would consider attractive, I must admit.

I put in my paperwork for retirement, thinking July would be a good time to hang it up. After submitting all the paperwork, reviewing it I caught a huge mistake, finding that December of 2006 would be the right time. I had to undo all the paperwork and start again. Most everything got screwed up due to my changing the retirement date. What a nightmare it had turned into! I never realized the red tape and hoops you have to jump through! I had to deal with my city retirement, Social Security, Medicare, Long-term care; funds that had to be borrowed from savings, so I could afford to live; paying back the retirement fund after I drew out my money, back when I had moved to Palm Springs; which, by the way, was a BIG MISTAKE and cost me thousands of dollars to pay back, because the longer I waited, the more it cost.

In order to be able to collect my social security I needed one quarter. I earned this by starting up a pet sitting business in my neighborhood, and did quite well, earning that quarter quickly. My love for animals made this a pleasure, though I did encounter an unfriendly one or two, but it worked out in the end. I think of the other businesses I attempted, a home cleaning service, the garment swap meet venture, and the calendar fiasco. I even thought of the pet rock craze before it happened, but never got it off the ground. I also tried to convince friends of mine in the early seventies to open a pet hotel, but to no avail. Not having the funds to start a business makes it next to impossible. But I did try more than once, anyway.

Everyone who has been there, knows that after fifty five, the days seem to go by in a blur. You may feel that your mind might still be 30 or 40, but your body sure lets you know: It ain't so! Your body seems to change on a daily basis, sometimes causing you to look in the mirror and wonder who it is looking back at you. If you haven't yet reached this stage in your life, take this as fair warning of things to come. You wake up and wonder: What happened? Where did that new wrinkle come from? When did that body part start sagging? It wasn't like that yesterday, but there it is today, staring me in the face!

In your sixties it is a total patch job. Your social life starts revolving around your next visit to the doctor or dentist. No matter how much care you've given to your teeth during your lifetime, they, too, start failing you. Aging is a challenge! Definitely not for the faint of heart. Whoever came up with the phrase "The Golden Years" either had to be insane, or 30 years old! There is nothing "golden" about the aging process, and as a dear 91 year old friend of mine used to say, "they can take the golden years and shove 'em!" But with that said, it's still better than the alternative.

A small portion of the population may be endowed with good genes, and may not experience the sudden drooping of chins, boobs, and skin. One day you're feeling pretty good about yourself, still wearing short skirts and sleeveless tops, and then without any warning, gravity strikes! Gone are the once firm and perky breasts, replaced by what I refer to as "flopsy and mopsy", gone is the once round taut behind, replaced by a flat almost non-existent derriere, gone are the firm muscular arms, replaced by sagging creped skin.

I recall turning on my side one evening and feeling a flopping sensation. To my surprise, it was my thighs! It seemed like they were no longer part of my body. They were firm yesterday, and I could show off my long legs with confidence in a pair of shorts or swim suit, but in the blink of an eye that was all gone, out went the shorts and mini-skirts, it was time for a new, much more conservative, skin covering wardrobe.

I also started out at 5'9" and now am a mere 5'3" in height. Take heed! There are many bone diseases that can rob you of your perfect posture. Thirty percent of bone loss occurs when you diet to the extreme as I did. Anorexia Nervosa not only takes a toll on you psychologically, practically ruining your nervous system, but affects every part of your physical being. There was no turning this around. There are some dietary changes that can affect the bone mass as well as supplements, but you never totally regain your former bone strength. I look around at some of my old buddies and I don't see such drastic changes going on with them. I can only surmise that the majority of my physical ailments are a result of being anorexic in my younger years.

And now I must remark on the physical appearance of some of the folks at my fifty-year high-school reunion. The ladies who were attractive in their teens still looked pretty good. It was also apparent that a few had gone under the knife a time or two. Most of the students at Harbor High School in Newport Beach came from affluent families, which most likely filtered down to this generation. They could afford whatever it took to keep their chins and boobs firmly in place.

The men, on the other hand, did not fare so well. There were lots of bald heads, totally acceptable and somewhat sexy on the right heads, but most of these men definitely did not have the right heads to wear bald well. And there were beer bellies galore! The two or three men I had looked forward to seeing again were on the deceased list, which made me quite sad. Back in those days they had been the "studs" of Newport Harbor High. I had dated one after we had reconnected at our twenty-year reunion. He was the star football player in school, and of course, he was hotly pursued by all the girls. He had married one of his high school sweethearts, but was soon divorced, after he traded in football for drinking as his sport of choice. I learned at our 50 year reunion that he had passed away after sousing his liver with vodka. We only dated a few times, because each and every time he got totally bombed, so I finally decided that he wasn't worth dying for in a horrible car crash; I'm actually surprised that's not what killed him. My guardian angels were really working overtime when I was with him. I remember preaching to him about getting behind the wheel in his condition, but he managed to smooth talk me several times, convincing me that he had it under control. When he was sober and would call me from work, he was so wonderful. He would tell me, I was the best thing that had happened to him in a long time, and he wanted to pursue our relationship as he was very serious about the two of us being together. I knew I would never be able to handle his over-the-top drinking problem; and as time went on, I didn't see it getting any better. So I ultimately ended our short romance. Bill was a terrific guy, but his demons got the better of him. At our twenty year reunion, the girls who had pursued him in school, were very surprised that he dated me, as I was not one of the socialite types he mingled with in school. I recall feeling like I had one up on them finally.

I probably was the most unrecognizable person at our twenty year reunion. My appearance had improved remarkably from the overweight unattractive girl I was in school, and that night I enjoyed the attention of several guys, including Bill. I reveled in all the attention, and felt like giving the bird to all my former classmates who had pretty much shunned me, or do something similar to it, but I pride myself on being classier than that, so I kept my gloating to myself.

All of my unhappy experiences in high school had caused so much self-loathing, and drove me to my near self-destruction. I felt, I had to prove to all those unkind people who shunned me for those miserable four years that I could look and be better than they ever dreamed of being.

Once I deluded myself into believing, that if I became thin enough, I could have any guy I wanted, starvation set in and the road to my self-destruction began. Nothing could stop my neurosis at this point in time, and no one could convince me to change this destructive path I was on. Reflecting back on my past, it was a waste of precious life. You have to overcome focusing on YOU and gear your thoughts to others, and to what you can contribute to society. One has to work on one's inner beauty, and let loose of what the secular society thinks you should be or strive for. I'm not saying to let your physical appearance go, but make the most of what you have from within. Sounds corny and trite and of course we all have heard this a zillion times, but age and life experience has taught me that this is indeed the way it is! You will want to eat, drink and exercise sensibly; whatever it takes to maintain good health.

This all sounds good... but not so easy to accept and actually implement it in your own life, when you are caught up in the clutches of self-destruction that anorexia is. But then, when you manage to start on the road to recovery, you will feel good about yourself and be motivated to go out and do good deeds and feel accomplishment in whatever you choose to do in life. I'm not there by any means, as it is a daily challenge to try and love most folks out there, and do the right thing by them, but I try.

I found that drinking removes one's will. It is short term relief for long term pain. I may have used this term earlier in my writing, but it is so truly profound. My relying on booze to get me through uncomfortable times, such as traveling or facing undesirable situations, only masked my phobias. It helped for a short time, but ultimately just made matters worse, physically and emotionally.

Experiencing a heart attack and having a stent implanted finally got my attention. I had suffered prior to the operation with arterial fibrillation, and was, and still am on prescription drugs for this problem. Not only did I have a heart attack, but at the same time experienced toxicity of the chest area, phlebitis, and deep vein thrombosis. It was a scary time, but the good lord got me through it once again. My doctor told me, I was one tough lady and I liked hearing that, because I had never really seen myself that way at all. In fact, I had always viewed myself as weak, because of my illness and my dependence on alcohol to handle stressful situations. I no longer drink, and must say I do not miss it, although once in a blue moon I would like the taste of a yummy exotic concoction. When that urge presents itself, I order a virgin drink. In the past few years since suffering all of my health issues, I've probably had only a sip or two and that's been it. It's not worth the headaches and the feeling of being unplugged. When you don't partake, you don't miss it. When you are with a group that is getting hammered, you realize that you too have made a fool of yourself a time or two while overindulging. I suddenly noticed when someone has one too many, they constantly repeat themselves to the point of being extremely annoying. The whole scene is nerve wracking when you are the sober one.

Walking into a club where there is live music and dancing, is intimidating when you are not partaking of the bubbly. The excitement pales, when all that's sitting in front of you are Shirley Temples, but at least you will be in much better shape the next day, not losing another day suffering the after effects of a night of intoxication. I have learned to dance without liquid courage, and still manage to have a good time; probably better, because now I remember what I did or did not do, I don't have to wake up dreading the stories I'm going to hear about the stupid things I did. I do wonder how many brain cells I've destroyed over the course of my drinking years; maybe I don't want to know.

With Joe by my side, taken in 2003

My life is pretty predictable today, and that's okay with me. I've had enough drama in my life to last two lifetimes. It is now time for simple pleasures, such as walks on the beach, which I have always cherished. Living close to the ocean all my life puts me on the blessed list. Searching for shells is like a treasure hunt; it's fun, it's free, and I get great pleasure and peace from it. The ocean's roar and salty air is revitalizing and good for my soul. Sticking my feet in the water and splashing around reinvigorates me each and every time. Whenever I can talk anyone into taking a whale watching trip with me, I'm out the door and ready for some big swells. Luckily I have never been subjected to sea sickness, so this is the ultimate experience, to be on a boat inhaling all that salt air and catching sight of sea creatures, large and small. I often ask God why I have been so fortunate to live where I have all my life and to live so well on very little.

My retirement pension gets me by each month, though there is not a lot to go around. But still, I somehow make it work. I trust in God to care for me, and I have learned to hand over all my worries and cares to the Lord. I adhere to this philosophy most every day and have learned that it works if you put him in charge.

I think of how totally out of kilter this world is. I thank God every day, too, as I do not live in a third world country where famine and horrific acts against humanity occur as a daily way of life. I do not deserve to have what I possess, and wonder why I am so blessed; why me? I have done things I am ashamed of, and would never think of behaving today as I did in the past. I despise some of my past actions and regret many of the choices I made. I starved myself nearly to death in search of something as superficial as exterior beauty, thinking that was the only way to be admired and loved. As a result, I developed so many phobias and my world changed and shrank around me because of them. Even though I wouldn't wish a heart attack on anyone, I think in my case it was God's way of opening my eyes and getting me back on a more spiritual track before it was too late. Years ago, I threw away all the medications, as they no longer helped; only making me more paranoid.

I still adhere to some of my anorexia behavior. I have to weigh in twice a day, mostly because I do not have much of an appetite, and want to make sure that I maintain a decent weight and make myself eat something to stay alive and well. I am a bit underweight, and have tried to gain a couple of pounds, but the old mindset is still there, that once I start putting it on, I may not be able to stop. In spite of all the progress I have made, it seems as though some of my neuroses will never go away. I remember all too vividly how ill I was from my starvation diet, and never want to experience such a nightmare again. But I'm also terrified of ever getting up to 180 lbs.

again. I hope I am older and wiser, and will be able to maintain a healthy weight and not become a butterball again.

29 CLOSING COMMENTS

The whole point to my writing this book has been to help those who may contemplate starving themselves in search of that perfect size 2 body and finding Mr. Right. Dieting should be under the care of a physician as everyone should know by now. If there was any magic pill or diet that was healthy and would make you skinny, everyone in the world would be skinny! A doctor would tell you to eat smaller portions, eat healthy food, exercise, and be sure to enjoy from time to time comfort foods to maintain a happy level of existence. Leave the table feeling comfortable, not stuffed. Not everyone should be a size 2, and too skinny is no more attractive than morbid obesity. And believe me, as one who knows from experience, there is no guarantee that it will buy you love.

Some men are actually attracted to ladies "built for comfort, not speed". Working on attitude is what it is really all about. If you go to extremes such as I did, and are fortunate enough to survive, you will suffer physical and mental torments almost insurmountable to deal with. There is so much in this world to do and to accomplish. Starving yourself will incapacitate you to the point of missing the true value of who you are, and what you can do to contribute to life and to those around you.

Again, I was blessed with wonderful friends and family who supported me through all these tough years; who did not desert me when I needed them most. Some people I know, got real fed up with my excuses of not being able to drive to meet them somewhere, and some of them wearied of picking me up if we were planning a get together, but not my real friends. I sure can understand the imposition those felt by my neurosis. It is most difficult for people, who have never been inflicted with these types of illnesses, to relate to such boundaries and restrictions created by daily phobias that rule my life. God knows how much effort I have put into overcoming them and attempts to conceal them.

It is a good thing that I do not like to travel, particularly in this day and age of crazies running amuck; otherwise I would be more distraught about my limitations. When I was younger, it did eat me up alive, that I just could not be a normal person, hop on a plane or whatever, and enjoy the experience of new places. I always had to have my meds or booze to get me out the front door. All the money I spent on therapy to overcome my numerous phobias, could have bought me a mansion; well almost! None of it was a cure, and actually of very little help. The drugs made me a total zombie, and took the joy out of each day. I hated the feeling of being unplugged, and to this day I resist taking any of the so called "wonder drugs". There is always a trade-off, as I learned from past experiences. No, Virginia, in life there are no free rides!

Often, through the years, I have wondered what my life would have been if I could have traveled with Steve, or gone on tour with Sharon and Eddie. I think, too, that Michael, who got me started in the modeling business, and insisted that I keep losing more weight, might not have dumped me because I resembled a Prisoner Of War, and became ill. Would he have treated me differently? Our breakup devastated me at the time, as I was so vulnerable and wanted desperately to have a man to lean on during this time in my life.

In the end, it worked out far better than I could have dreamed. I prayed for a good and decent man, and I have been with one for the past twenty plus years. God did reward me far beyond what I deserved. I had a terrific job for the thirty-seven years that I looked forward to each day; well almost... particularly in the beginning, when the department was not so politically correct. Most all the cops were and are people of integrity and values, and do a job that most would not be willing to do. Most of the time they receive little thanks, and put themselves out there where God only knows what can happen to them. I have the utmost respect for the officers and the department that I worked for most of my adult life.

We live in a wonderful neighborhood, within walking distance from the ocean that I love. There are stores within my two mile driving range, so I can get out and about on my own and not be confined to the house when no one is available to come out and play with me. I still have days where it can be nerve wracking to get behind the wheel and take off on my own. Actually, each time I step out the door, I have to psych myself into a positive mindset and say prayers. On those occasions when I don't get proper rest, my demons take over and I become hesitant to leave the house, something that could lead to such a severe case of agoraphobia that I might never leave the house again, so if it takes 10 hours in bed and then a nap, so be it, I will do anything to never be in that situation again. Whatever it takes, in order to function, that's what I will do; I can never allow myself to fall back into the old habits that almost destroyed my life.

When all is said and done, I am so very grateful for all of the remarkable experiences I have had and the amazing people I have encountered during my lifetime. Most people do not get to grow up living at the beach, or rub elbows with so many famous entertainers, or enjoy the support and love of so many dear friends. The single, most important change in my life was discovering my true spirituality before it was too late.

Despite my handicaps, I have lived and continue to live a good life and cannot express how fortunate I am, but that doesn't mean that I won't always have those "what if"-s in the back of my mind: What if I had not starved myself almost to death for love? How much different would my "normal" life have been?

I will never have the answers to those questions. So I've grown to accept that I've lived the life God meant for me to live.

And I'm eternally grateful for it.

About the author

Norma Jeanne Bent-Johnson was raised in Balboa, California, a beautiful beach town South of Los Angeles. Raised by a single mom, they were very poor, five people sharing a one bedroom cottage.

Growing up in Balboa during the 1950's was a simpler, but also a challenging time for the young impressionable girl whose role models were Marilyn Monroe and Lana Turner.

Believing that in order to find true love, she had to look like the famous movie stars of the era, led her to anorexia, excessive drinking and addiction to prescription medications. It may have been the lack of a father figure in her early life that caused her obsession with men and finding love.

She went to work for a local police department, leading to a career of four decades in law enforcement as a civilian investigator. She is now retired and resides in Southern California with her husband, spending much of her time working for animal rights.

She hopes her tale of obsession, addiction and anorexia, all in the name of love, will help other women avoid going down a similar path, leading to disaster.

Love can, and should be a beautiful thing; it does not have to be disastrous.

Made in the USA
San Bernardino, CA
31 January 2020